Tourism and
Political Change

Tourism and Political Change

Edited by

Richard Butler
and
Wantanee Suntikul

(G) **Goodfellow Publishers Ltd**

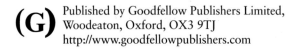

Published by Goodfellow Publishers Limited,
Woodeaton, Oxford, OX3 9TJ
http://www.goodfellowpublishers.com

British Library Cataloguing in Publication Data: a catalogue record
for this title is available from the British Library.

Library of Congress Catalog Card Number: on file.

ISBN: 978-1-906884-11-6

 Design and typesetting by P.K. McBride, www.macbride.org.uk

Printed by Marston Book Services, www.marston.co.uk

Cover design by Cylinder, www.cylindermedia.com

Cover images: © www.istockphoto.com

Contents

Figures   vii

Tables   viii

Contributors

About the editors

1   **Introduction**   1
     Wantanee Suntikul and Richard Butler

2   **Politics and Tourism: Interdependency and Implications in
     Understanding Change**   7
     C. Michael Hall

Part I: Unification/Reunification   19

3   **German Reunification and Tourism in Berlin**   21
     Wantanee Suntikul

4   **The European Union: Between the Global and the National, and
     Between Neo-Liberalism and Interventionism**   33
     Allan M Williams and Vladimir Baláž

5   **The Implications and Effects of the Handover of Colonies – Macau**   45
     Glenn McCartney

Part II: Increasing Autonomy   55

6   **Devolution – Towards Independence: Tourism in Scotland in
     the 21st Century**   57
     Rory MacLellan

7   **Political Change and Tourism in Arctic Canada**   68
     Emma J. Stewart and Dianne Draper

8   **Central and Eastern Europe: the End of the Soviet Union and its
     Satellites**   82
     Derek Hall

Part III: Normalisation/Opening   95

9   **Tourism as an Instrument of Foreign Policy: the U.S Trade
     Embargo on Cuba**   97
     Tom Hinch

10   **Arab Politics and Tourism: Political Change and Tourism in the
     Great Socialist People's Libyan Arab Jamahiriya**   108
     Eleri Jones

11   From Apartheid to a 'Managed Revolution': Tourism Development
     and the Transition in South Africa   120
     Peter U.C. Dieke

12   Tourism and Political Transition in Reform-Era Vietnam   133
     Wantanee Suntikul

Part IV: Political Unrest   145

13   Tourism and Political Change in Nepal   147
     Sanjay Nepal

14   Political Change and Tourism: Coups in Fiji   160
     David Harrison and Stephen Pratt

15   Iran or Persia: What's in a Name? The Decline and Fall of
     a Tourism Industry   175
     Tom G Baum and Kevin D O'Gorman

Part V: Changes in Political Relations   187

16   Does Tourism have a Role in Promoting Peace on the Korean
     Peninsula?   189
     Bruce Prideaux, Jillian Prideaux and Seongseop Kim

17   The Opening of the Ledra Crossing in Nicosia: Social and
     Economic Consequences   199
     David Jacobson, Bernard Musyck, Stelios Orphanides
     and Craig Webster

18   Politics on Ice – Tourism in Antarctica   208
     Thomas G Bauer

Conclusions   219

19   Conclusions   221
     Richard Butler and Wantanee Suntikul

     Index   227

Figures

4.1 Value added, employment, productivity and labour costs in tourism in the EU, 1995–2007   36

4.2 Nights spent in hotels and similar establishments in the EU27, 1994–2007 (millions)   39

4.3 Assistance to tourism under Cohesion policy in 2007–13, shares of main targets   42

7.1 Map of Nunavut   69

7.2 *Kapitan Khlebnikov* on a Northwest Passage tour, near Cambridge Bay   73

7.3 Bylot Island from Pond Inlet   75

7.4 *Hanseatic* in Pond Inlet (2007)   76

9.1 International visitors, phases of Cuban tourism and highlights of US foreign policy   98

10.1 Map of Libya   109

13.1 Tourist arrivals to Nepal between 1962 and 2008   147

13.2 Tourist arrivals by major regions – 1990–2008   155

13.3 Tourist arrivals by purpose of visit – 1990–2008   155

13.4 Protected area visitors between 1990 and 2008   156

13.5 Tourist arrivals by major airlines – 1990–2008   156

13.6 Foreign exchange earnings from tourism   157

14.1 Fiji tourism arrivals and tourism earnings: 1980–2008   163

14.2 Imputed impacts on tourism arrivals   164

14.3 Tourism Fiji's marketing budget: 1993–2009   168

18.1 1992-2007 Antarctic tourist trends   216

Tables

2.1	Conceptions of the public policy process	14
5.1	Macau visitor arrivals and gross gaming revenues (in Macau Patacas (MOP)	48
6.1	Tourist visits to Scotland 2008	58
8.1	CEE international tourist arrivals, 1990-2007	86
8.2	CEE international tourism receipts, 1990-2007	87
10.1	Ten-year predictions for the contribution of tourism to the Libyan economy	109
11.1	Overseas visitor arrivals to South Africa, 1987–1997	124
13.1	Tourism development and political events in Nepal–Era I	149
13. 2	Tourism development and political events in Nepal–Era II	151
13.3	Tourism development and political events in Nepal–Era III	153
13.4	Tourism development and political events in Nepal–Era IV	154
14.1	Macroeconomic indicators for Fiji, 1971–2008 (%)	162
14.2	Average annual arrivals and earnings: growth rates by decade	162
14.3	Arrivals and earnings in the years of the coups and surrounding years	164
14.4	International arrivals to Fiji, actual and forecast: 1986–2008	165
14.5	Summary of estimated losses in arrivals and earnings	166
14.6	Emigration from Fiji: 1978–2008: Selected years	169
14.7	UNDP human development position of selected countries: 1991–2007/08	170
14.8	Tourism in the South Pacific, 1985-2008: selected years	171
15.1	Iranian monuments inscribed on the World Heritage List	177
17.1	Crossings through Ledra Street/Lokmaci checkpoint	200
17.2	Crossings through the Green Line	203
18.1	Total preliminary visitor estimates for 2009-10 season	216

Contributors

Allan Williams, London Metropolitan University, London, UK.

Bernard Musyck, School of Economic Sciences and Administration, Frederick University, Cyprus

Bruce Prideaux School of Business, James Cook University, Brisbane, Australia

Craig Webster, School of Humanities, Social Science and Law, University of Nicosia, Cyprus

Eleri Jones, University of Wales Institute, Cardiff, UK,

Emma J. Stewart, Environment, Society & Design, Lincoln University, Christchurch, New Zealand

David Harrison, School of Tourism and Hospitality Management, University of the South Pacific, Suva, Fiji Islands

David Jacobson, Professor of Economics, Dublin City University Business School, Dublin City University, Ireland

Derek Hall, Seabank, Ayrshire, Scotand.

Dianne Draper, Department of Geography, University of Calgary, Calgary, Alberta Canada.

Glenn McCartney, University of Macau, Macau, China

Jillian Prideaux, University of Queensland, Brisbane, Australia.

Kevin D O'Gorman, Strathclyde Business School, University of Strathclyde, Glasgow, UK

Michael Hall, Department of Management, University of Canterbury, Christchurch, New Zealand

Peter Dieke, George Mason University, Manassas, VA, USA

Rory MacLellan, Napier Business School, Napier University, Edinburgh, UK

Sanjay Nepal, Department of Recreation, Park and Tourism Sciences, Texas A&M, USA

Seongseop Kim, Department of Hospitality and Tourism Management, Sejong University, Seoul, Korea

Stelios Orphanides, Indpendent Consultant, Nicosia, Cyprus

Stephen Pratt, School of Tourism and Hospitality Management, University of the South Pacific, Suva, Fiji.

Thomas Bauer, School of Hotel and Tourism Management, The Hong Kong Polytechnic University, Hong Kong SAR, China

Tom Baum Strathclyde Business School, University of Strathclyde, Glasgow, UK

Tom Hinch, Faculty of Physical Education and Recreation, University of Alberta, Edmonton, Canada

Vladimir Baláž, Insitute of Forecasting, Slovak Academy of Science, Bratislava, Slovakia

About the editors

Professor Richard Butler is Emeritus Professor in the Strathclyde Business School of the University of Strathclyde in Glasgow, Scotland.

He has published widely in tourism journals, and produced eleven books on tourism and many chapters in other books. His main fields of interest are the development process of tourist destinations and the subsequent impacts of tourism, issues of carrying capacity and sustainability, and tourism in remote areas and islands. He is currently editor Emeritus of 'The Journal of Tourism and Hospitality Research'.

Dr Wantanee Suntikul is Assistant Professor in Tourism Planning and Development at the Institute For Tourism Studies in Macao, China.

Besides teaching and researching, Wantanee has also been involved in several tourism related consultancy projects in Southeast Asia. Her core research interest and expertise are in the political, social and environmental aspects of tourism planning and development and poverty alleviation.

Acknowledgements

We wish to acknowledge our great thanks to our fellow contributors to this volume, both for their chapters and for their cooperation, understanding, and support for the volume. They have responded to our comments and queries with patience and alacrity, and we hope that they feel their efforts have been justified and that we have not abused their discretion and good will.

We are also grateful to the staff at Goodfellow, our publishers, for their assistance and support during the publication of this work, particularly Sally North who has been with us from the beginning, and whose patience and understanding we really appreciate.

Dedications

This book is dedicated to my dear late father, who passed on his knowledge and passion for politics to his admiring daughter. Thank you for leading me on the first steps of the journey of discovery that inspired this book.

To my late mother, for her support and encouragement, and for convincing me of the value of education and learning, not only for a career but also for life itself.

Wantanee Suntikul

To Margaret, my thanks for help and encouragement during the preparation of this volume, and for your support in so many other ways.

To Tim, thank you so much for teaching me how to remain patient and positive through all the rough spots. My discussions with you have fueled my passion for research and I look forward to many more such discussions with you in the future.

Richard Butler

1 Introduction

Wantanee Suntikul and Richard Butler

This volume addresses an issue that is of great current relevance, and which will only continue to increase in importance in coming years. Tourism has been proclaimed the largest industry in the world. According to the World Tourism Organization, international tourist arrivals reached 922 million worldwide in 2008 and are forcasted to reach 1.6 billion by 2020. As such, tourism is acknowledged as an important economic sector for many countries. However, the impacts of a complex economy of social contact and exchange like tourism go well beyond the economic realm, and there is a growing acknowledgement that tourism is a human activity with undeniable political dimensions, which enters into relations with other political factors at all scales.

The political dimensions of tourism are many. The increasingly global nature of tourism patterns and tourism-related enterprises is bringing tourism into the realm of global politics. Not only is tourism affected by global economic and political trends and relations between nations – but the role of tourism in influencing international diplomacy is becoming increasingly apparent. Tourism is also intrinsically enmeshed in national, regional and local political milieus, and is an inextricable aspect of the micro-politics of society at every destination.

Tourism has become more closely implicated in political action and activism in recent years, with tourism being seen and used as a tool for political and economic change. Calls for tourist boycotts of countries with undesirable political regimes, the use of tourism to initiate political discussions, increased pressure for fair trade, the potential of tourism for poverty reduction and the role of GATT in tourism all reflect the clearly apparent growing link between these two fields.

The greater politicisation of tourism is happening within an increasingly complex political context. Over the past two decades the number of independent nation states has continued to increase and what were once regarded as fixed institutions, such as the Soviet Union, have disappeared or changed beyond all recognition and expectation. The economic and social consequences of the fall of Communism in Eastern Europe and the adaptive re-invention of Communist societies in Asia continue to have repercussions on the global stage and at the level of specific destinations within these regions , as does the rapid and sizeable expansion of the European Union. Complex practices emerge at the interface between global culture and local societies. Former colonies struggle with issues of political identity. New political constellations emerge with the shifting economic fortunes and political affiliations of countries around the world, and xenophobic religious fanaticism ascends to the global political stage. The bombings of tourist nightlife venues in Bali in 2002 and the use of commercial jets to destroy New York's World Trade Center in 2001 are indicative of the tourism industry's attractiveness and vulnerability as a target for politically-motivated terrorist attacks.

Research on the links and relationships between tourism and politics does not have a long or extensive history, but it is a subject area which has grown considerably since Richter pioneered research on the relationship between politics and tourism, notably in her book The *Politics of Tourism in Asia* (Richter, 1989), in which she discusses the influences on, and effects of, tourism policy in ten Asian countries. Her writings, in particular, have encouraged scholars in the social sciences to take more interest and action in understanding and influencing tourism policy. In his *Tourism and Politics: Policy, Power and Place* (Hall, 1994), Hall introduced the discourse of political theory into tourism and reflected on the role of the political dimension in tourism at scales ranging from the personal to the global.

To some extent this theme was continued by Elliott (1997), who presents a primer on the roles of government in regulating and supporting tourism. A practical point of view on the relation of politics and tourism was taken by Poirier (1997) in his investigation of the uses of political science to determine the political risk of foreign direct investment in tourism. Timothy (2001) and Wachowiak (2006) have both produced books on political boundaries and tourism, while the symbolic and political aspects of passports within the system of cross-border tourist movement are elaborated upon by O'Byrne (2001). The literature in this area also contains works examining the politics of tourism as actually practiced and experienced in specific contexts including Myanmar (Philp and Mercer, 1999; Henderson, 2003), Indonesia (Dahles, 2002), North Korea (Kim *et al.*, 2007), Tobago (McLeod and Airey, 2007), the Arab World (Hazbun, 2008) and China's Yunnan Province (Su and Teo, 2009). A current general overview of the recent state of research into the relation between politics and tourism is well represented in Burns and Novelli's (2007) edited compilation *Tourism and Politics: Global Frameworks and Local Realities*.

In their linking of socio-political changes to changes in tourism patterns and policy, a handful of earlier researchers, such as Jaakson (1994) and Leheny (1995) prefigure some of the themes of this book. Political change is also included among the modes of change discussed in books dealing with issues of change in tourism (e.g. Butler and Pearce, 1995; Laws *et al.*, 1998). However, a broad awareness of and attention to the interrelation between political change and tourism is a more recent trend, as represented by Hall (2004), who elaborates on tourism in countries undergoing political transition. In recent years, a number of researchers have been turning their attention to the analysis of the interrelation between political change and tourism, both from the historical perspective – such as Pack's (2007) book chapter on the effects of political change on tourism during the fascist Franco regime in Spain – and in contemporary case studies like George *et al.*'s (2009) study of the political changes that arrived through tourism development in several rural communities in Canada. Altinay and Bowen's(2006) work identified barriers and challenges to planning for a consolidated tourism industry on Cyprus within the scenario of potential closer political integration of the two halves of the politically divided island under a 'federation' arrangement – a subject taken up later in this volume (Chapter 17).

Other recent work on tourism and politics (e.g. Church and Coles 2007, Hall, 2008) has focused on issues of power, implications for involvement and empowerment, political ideologies, governance and, particularly, policy. However, the specific focus on tourism's relation to political change at different levels in different political and geographical locations has not been examined in detail before.

Structure of the book

This volume builds upon the foundation established by the aforementioned writers by discussing in concrete terms the specific ways in which the interrelationship between politics and tourism is playing out in a number of different situations involving political changes at different scales in recent years in many parts of the world, including the ending of the Cold War, the decline of Communism (glasnost, perestroika), the end of apartheid in South Africa, the apparent thawing of relations in the divided pseudo-states of Korea and Cyprus, the opening up of Vietnam and China to tourism, the handover of the former colonies of Hong Kong and Macau to China, the redrawing of the map of Europe through the re-unification of Germany and the fragmenting of several Eastern European nations.

Tourism has caused and experienced various impacts as a result of these changes but the implications of political change on tourism have not been fully explored. This book is the first to provide a compilation of in-depth, focused and scholarly discussions dealing with the interaction between political change and tourism in individual specific cases. Out of these individual cases it builds a grounded understanding of the political dimensions of tourism, both in terms of a comprehensive survey of the different manifestations of this phenomenon across the world and the proposition of a conceptual framework within which these individual examples may be brought together.

The body of this book, between this introduction and the concluding chapter, begins with a piece by Michael Hall (Chapter 2) on the aspects of politics and policy that influence tourism, in which he posits that change is the rule rather than the exception in tourism politics and policy, and calls for increased attention in tourism research to the multilayered and changing environment of policy that constrains and guides tourism planning and development. This chapter is followed by five thematic parts, each comprised of several chapters on tourism in specific contexts characterised by a certain mode of political change. The subtopics by which chapters are grouped are Unification/Reunification, Increasing Autonomy, Normalisation/Opening, Political Unrest, and Changes in Political Relations.

The three chapters that make up the first such part, *Unification/Reunification*, elaborate on tourism developments in three contexts – at the urban, national and international scale – in which formerly separate political entities have been united into one. Suntikul's chapter (3) details the ways in which political differences between East and West Germany gave form to very different models of tourism in the two halves of pre-Reunification Berlin, and chronicles the process of transformation in tourism patterns and development that has accompanied the growing-together of East and West Berlin. Williams and Baláž (Chapter 4) examine the place of tourism in the pan-European process of political integration within the European Union, and specifically the role of tourism policy in achieving specific EU goals. In a very different spatial and cultural setting, the former Portuguese colony of Macau was returned to China in 1999. In the final chapter (5) of Part I, McCartney writes on the challenges in developing Macau as an international tourism destination, focused on its burgeoning gaming industry and UNESCO World Heritage sites, within the 'one country, two systems' policy by which Macau (like Hong Kong) has maintained as an exceptional political entity within China.

Increasing Autonomy is the second thematic part, and comprises three chapters looking at the tourism aspects of nations, and semi-autonomous regions within nations, which in recent years have gained increasing political self-determination after a history of domination by a stronger central political power or ideology. MacLellan's chapter (6) examines the successes and struggles in the development of Scotland's tourism image and tourism industry since the region's increased political autonomy heralded by devolution of powers and the founding of the Scottish Parliament in 1999. Stewart and Draper (Chapter 7) discuss an analogous context – that of the Inuit region of Nunavut in Arctic Canada, which also attained political legitimacy as a semi-autonomous territory in 1999, but which has not yet achieved a unified tourism vision or policy requisite to its political unity. Lastly, Derek Hall (Chapter 8) discusses the differing developmental paths of post-Cold War tourism in the former Communist nations of Central and Eastern Europe and the issues arising from the political change in that region.

Part III, Normalization/Opening offers four chapters on tourism in four parts of the world which are undergoing or have undergone a transformation in their political relations within the international community of nations, usually as a result of internal political changes and/or changes in their international relations stances. Hinch contributes a chapter (9) on the part played by tourism in the history of US/Cuban political relations in the context of the long-standing US trade embargo on Cuba and its likely future developments during Obama's presidency. Jones (Chapter 10) writes on the tourism dimension of Libya's cautious opening up to the developed world, both as a promising but underdeveloped destination and as a potentially lucrative but idiosyncratic place for foreign investment in tourism development in somewhat unique political setting. At the other end of the African continent, Dieke (Chapter 11) elaborates on the barriers to the development of the tourism industry in post-apartheid South Africa posed by the legacy of inequitable practices of tourism development and government neglect of the country's tourism industry during its years of isolation through trade and travel embargoes, and the progress made to date. Part III is rounded off by Suntikul's chapter (12) on the changes in the Vietnamese government's position on, and involvement in, the development and regulation of tourism, seeking a balance between socialist ideals and the country's rapidly emerging free market economy following the adoption of the *doi moi* policy.

Part IV, *Political Unrest*, observes historical and recent political instability in three nations and analyses the relations between such disturbances and tourism patterns in these nations. Sanjay Nepal begins the section with a chapter (13) that describes the development of tourism in Nepal during the past 60 years, and how it has survived that country's perennial political upheavals. Harrison and Pratt (Chapter 14) venture to quantify the effect of incidents of political unrest in the form of a number of coups in Fiji on tourist traffic to that island nation, while also delving into the ways in which tourism has become intertwined with the racial and social roots of such unrest. Baum and O'Gorman's chapter (15) traces the changes in Iran's ideology and political alignment, and the effects of such changes on tourism in the country, primarily in terms of the interruption or diversion of 'normal' processes of tourism growth by radical political transformations in a destination country. To some degree the issues mirror some of those discussed in Jones' chapter on Libya, with both Libya and Iran facing problems deriving from mostly Western Christian tourists potentially bringing change to conservative Muslim societies.

In the fifth and final part, *Changes in Political Relations*, three chapters address the effects, or lack thereof, of political relations between nations on tourism patterns. Two of the chapters deal with divided quasi-states while the third deals with the world's (ostensibly non-politicized) most remote continent. Prideaux, Prideaux and Kim (Chapter 16) discuss the role that inter-Korea tourism has played and continues to play in changes in political relations between North and South Korea, and demonstrate how tourism policy has been used by the governments of both Koreas to pursue their respective political ends. Jacobson, *et al.* (Chapter 17) describe how the improvement of tourism flows between the two halves of the divided city of Nicosia in Cyprus has led to a restoration of interrupted tourism flows that has benefited the tourism industry in both the (Greek Cypriot) southern part of the city and the (Turkish Cypriot) northern part. Bauer (Chapter 18) recounts the history of nations' political claims on the nominal 'no-man's land' of Antarctica and the effects on tourism there. In contrast to the hyper-politicized Korean example, Bauer remarks on the exemplary international and public/private cooperation that surrounds the practice of tourism in this fragile and remote destination, despite vast changes in the political climate in the world at large and between the 'ruling' states in Antarctica.

Conclusion

The chapters cover a variety of political changes in many different parts of the world at different scales. The emphasis throughout is on change in the relatively recent past, although in some examples it is clear that the origins of recent political changes are found in past events and policies that are likely to have repercussions and further developments well into the future.

The breadth of geographical scope of the content of this book is matched by the geographical span of its contributors. The authors in this book represent institutions of higher learning in nine different countries or regions in four continents and the South Pacific. All are established researchers who have published in the academic literature on tourism in journals and books. This book has given these authors a venue to explore in detail the specific nature of the relationship between political change and tourism within the areas of their research focus and experience.

The political changes discussed in this book are those which have had, or are currently having, significant consequences for tourism. These changes, and their relation to tourism, will continue to be important and relevant even as future political changes exert their influence on tourism, and future tourism trends make their impression on local, national, regional and global politics. Indeed, the discussion presented in this volume can give a perspective from which future developments can be understood and contextualised and the writings herein will have continued implications for further study of the relationship between tourism and politics as world events unfold.

The principal common themes and threads in the relationship between tourism and political change that run through the various situations discussed in the following chapters are delineated and discussed in the concluding chapter.

References

Altinay, L. & Bowen, D. (2006) 'Politics and tourism interface: the case of Cyprus', *Annals of Tourism Research*, 33(4), 939-956.

Burns, P. & Novelli, M. (eds.) (2007) *Tourism and Politics: Global Frameworks and Local Realities*, Oxford: Elsevier.

Butler, R. & Pearce, D. (eds.) (1995) *Change in Tourism: People, Places, Processes (Issues in Tourism)*, London: Chapman and Hall.

Church, A. & Coles, T. (2007) *Tourism, Power and Space*, London: Routledge.

Dahles, H. (2002) 'The politics of tour guiding: image management in Indonesia', *Annals of Tourism Research*, 29(3), 783-800.

Elliott, J. (1997) *Tourism: Politics and Public Sector Management*, London: Routledge.

George, E.W., Mair, H. & Reid, D.G. (2009) *Rural Tourism Development: Localism and Cultural Change (Tourism and Cultural Change)*, Bristol: Channel View Publications.

Hall, C.M. (1994) *Tourism and Politics: Policy, Power and Place*, Chichester: Wiley & Sons.

Hall, C.M. (2008) *Tourism Planning: Policies, Processes and Relationships*, London: Pearson Prentice Hall.

Hall, D.R. (ed.) (2004) *Tourism and Transition: Governance, Transformation and Development*, Wallingford: CABI.

Hazbun, W. (2008) *Beaches, Ruins, Resorts: The Politics of Tourism in the Arab World*, Minneapolis: University of Minnesota Press.

Henderson, J. (2003) 'The politics of tourism in Myanmar', *Current Issues in Tourism*, 6(2), 97-118.

Jaakson, R. (1996) 'Tourism in transition in Post-Soviet Estonia', *Annals of Tourism Research*, 23(3), 617–634.

Kim, S.S., Timothy, D.J. & Han, H.C. (2007) 'Tourism and political ideologies: a case of tourism in North Korea', *Tourism Management*, 28(4), 1031-1043.

Laws, E., Faulkner, B. & Moscardo, G. (1998) *Embracing and Managing Change in Tourism: International Case Studies*, London: Routledge.

Leheny, D. (1995) 'A political economy of Asian sex tourism'. *Annals of Tourism Research*, 22(2), 367-384.

McLeod, M.T. & Airey, D. (2007) 'The politics of tourism development: a case of dual governance in Tobago', *International Journal of Tourism Policy*, 1(3), 217-231.

O'Byrne, D. (2001) 'On passports and border controls', *Annals of Tourism Research*, 28(2), 399-416.

Pack, S.D. (2007) 'Tourism and political change in Franco's Spain', in N. Townson (ed.) *Spain Transformed: The Late Franco Dictatorship, 1959-1975*, Houndmills Basingstoke: Palgrave Macmillan, pp. 47-66.

Philp, J. & Mercer, D. (1999) 'Commodification of Buddism in contemporary Burma', *Annals of Tourism Research*, 26(1), 21-54.

Poirier, R. (1997) 'Political risk analysis and tourism', *Annals of Tourism Research*, 24(3), 675-686.

Richter, L. (1989) *The Politics of Tourism in Asia*, Honolulu: University of Hawaii Press.

Su, X. and Teo, P. (2009) *The Politics of Heritage Tourism in China: a View from Lijiang*, London: Routledge.

Timothy, D.J. (2001) *Tourism and Political Boundaries* (Routledge Advances in Tourism), London: Routledge.

Wachowiak, H. (ed.) (2006) *Tourism and Borders: Contemporary Issues, Policies and International Research* (New Directions in Tourism Analysis), Farnham: Ashgate Publishing.

2 Politics and Tourism: Interdependency and Implications in Understanding Change

C. Michael Hall

Change is as normal in politics as it is in tourism. Yet the relationship between politics and tourism has been a small subfield of the social science of tourism, even though there are many examples of the way that political change has affected the patterns, processes and directions of tourism development. In developing the interconnections between political change and change in tourism this chapter outlines some of the elements of politics and public policy that are determinants or at least influences on tourism, as well as the interrelationships between them. It then highlights the importance of temporality to understanding public policy change. The chapter discusses three different models of policy-making to illustrate that different frameworks approach issues of policy and change in different ways. Finally, the chapter notes the importance of examining the interdependencies between politics and tourism at multiple scales and times.

Political concepts

Politics is concerned with both the exercise of power and influence in a society and in specific decisions over public policy. A common element in definitions is that 'public policies stem from governments or public authorities ... A policy is deemed a public policy not by virtue of its impact on the public, but by virtue of its source' (Pal, 1992: 3). Public policy is what officials within government decide to do or not to do about issues and problems that require government intervention. 'Government' is a term that refers to the legitimate institutions and associated political processes through which public policy choices are made. Unfortunately, the language used to discuss public policy is often confusing. Policy is more than just a written document, although that may represent an important output of a decision and policy making process, it is an extremely broad concept that covers such matters as:

- the purpose of government action;
- the goals or ends that are to be achieved;
- the means to achieve goals, usually referred to as plans, proposals or strategies;
- the programmes that are established to achieve goals, (the government sanctioned means); and

♦ the decisions and actions that are taken with respect to policy, including implementation.

In addition, it is also important to differentiate between public policy *outputs*, which are the formal actions taken by government with respect to policy from public policy *outcomes*, namely, the effects government policy outputs actually have. Thus public policy can be defined as 'a course of government action or inaction in response to public problems' (Kraft and Furlong, 2007: 5). The idea of inaction is a key concept in policy studies, for example, Dye (1992: 2) also defined public policy as 'whatever governments choose to do or not to do'. Such an approach is extremely significant as it is important to recognise that what a government does not do is as important as what it does do. Hall and Jenkins (1995) described tourism public policy as whatever governments choose to do or not to do with respect to tourism. Such state actions with respect to tourism are justified from a number of economic and political rationales including:

♦ improving economic competitiveness;

♦ amending property rights;

♦ enabling government decision makers to take account of economic, environmental and social externalities;

♦ providing widely available public benefits;

♦ reducing risk and uncertainty for investors;

♦ supporting projects with high capital costs and involving new technologies;

♦ encouraging social and economic development in marginal and peripheral areas;

♦ assisting specifically targeted and often marginal populations; and

♦ educating and providing information.

Tourism policy is therefore a course of government action or inaction in specific relation to tourism. It is specific so as to differentiate tourism policy from policies in other fields, such as environment, transport, and international relations that can have enormous impacts on tourism but are not developed as tourism policies *per se*. Such an understanding may, in fact be extremely important for understanding why tourism develops in some ways in some locations but not in others. For example, the creation of a favourable tax advantage for investors because of a government's foreign investment, taxation and profit repatriation policies may have far greater influence on why some destinations develop at a faster rate than others with intrinsically more attractive attributes for tourists. Similarly, decisions over the location of transport infrastructure, such as airports, railways and roads, which usually fall under the realm of transport policy, will also be critical to the competitive advantage of some locations in tourism development over others (Hall, 2008).

Policy is inseparable from politics. Lasswell (1958) described the situation well when he stated that politics is about 'who gets what, when and how'. In some political systems politics will also include the electoral processes, the policies of political parties, issue agendas, political ideologies, beliefs, values and philosophies. However, it is important to note that there are different political systems in which western democratic ideas and systems do not apply with respect to ideas of democratic representation and voting, transparency and accountability in government processes, legal standing of the individual in relation to government actions, and competing political parties. Of course this does not mean that such states cannot be studied with respect to change, but it is to note that some of these elements that may be important for political change in a western country, e.g. voters or the media, will not be so significant in other contexts.

Understanding change: connecting theory and public policy

One of the great difficulties in studying politics and change is the way that theories of politics and policy-making are inextricably linked to what is identified as important to understanding change. The idea that 'it is logically impossible to understand any reasonably complicated situation – including almost any policy process – without some theoretical lens ('theory', 'paradigm' or 'conceptual framework') distinguishing between the set of important variables and causal relationships and those that can be safely ignored' (Sabatier and Jenkins-Smith, 1993: xi) is well understood in political studies but seemingly not so explicit in accounts of policy in tourism studies (e.g. Edgell 1990; Edgell *et al.*, 2007). The relationship between policy and theory in both analysis and practice is fundamental to a conceptual understanding of the policy process, and therefore change in that process, given that 'policies imply theories':

> *Whether stated explicitly or not, policies point to a chain of causation between initial conditions and future consequences. If X, then Y. Policies become programs when, by authoritative action, the initial conditions are created. X now exists. Programs make the theories operational by forging the first link in the causal chain connecting actions to objectives. Given X, we act to attain Y.*
> *(Pressman and Wildavsky, 1973: xv)*

Majone (1980) similarly argued that policies can be viewed as theories from two related but different perspectives. First, as an analyst's rational reconstruction of a complex sequence of events. Second, from the point of view of actions, as doctrines which evolve from past decisions and actions, giving them stability and internal coherence. These perspectives are significant because as well as indicating ways in which policy and politics are understood, they also suggest that as theories of policies, such as the role of the state in society, change so too might the policies. Indeed, there is substantial evidence for that having been the case. For example, Hall and Jenkins (2004) suggest that the tendency to privatise and commercialise functions that were once performed by government, which has been almost universal in western nations since the early 1980s until the recent global economic crisis, has substantially affected the nature of many national governments' involvement in the tourism industry. According to Hall and Jenkins (2004) the economic reasons for such activities such as 'reducing debt' and 'greater efficiency' are themselves shrouded in political rationales that relate to broader philosophical perspectives which have most often been associated with a 'New Right', corporatist or neo-conservative economic agenda, labelled in various countries as 'Reaganism' (USA), 'Thatcherism' (UK) or 'Rogernomics' (New Zealand) and which reflected a change in philosophical and theoretical understandings of what the role of the state should be.

The role of government in tourism has, therefore, undergone a dramatic shift over a 25-year period, from a 'traditional' public administration model which sought to implement government policy for a perceived public good, to a corporatist model which emphasises efficiency, investment returns, the role of the market, and relations with stakeholders, usually defined as industry (Hall, 1999, 2008; Dredge and Jenkins, 2007). Corporatism, here, is used in the sense of a political philosophy in western society which claims rationality as its central quality and which emphasises a notion of individualism in terms of self-interest, rather than the legitimacy of the individual citizen acting in the democratic interest of the public good (see Saul, 1995). However, in many policy areas, including tourism, the changed role of the state and the individual's relation to the state provides a major policy quandary. On the one hand there is the demand for less government interference in the market and allowing industries to develop and trade without government subsidy or assistance while, on the other, industry interest groups still seek to have favourable government policy developed, frequently including the maintenance of government funding for promotion and development. This policy issue has generally been resolved through the restructuring of national and regional tourist organisations to (a) reduce their planning, policy and development roles and increase their marketing and promotion functions; and (b) to engage in a greater range of partnerships, network and collaborative relationships with stakeholders. Such a situation was described by Milward (1996) as the 'hollowing out' of the state in which the state's role has been transformed from one of hierarchical control (closely akin to traditional notions of government) to one in which governing is dispersed among a number of separate, non-government entities (related to the concept of 'governance'). This has led to increased emphasis on governance through network structures as a 'new process of governing; or a changed condition of ordered rule; or the new method by which society is governed' (Rhodes, 1997: 43).

The restructuring of public administration as a result of changed thinking with respect to the role of government involvement in tourism has been substantial (Dredge and Jenkins, 2007; Hall, 2008). For example, in the United States the Colorado state's tourism offices were abolished by voters, while Oregon and Virginia privatised their state offices in order to gain greater levels of private sector funding (Bonham and Mak, 1996). Similarly, in Australia, Canada and New Zealand, national and state tourism departments have been corporatised, with greater emphasis being given to the establishment of partnerships with industry in joint marketing and promotional campaigns. This has often involved splitting the policy and marketing function between different bodies, with policy being retained in a small ministry and marketing devolved to a separate agency, usually managed by a board of directors derived from the tourism industry, which although government funded and answerable to a minister is run at 'arm's length'. Such a situation clearly indicates that, far from being abstract, theories of government and policy may have very practical affects on tourism and stands in stark contrast to the prescriptive orthodox dichotomy between politics and public administration, well illustrated by Woodrow Wilson:

The field of administration is a field of business. It is removed from the hurry and strife of politics; it at most points stands apart even from the debatable ground of constitutional study... administration lies outside the proper sphere of politics. Administrative questions are not political questions. Although politics set the tasks for administration it should not be suffered to manipulate its offices.

(1887: 209, 210)

Understanding change: temporality

Even though the politics/public administration dichotomy may no longer be regarded as true with respect to 'real world' policy and politics, it still has enormous influences. Particularly because its prescriptive-rational approach is the very stuff that management (including tourism) textbooks, are made of. Conventional descriptions of prescriptive-rational decision-making identify the following aspects:

(a)   clarification of objectives or values,

(b)   survey of alternative means of reaching objectives,

(c)   identification of consequences, including side-effects of by-products of each alternative means, and

(d)   evaluation of each set of consequences in the light of objectives (Hirschmann and Lindblom, 1962: 215).

One of the advantages of the prescriptive-rational approach is that it is relatively simple to construct, yet as Kay (2006: 1) notes, 'any policy process is a complex system and dynamic models of complex systems are much more difficult to construct than static ones'. In tourism policy one of the difficulties is that there are typically several political processes occurring at different speeds at the same time. This also makes the separation of different time scales, such as the short, medium and long-term as essential to understanding change as it is to distinguish between different spatial scales (include scale of governance), as in the macro, meso and micro scales that are common in policy studies (e.g. Hall and Jenkins, 1995, 2004). Understanding change in tourism policy and politics, as in other areas of tourism and change, therefore requires an understanding of temporality (Hall and Lew, 2009).

Dynamic approaches and perspectives on policy will examine successive states of a policy system and the relationship between them. This can be contrasted with a comparative approach that does compare certain states of a political system over time but does not consider the relationship that links these states through time. Although it is possible to have a theory of change within a comparative perspective that provides reasons why some public policy states will change, Kay (2006) argues that two important elements will be missing. First, an account of the process of adjustment between the states. Second, the separation of any two states is in essence atemporal as they are being compared for reasons other then temporality, e.g. two significant political events. Temporal analysis, therefore, is 'systematically situating particular moments (including the present) in a temporal sequence of events and processes stretching over extended periods' (Pierson, 2004: 2) and is essential to understanding change.

There are four ideas involved in the notion of change (Kay, 2006):

(a)   an enduring thing;

(b)   its various possible states;

(c)   the identification of an initial and a final state by the temporal index; and

(d)   the characterisation of these states.

A thing's potential to change is limited by the range of possible states admissible for the type set of which it is a member. This is not as abstract as it sounds and is a critical issue in explaining policy change with respect to changes in things and changes in kind (Majone, 1980). If the 'thing' is tourism policy, for example, only certain policy states are possible; that is, only certain 'things' can be tourism policy. If the boundary is over-stepped, the 'thing' (tourism policy) becomes another 'thing' (another policy field – e.g. environment), rather than a different value of the same thing. However, the identity of the 'thing' through time, its endurance, raises a troublesome philosophical question: 'if a changing thing really changes, it cannot literally be one and the same thing before and after the change: however, if a changing thing literally remains one and the same thing (that is, it retains its identity) throughout the change, then it cannot really have changed' (Kay, 2006: 6). Again this is not philosophical or abstract irrelevance as many debates over public policy are debates about things and values that are politically contested, for example, representation of women and the body in tourism advertising and promotion or modernisation of heritage cities. This identity through time is even more complex when the thing is composite and in flux, as in the case of policy. For example, is tourism policy under a Keynesian welfare state a different thing from neoliberal tourism policy, or is it a different value of the same thing? In addition it is important to try and appreci-ate that public policy consists of a multitude of processes operating at different speeds. Therefore, in seeking to understand change it is as important to distinguish between the role of events (an abrupt change) and process (a more gradual change). Much of the focus in research on tourism and political change is often on the role of high-profile high-magnitude political events in instigating change, however the role of process is just as, if not much more, important in understanding changes between policy states in either composition or time.

Three frameworks

The above discussion brings us back to understanding public policy as something that both changes and endures over time and the need to explain why change or stability occurs. The prescriptive orthodox or classic view of policy is that public policy is a choice that occurs as a result of a rational process. According to Stone (2001: 7) 'the model of policy making in the rationality project is a production model, where policy is created in a fairly ordered sequence of stages, almost as if on an assembly line'. Such ideas have an enormous 'textbook' influence, particularly in tourism management texts. However, the notion of a 'policy cycle' which imagines the policy process as an endless cycle of policy decisions, implementation, and assessment has its base in Easton's (1966) systems model of politics which specified the functioning input, throughput, output, and feedback mechanisms operating within broader 'environments' (ecological, biological, social, personality). Undoubtedly, such models which have diffused through the policy literature (e.g. Hogwood and Gunn, 1984) have been a useful heuristic device, primarily because such 'stages' models have helped to stress the importance of process in public policy making that operates across various institutions rather than just concentrating on single institutions, e.g. parliament or public opinion, significant as these might be. Nevertheless, such models have significant weaknesses.

Policy cycle models fail to embrace the complexity of the policy making process and the reality that policy rarely, if ever, develops in a linear progression. Stages are often skipped or compressed and the idiosyncrasies, interests, preset dispositions, policy paradigms or mental maps of the actors involved often usurp the sense of a smooth process. There are a multitude of different processes at different scales and at different speeds occurring simultaneously.

(Kay, 2006: 9)

The complexity of tourism politics and policymaking and its seeming irrationality has been conveyed in a number of studies (e.g. Hall, 1994, 2002, 2008; Dredge and Jenkins, 2007). Nevertheless, rational models still tend to be strongly supported by tourism policy actors such as governments and the UNWTO (Hall, 2008). Jenkins-Smith and Sabatier (1993) identify six serious limitations with the stages model in explaining change:

1. Most importantly, the stages model is not causal at all.

2. Because it lacks causal mechanisms it does not provide a clear basis for empirical hypothesis testing.

3. There is a descriptive inaccuracy in the sequencing of stages starting with agenda setting and passing through policy formulation, implementation, and evaluation as deviations are frequent.

4. It suffers from an inherent top-down focus that neglects other actors in the policy process.

5. The approach inappropriately emphasises the policy cycle as the temporal unit of evaluation. Policy evolution usually involves multiple cycles that interact with each other across multiple levels of government.

6. It fails to provide a good vehicle for integrating the roles of policy analysis and policy-oriented learning throughout the public policy process.

The latter point is especially significant for tourism because policy initiatives in one country or jurisdiction may be copied by another (Hall and Williams, 2008). Given this criticism of the classic rational model of public policy making what other frameworks may be available?

Table 2.1 outlines three conceptions of the policy process including the rational stages model as well as the advocacy coalition framework (ACF) approach and the argumentative turn (AT). Although work associated with the argumentative turn entails an outright rejection of what is seen as the fundamental positivism of the stages model, the ACF represents something of a bridge between the two, recognising the fact of advocacy and trying to account empirically for success or failure in advancing their preferences and achieving policy change (Burton, 2006: 179).

The ACF approach understands policy change over time as a function of three sets of processes. In the first set of processes change arises from the interactions of competing *advocacy coalitions* within a policy system. An advocacy coalition consists 'of actors from a variety of public and private institutions at all levels of government who share a set of basic beliefs (policy goals plus causal and other perceptions) and who seek to manipulate the rules, budgets and personnel of government institutions in order to achieve these goals over time' (Jenkins-Smith and Sabatier, 1993: 4). In tourism there is usually a very strong coalition between various tourism businesses as an advocacy coalition for benefits for the tourism industry (Hall, 1999; Dredge and Jenkins, 2007).

Table 2.1: Conceptions of the public policy process

Model	Rational stages model	Advocacy coalition framework	Argumentative turn
Understanding of policy making	Policy is made through a logical series of stages by legitimately elected decision makers.	Policies are the product of competition among advocacy coalitions in which the rules of the game are determined by relatively stable political, social and economic structures.	Policies should be the product of democratic deliberation.
Notion of how change occurs	Evidence enters at every stage, from problem framing, through solution generation and alternative testing, to evaluation.	The most powerful collection of interests will have the greatest influence on determining the direction and nature of change.	Development of shared understanding of issues, problems and ways of solving them.
Exemplars	Easton, 1966; Hogwood and Gunn, 1984	Sabatier and Jenkins-Smith, 1993, 1999	Fischer, 2003

The second set of processes concerns *changes external to the subsystem*, e.g. socio-economic conditions, external shocks, system-wide governing coalitions, and output from other subsystems that provide opportunities and obstacles to the competing coalitions. Examples here would include the impact of the September 11 terrorist attacks in the United States on the management of tourist entry into the United States or the impact of financial and economic crisis on policy making in general. Sabatier and Jenkins-Smith (1999: 123) argue that policy-oriented learning tends only to affect the secondary belief systems of policy actors, while their core beliefs only change in the face of external shocks or 'non-cognition factors external to the sub-system'.

The third set of processes concerns the effects of *stable system parameters*, e.g. constitutional rules, political culture, on the constraints and resources of the various subsystem actors. For example, in the United States the political and legal culture allows a far greater opportunity for environmental and public interest groups to legally challenge tourism development proposals on environmental grounds or to mount public protests as compared to authoritarian regimes where protests may be banned and there is little or no legal recourse to oppose development. Under the ACF approach therefore:

> *Policy is more like an endless game of monopoly than sewing machine repair. Hence the common complaint that policies never seem to solve anything. The process of choosing and implementing the means of policy is political and contentious. The actions we commonly call 'new policies' are really somebody's new move, and in politics, as in a good game, nobody's move completely determines anybody else's future move.*
>
> *(Stone, 2001: 208)*

Although the ACF goes beyond the limitations of the stages model and some of its questionable assumptions of political neutrality and rational behaviour, for many researchers in public policy it still does not go far enough in acknowledging the social construction of reality in policy processes and the epistemological impossibility of objective knowledge (Burton, 2006). Therefore, in the late 1980s and 1990s public policy analysis took an 'argumentative turn' (AT) in which the importance of rhetoric and debate was high-lighted (Fischer and Forester, 1993). For Fischer (2003) public policy analysis should not serve 'intentionally or unintentionally to facilitate and bolster bureaucratic governance' nor 'serve as an ideology that masks elite political and bureaucratic interests' (2003: 14), but should instead 'provide access and explanation of data to all parties, to empower the public to understand analyses, and to promote serious public discourse' (2003: 15).

Each framework provides different insights into tourism politics and public policy. Theory choice is ultimately driven by the questions posed and answers sought by the policy analyst (Majone, 1989; Hall, 2008). However, the selection of theory and assumptions that are used will also determine the answers that are found with respect to explaining change. For example, Allison's (1971) classic study of the Cuban Missile Crisis developed two new theoretical approaches, an organisational process model and a bureaucratic policy model, to compete with the then prevalent rational actor model of foreign policy making. Allison illustrated how each approach could provide an equally coherent basis with which to explain the processes and events in political and policy-making terms. Therefore, in many cases and depending on the circumstances, different models of policy-making may provide equally good accounts of explaining change. Ideally, students of tourism who wish to examine and explain why and how change has occurred need to be familiar with a range of different theoretical approaches. Nevertheless, what the different approaches also do is focus on particular variables as part of the explaining change. For example, with reference to the frameworks discussed above, the ACT emphasises the role of interest groups and individuals and their relative power in explaining change as well as the role of external shock. The AT focuses more on communication and the creation of space for knowledge transfer and participation, though it also acknowledges the role of power. In contrast, the stages approach empha-sises rational decision-making by key actors and institutions.

Tourism and politics as an 'endless game of monopoly'

If tourism politics and policy are more like an endless game of Monopoly it surely becomes important for researchers to try and understand the way in which the rules of the game are structured and how this might affect policy discourse (including the relative influence of different researchers and research approaches) as well as who are the winners and losers. Unfortunately, this is not something that is done very effectively. Most accounts of tourism-related political change actually fail to account for the mul-tiple levels at which public policy operates, which means that not only are the different temporalities of change not sufficiently appreciated but that the potential multiple influences and reasons for change are not addressed. For example, Hall (2002) argued that the impacts of the September 11 terrorist attacks on tourism policy needed to be understood within the context of how issues get to be on the policy agenda as part of the issue–attention cycle (Downs, 1972). This means addressing how tourism security issues are then 'solved' given that the stringency of application of security measures has previously ebbed and flowed in light of responses to terrorist attacks and hijackings and perceptions of risk and security and subsequent commercial and consumer pressures for convenient and cheaper travel (Hall, 2002).

This chapter has utilised an understanding of public policy theory to emphasise that change is actually the norm in politics and policy, including in tourism. While the focus is often on external events or shocks to the tourism policy system as a change factor, the reality is that the multi-layered levels of policy processes are probably more important in explaining change. This is especially the case given that tourism policy and politics represent only a small subset of the wider field of political arenas and policy advocacy coalitions that will actually affect tourism. Moreover, many studies of change actually do not consider fully the way in which temporality will affect understandings of change nor the importance of the selection of a theoretical framework, especially if it is implicit in policy structures. The changing interplay of tourism and politics and policy means that it is vital for students of tourism to understand the rules of the game by which they are played and how, even if the rules are different from one location to another, the game still goes on.

References

Allison, G. Jr. (1971) *Essence of Decision: Explaining the Cuban Missile Crisis*, Boston, MA: Little Brown.

Bonham, C. and Mak, J. (1996) 'Private versus public financing of state destination promotion', *Journal of Travel Research*, **35** (2), 2–10.

Burton, P. (2006) 'Modernising the policy process. Making policy research more significant?' *Policy Studies*, **27** (3), 173–195.

Downs, A. (1972) 'Up and down with ecology: the issue-attention cycle,' *The Public Interest*, **28** (Summer), 8–50.

Dredge, D. and Jenkins, J. (2007) *Tourism Planning and Policy*, Wiley.

Dye, T. (1992) *Understanding Public Policy*, 7th edn, Prentice Hall.

Easton, D. (1966) *A Systems Approach to Political Life*, West Lafayettte, IN: Purdue University Press.

Edgell, D.L. (1990) *International Tourism Policy*, New York: Van Nostrand Reinhold.

Edgell, D.L., Allen, M.D., Smith, G. and Swanson, J. (2007) *Tourism Policy and Planning: Yesterday, Today and Tomorrow*, Oxford: Butterworth-Heinemann.

Fischer, F. (2003) *Reframing Public Policy: Discursive Politics and Deliberative Practices*, Oxford: Oxford University Press.

Fischer, F. and Forester, J. (eds) (1993) *The Argumentative Turn In Policy Analysis and Planning*, Durham, NC: Duke University Press.

Hall, C.M. (1994) *Tourism and Politics: Power, Policy and Place*, Chichester: John Wiley.

Hall, C.M. (1999) 'Rethinking collaboration and partnership: A public policy perspective', *Journal of Sustainable Tourism*, **7** (3/4), 274–289.

Hall, C.M. (2002) 'Travel safety, terrorism and the media: The significance of the issue-attention cycle', *Current Issues in Tourism*, **5** (5), 458–466.

Hall, C.M. (2008) *Tourism Planning: Policies, Processes and Relationships*, 2nd edn, Pearson Education.

Hall, C.M. and Jenkins, J.M. (1995) *Tourism and Public Policy*, London: Routledge.

Hall, C.M. and Jenkins, J.M. (2004) 'Tourism and public policy', in Lew, A., Hall C.M. and Williams, A.M. (eds), *Companion to Tourism*, Oxford: Blackwells, pp. 525– 40.

Hall, C.M. & Lew, A. (2009) *Understanding and Managing Tourism Impacts: An Integrated Approach*, Routledge, London.

Hall, C.M. and Williams, A.M. (2008) *Tourism and Innovation*, London: Routledge.

Hirschmann, A.O. and Lindblom, C.E. (1962) 'Economic development, research and development: some converging views', *Behavioural Science*, 7, 211–222.

Hogwood, B.W. and Gunn, L.A. (1984) *Policy Analysis for the Real World*, Oxford: Oxford University Press.

Jenkins-Smith, H.C. and Sabatier, P.A. (1993) 'The study of public policy processes', in Sabatier, P.A. and Jenkins-Smith, H.C. (eds), *Policy Change and Learning: An Advocacy Coalition Approach*, Boulder, CO: Westview Press, pp. 1–9.

Kay, A. (2006) *The Dynamics of Public Policy: Theory and Evidence*, Cheltenham: Edward Elgar.

Kraft, M.E. and Furlong, S.R. (2007) *Public Policy: Politics, Analysis, and Alternatives*, 2nd edn, CQ Press.

Lasswell, H.D. (1958) *Politics: Who Gets What, When, How*, Gloucester, MA: Peter Smith Publisher.

Majone, G. (1980) 'The uses of policy analysis', in Raven, B.H. (ed.), *Policy Studies Review Annual*, Vol. 4 pp. 161–180, Sage.

Majone, G. (1989) *Evidence, Argument and Persuasion in the Policy Process*, Yale University Press.

Milward, H.B. (1996) 'Symposium on the hollow state: capacity, control and performance in interorganizational settings', *Journal of Public Administration Research and Theory*, 6 (2), 193–195.

Pal, L.A. (1992) *Public Policy Analysis: An Introduction*, Toronto: Nelson.

Pierson, P. (2004) *Politics in Time: History, Institutions and Social Analysis*, Princeton, Princeton University Press.

Pressman, J.L. and Wildavsky, A.B. (1973) *Implementation*, Berkeley: University of California Press.

Rhodes, R.A.W. (1997) 'From marketisation to diplomacy: It's the mix that matters', *Australian Journal of Public Administration*, 56 (2), 40–53.

Sabatier, P.A. and Jenkins-Smith, H.C. (eds) (1993) *Policy Change and Learning: An Advocacy Coalition Approach*, Boulder, CO: Westview Press.

Sabatier, P. and Jenkins-Smith, H. (1999) 'The advocacy coalition framework: an assessment', in Sabatier, P. (ed.), *Theories of the Policy Process*, Boulder, CO: Westview Press, pp. 117–66,

Saul, J.R. (1995) *The Unconscious Civilization*, Toronto: House of Anansi Press.

Stone, D. (2001) *Policy Paradox and Political Reason*, 3rd edn, New York: W.W. Norton and Company.

Wilson, W.W. (1887) 'The study of administration', *Political Science Quarterly*, 2, 197–222.

Part I
Unification/
Reunification

3 German Reunification and Tourism in Berlin

Wantanee Suntikul

Introduction

Perhaps more so than any other city, Berlin has been affected by most major global political events of the 20th century. The two World Wars, the Cold War, and the rise and fall of Communism were experienced with unusual immediacy in the city. Berlin's development from the Second World War until German Reunification in 1990 was largely determined by Germany's membership in two anomalous 'families' of political units symptomatic of the global political map of the time: quasi-states and Soviet satellite states. Since German Reunification, Berlin has experienced an unprecedented phase of growth, accompanied by an increase in popularity with tourists, both German and foreign. With more than 17 million overnight stays in 2008, Berlin has become one of Germany's most-visited tourist destinations (http://www.visitberlin.de/reiseindustrie/index.en.php? seite= ueberuns_btm).

The focus of this chapter is to examine the relationship between political differences and change and tourism development in Berlin. This involves a comparison of patterns of tourism in the two halves of the city in the period preceding the fall of the Berlin Wall, especially the decade immediately preceding 1990, and noting how patterns have changed in each of the two halves in the two decades since reunification.

Tourism development

Both East Berlin and West Berlin were fragments of a previous whole, and both claimed to be the true heir of the pre-war metropolis of Berlin. West Berlin had lost its importance as the economic, commercial and political centre of Germany (commerce moving to Hamburg, finance to Frankfurt and the government to Bonn) and found itself in need of a new definition. East Berlin retained the central function which greater Berlin had had in Hitler's Reich, making a 'rewriting' of the symbolic significance of the city even more important (Merritt, 1986). Berlin increasingly became the subject of competing claims of proprietorship over its parts and its future. West Berlin was advertised as the *Bollwerk der Freiheit* (bulwark of freedom) while East Berlin depicted itself as a *Stadt des Friedens* (city of peace). Tourism development and marketing in both halves of Berlin can be seen as components and expressions of these two political and economic visions of the city.

Tourism development in West Berlin

The tenuous position of West Berlin and its dependent relationship with West Germany (also called the Federal Republic of Germany (FRG)) and the Western international community was illustrated by the Soviet blockade of the city and the Berlin airlift of 1948/49. The Berlin Traffic Authority (Verkehrsamt Berlin) was founded in West Berlin after the lifting of the Soviet blockade in June 1949 and entrusted with the rebuilding of a functioning transport network in West Berlin, and also with marketing the city as a safe, normal, world-class city comparable with London or New York (Poock-Feller, 1996).

The first marketing campaign for West Berlin was aimed at the US market and brazenly presented the difficult situation of the city as its unique selling point: the chance to experience first-hand the confrontation between two systems and ideologies which defined the global political geography of the time. The view over the Berlin Wall was a central experience of any West Berlin visit. Publicity measures within West Germany, however, concentrated on attracting meetings and conferences (Heineberg, 1977). Thus, the Wall played an ambivalent role in the tourism image of West Berlin. It was a universally recognised landmark and the most visible manifestation of the city's unique selling point, while at the same time standing as the most blatant contradiction of any pretence of 'normality'.

Eberhard Diepgen, mayor of West Berlin (1984–89) and of reunified Berlin (1991–2001) attributed a high political significance to tourism, equating an increase in tourism figures with an improvement in the perceived image of the city, and acknowledging Berlin's isolated condition and the need to always give tourists new reasons to visit the city. The status of the city as a conference and fair centre was crucial in providing such incentives for return visits and new guests. This meant as well that the fortunes of the entire Berlin tourist market were largely dependent on an ever-renewing string of events to attract visitors. The path of tourism development in West Berlin from the division of the city until reunification must be judged as successful, especially in light of the geographical and political handicaps that had to be overcome. In 1963, West Berlin ranked seventh among the FRG's cities in terms of tourist arrivals. By 1988 it was second.

Tourism development in East Berlin

The tourism industry of East Germany (the German Democratic Republic, orGRD) fell under the control of a small number of government monopolies. The controlling body for tourism in the GDR was the Ministry of Transport. The Reisebüro der DDR (Travel Office of the GDR) was the organ within the Ministry of Transport, which had direct jurisdiction over tourism planning and development for the entire country. The Reisebüro itself controlled the booking of only the more exclusive travel and accommodation. The Handelsorganisation or HO (Commercial Organisation) ran hotels and other establishments such as restaurants, bars, cafés and nightclubs. The Interhotel Association offered high-end accommodation, aimed mainly at the foreign market. There were also Intershops and Intercamping facilities, which attracted hard foreign currency by offering higher quality goods and services than were normally available in the GDR.

Coordinated marketing of East Berlin as a destination began in 1957 with the founding of the city marketing authority Berlin-Werbung Berolina. Poock-Feller (1996) has described tourism marketing in the early days of East Berlin as a component of the conception of the city itself as a propaganda tool and showplace for the success of socialism. An attempt in the 1960s to reduce the pedagogical tone of city marketing in East Berlin and communicate a more visceral, less cerebral, image of a bustling, exciting metropolis, was short-lived. In 1967, city marketing was re-integrated into the propaganda apparatus in a conscious effort to distinguish East Berlin from the capitalist West.

The Reisebüro der DDR organised tours in East Berlin for foreign groups, often with themes addressing special cultural or professional interests. To this end, the Reisebüro entered into co-operation with Berlin's Interhotels, the state airline Interflug and attractions such as the Television Tower (Fernseheturm). About a third of all tours in East Berlin, however, originated in non-socialist countries or West Berlin (Bräuninger, 1986). Most Western visitors to East Berlin came as part of such a package tour, individual travel having been discouraged by the GDR authorities.

Excursions into East Berlin by Western tour operators in the 1950s tended to feature areas of the capital which were less than flattering to the GDR, such as areas where the rubble from the Second World War had not yet been cleaned up, confirming a condescending view of the East harboured by many Westerners. The Eastern authorities reacted by regulating and then forbidding the tour operators from including such sites on their routes.

The fall of the Wall

On November 9, 1989, the East German government announced the lifting of all exit requirements and guaranteed the granting of exit visas upon request at all border crossings. Within a week of the announcement of this policy, the border police had granted 8,626,047 visas and 14,669 permits for permanent emigration out of the GDR (Neues Deutschland, 10/11/89, 19/11/89). The loosening of travel restrictions brought about the greatest and most sudden change in tourism patterns in the history of the GDR, not only in volume of travel but also in the internal re-organisation of the country's tourism policy. A GDR Ministry of Tourism was established for the first time in November 1989 to address the great increase in both incoming and outgoing travel and to realise the economic potential of tourism by overseeing its change from a centrally planned activity to a growing sector in a market economy. This task, which included the preparations for the privatisation of the GDR's tourism enterprises, was undertaken in cooperation with the West German Ministry of Economics (Benthien, 2000).

Tourism development in post-reunification Berlin

The merging of the tourism infrastructures and markets of the two Berlins, and the two Germanies, was not immediate. Many established patterns remained, even in the absence of the constraints that had generated them. During the first years of the reunited Germany, for instance, curious Western tourists tended to stay in hotels in West Berlin and visit the East on day excursions, discouraged by the perception of an inferior tourism infrastructure in the East. Other patterns, however, were changed radically by Reunification. In 1989, 6.5 million of the 8.8 million guests arriving in the GDR came from socialist countries, but in 1990, only one million visitors arrived from socialist countries, the introduction of the Western Deutschmark having made prices prohibitively high for many in this target group (Hill, 1993).

The process of developing the tourism infrastructure in the East received extensive financial support from the German federal government. In 1991, 500 tourism projects in Germany were assisted financially, 80% of which were also eligible for ERP (European Recovery Program) loans of up to 40% of total investment (Schnell, 1998). Between 1990 and 1998, 7.6 billion marks (US$4.3 billion by 1998 exchange rate) out of a total 20 billion marks (US$11.4 billion) invested in tourism development in the former East Germany came from government funds. It is estimated that this development created or protected about 43,000 jobs in the hotel and catering trade and about 7000 jobs in other tourism-related services (Benthien, 2000). Besides financial support, the tourism industry in the eastern states of Germany needed to be improved to Western standards and practices. Godau (1991) saw the transfer of such knowledge as the most important requirement for the development of tourism in the new *Länder* (German states).

Berlin enjoys a reputation as a young city: new in itself and attractive to young people. As the 5th largest economic sector in Berlin, tourism is of great importance to the city's economy and image, and 7.7 billion marks in yearly sales and 50,000 jobs in Berlin are attributable to tourism. The image of Berlin has benefited from Reunification. The optimism and dynamism of a city-on-the-make has led to the phenomenon of 'Reunification tourism' (*Vereinigungstourismus*), comparable to the 'Wall tourism' (*Mauertourismus*) in West Berlin until 1989. As the situation in the city has normalised, however, Berlin has been faced once again with the question of how to position itself in the world market in the long term (Schloemp, 1994). To this end, the city marketing firm Berliner Tourismus Marketing was established in 1993.

Air transport in divided Berlin

After the Second World War, the German aviation industry was outlawed and only the occupying allies flew into and out of Berlin. Each of the Western occupying powers had its own airport, at Tempelhof (American sector), Tegel (French) and Gatow (British) respectively. Three air corridors set up for allied flights between Berlin and Hamburg, Hanover and Frankfurt as part of the 1946 Air Safety Agreement between the four occupying powers remained in effect until the Reunification, attaining their greatest importance during the Berlin airlift of 1948/49. Because airlines required nomination by the Western allies to fly these corridors, only American (Pan Am), French (Air France) and British (British (European) Airways) carriers served West Berlin. Even Lufthansa was excluded from West Berlin's airports (Elkins and Hofmeister, 1988, Treibel, 1992). The Soviet occupying forces used an airfield to the southeast of the city at Schönefeld. This airport was officially handed over to the GDR on April 1995 and became the hub of the East German national airline Interflug, served by most of the world's socialist state airlines as well as carriers from the Middle East and some non-socialist European countries such as Austria, Finland and Belgium.

During the division, the airports of West Berlin were 'dead ends'. With the air corridors all leading westwards to the Federal Republic of Germany, a function as a transfer point became all but impossible. Interflug and state airlines from other socialist countries offered flights from Schönefeld at dumping prices as low as 25% of the fare proscribed by the IATA (International Air Transport Association), which had to be respected by the Western airlines but of which Interflug was not a member (Verkehr in Berlin, 1990; Bericht IHK, 1982; Bundesministerium für innerdeutsche Beziehung, 1985). Shuttle buses were provided between Schönefeld and West Berlin to expedite connections for Western tourists (Interflug, 1985) and an Interflug ticket office was set up in the part of the Friedrichstraße train station, which was accessible only to West Berliners (Bericht IHK, 1985). There was a special control point at Waltersdorfer Chaussee in West Berlin's southeast for access to Schönefeld. In 1985, nearly 400,000 people crossed at this point to and from the airport (Bericht IHK, 1986). In seeming contradiction to this discrepancy in Schönefeld's favour, however, only 2.1 million passengers passed through Schönefeld in 1981 compared to 4.4 million who used Tegel, indicating the far greater propensity for West Germans to travel, compared to East Germans (Elkins and Hofmeister, 1988) reflecting also East German government restrictions on its citizens' movement.

Air transport in post-reunification Berlin

With Reunification, Germany regained jurisdiction over all of Berlin's airports and airways. In an agreement whereby German carriers were to take over all domestic flights to and from Berlin by 1993, Lufthansa was granted all the routes formerly flown by Pan Am, which constituted the majority of flights. The former East German airport at Schönefeld experienced a 31.6% decrease in passengers in 1990. The introduction of the West German mark in the former East led to an increase, in real terms, in the cost of travel for the primarily Eastern European customer base of the airport and discouraged travel. The growing tendency of East Germans to travel to the West caused a shift to the more westward-oriented Tegel.

In 1990, the German federal government recommended the termination of Interflug, rather than spend the estimated 200 million marks needed to keep the decaying airline operating until the end of 1991. Interflug stopped operations in 1991 (Bericht IHK, 1991; Treuhandanstalt, 1994). Schönefeld was privatised in 1994 with a new Board of Directors (Treuhandanstalt, 1994).

Accommodation in West Berlin

After the Berlin airlift the Western half of Berlin enjoyed a special status and relied on subsidies from local and national government bodies for its very existence and the maintenance of a symbolic semblance of Western urban normality in defiance of its isolated 'island' location. This can be said for the development of the accommodation sector in particular, in which practically every major trend between the 1960s and German Reunification coincided with a governmental initiative or programme.

Until the Second World War, the Western part of Berlin was not an important location for hotels, most of which were concentrated around the city centre in what was to become East Berlin. Even until the mid-1950s, West Berlin had fewer than 6000 hotel beds with an occupancy rate of only 39% (IHK, Die Berliner Wirtschaft, Nr. 25, 1972 quoted in Heineberg, 1977:85). The Berlin Internationale Bauausstellung (IBA or International Building Exhibition) of 1959, served as an impetus for the development of both the tourism industry and the built environment of the city. Fifteen million marks in credits made possible an increase to a total of over 8000 beds and an improvement in existing facilities (Heineberg, 1977; Elkins and Hofmeister, 1988). Hotels and other businesses in West Berlin also benefited from tax breaks simply by virtue of their location in the city.

A Senate-sponsored hotel-building programme in the early 1970s foresaw the creation of another 1500 beds by 1975 (Der Senat von Berlin, 1973 quoted in Heineberg, 1977). Between 1950 and 1973, the number of overnight stays in West Berlin grew fivefold, before levelling-off around one million in the early 1970s (Heineberg, 1977).

The city was a popular destination for short breaks, and a sizeable number of students and workers occupied the less costly hotels during the week and returned to their homes in West Germany for the weekend (Elkins and Hofmeister, 1988). Hotels in West Berlin were also used as a base for Western tourists visiting East Berlin on a day trip. Following the release of an unfavourable assessment of West Berlin's hotels in a consumer report (*Stiftung Warentest*) of 1985, the Berlin Senate once again offered support in the form of favourable interest rates for financing modernisation measures (Bericht IHK, 1986).

Accommodation in East Berlin

Like all aspects of tourism, and all facets of society in the GDR, the supply and structure of the accommodation market was centralised and highly politicised. The government tourism agencies – the Free German Trade Union Association (FDGB) and the Reisebüro der DDR – had a monopoly on the booking of the complete accommodation network for GDR citizens as well as for foreigners.

One-third of the FDGB-booked rooms were in lodgings owned by the FDGB. The other two-thirds were in contractually administered recreation homes (*Betriebserholungsheime*), hotels and high-end Interhotels. In 1979, a night in an FDGB establishment cost between 30 and 170 marks for trade union members and 120 to 250 marks for others, who were able to stay only as family members of a trade unionist. Places in FDGB accommodations were highly subsidised. This, combined with limited supply and relatively high prices of hotels, was part of the state policy of discouraging individual travel and keeping citizens in the controlled, supervised environment of group tourism homes (Mellor, 1991: 150).

From 1980 until 1987, there were only three years in which the Travel Office of the GDR organised accommodation for East German citizens in Berlin, and the numbers from these years were negligible (29 guests in 1983, 45 in 1984, and 119 in 1987). Despite a steep increase during the next two years (841 guests in 1988, and 1771 in 1989) (Statistische Zentralverwaltung für Statistik, 1980-1988, Zahlen und Fakten, 1990), the figures never grew to represent an appreciable percentage of the city's capacity. The Reisebüro der DDR offered higher-standard luxury accommodations. Although East Germans were not explicitly excluded from most of the hotels booked by this office, the prices were prohibitively high for the majority of GDR citizens, and most of these luxury accommodation places were reserved for foreigners paying with convertible currencies.

A distinction was made between public and non-public (*öffentliche* and *nicht öffentliche*) types of accommodation, i.e. between establishments open to all people and those intended specifically for a certain narrowly-defined group, such as quarters owned and run by specific trades or enterprises for their own workers. Most public accommodations were run by the state Commercial Organisation (HO) or local government administrations. Five-star class hotels (Grand Hotel, Hotel Metropol and Palast Hotel) were administered by the Interhotel Association. Western standard hotels in East Berlin realised an advantage from the city's adjacency to West Berlin. On the occasion of important popular fairs in West Berlin, such as the *Grüne Woche* (Agricultural Fair) or the *Funkausstellung* (Telecommunications Fair), hotels in the East benefited from excess visitors unable to find a room in the overbooked accommodation network of the West Berlin (Vetter, 1984, quoted in Elkins and Hofmeister, 1988:155).

Accommodation in post-reunification Berlin

The year 1990 saw a shift of most GDR tourism enterprises from government to private hands (Bericht IHK, 1991; Benthien, 2000). The Treuhandanstalt, the agency responsible for the privatisation of East German property, administered around 300 former HO hotels, 1700 state vacation establishments and 800 union holiday homes in East Germany. International hotel chains and private developers were quick to recognise the opportunities presented in the freshly opened eastern *Bezirke* (districts) of the city. The city government also gave high priority to development in the accommodation sector and a working group was formed to expedite building projects. Despite this development-friendly climate, many projects were delayed by the bureaucracies of the individual *Bezirke* and complications in building permit review and approval (Bericht IHK, 1992).

At the end of 1991, 22 hotels and hotel extensions were under construction in Berlin, with a further 59 pending permit and 26 more submitted for pre-permit approval, which would add a total of around 5000 rooms (Bericht IHK, 1992). At the beginning of 1993, Berlin had a supply of over 42,500 beds in 453 accommodation facilities, which grew in the 1990s, to 504 facilities and nearly 56,000 beds in 1999 (Statistisches Monatsschrift, 2000). The prevalence of large units, already present on both sides of the Wall in the 1980s, continued to hold true, with 14 hotels with 500 beds or more accounting for a quarter of Berlin's beds in 1994 (Schloemp, 1994, Tourismus in Berlin, 1990). By April of 2009, Berlin had 101,500 beds in 668 accommodation facilities (Berlin Tourismus: Press Information: 16 June 2009).

Government tax incentives were offered to spur hotel development throughout Germany, especially in the East. Critics claimed that this would lead to an overcapacity, as seems to be the case in the Eastern *Bundesländer* as a whole, where a 22% increase in capacity between 1992 and 2000 far exceeded the actual growth in overnights of 1.4%. The consequences are visible in the fall of the occupancy rate from 40.3% in 1992 to 32.2% in 1998 (Marvel, 2000). The rapid expansion in the accommodation sector has also been present in Berlin, and oversupply has led to a decrease in the average room price in past years. However, even within the economic downturn at the time of this writing, the number of accommodation beds in Berlin increased 8.3% from April 2008 to April 2009, with an occupancy rate of 51.9% (ibid.).

Attractions in West Berlin

Except for conferences and fairs, West Berlin had little business tourism. The city also lacked the benefit of a mutually supporting relationship with its surrounding area, in terms of attracting and providing for tourists (Elkins and Hofmeister, 1988). West Berlin had more of a reputation as a peripheral area than as a centre, which made it an attractive destination for youth and those travellers who saw themselves as a members of a counterculture, as well as those seeking to experience first-hand the extreme geopolitical situation made so tangible in West Berlin by the Berlin Wall.

By 1987, the 'Berlin Programme' city entertainment guide contained listings for fifty different museums and thirty-five special exhibitions in West Berlin, and many smaller private and independent galleries. Initially, though, West Berlin lacked the inheritance of museums, buildings, and cultural institutions present in the East and had to construct the edifices of its cultural landscape over the years. Berlin's 'Culture Forum' (Kulturforum) is a cluster of freestanding modern structures housing the New National Gallery, the Philharmonic Hall and Chamber Music Hall, the State Library and the Museum of Applied Arts lying adjacent to the former site of Postdamer Platz, on the 'edge of Berlin'.

Although a theatre scene emerged in West Berlin after the war, it could never regain the national pre-eminence of Berlin theatre in the lively pre-war period. In 1987, West Berlin's 19 theatres played to combined yearly audiences of over 2.3 million. Even the city's private theatres were government-subsidised. Government subsidies of theatres in West Berlin amounted to more than 100 million marks yearly (750 Years Berlin, 1987).

West Berlin's zoo (*Zoologischer Garten*) opened in 1844 as one of the first public zoos in the world. After decimation of the zoo's animal population in the Second World War, the zoo was slowly restored once more to world prominence. Benefiting from its proximity to its namesake central train station of the city, *Bahnhof Berlin Zoologischer Garten*, this remained a must-see attraction, housing more than 4,500 animals and receiving over 2,600,000 visitors in 1989, the year before Reunification (Statistisches Jahrbuch der DDR, 1990).

The Berlin Wall was the star attraction on the West Berlin tourist circuit. The Museum at Checkpoint Charlie, with its exhibits about the Wall and the various escape attempts and successes from East to West Berlin, was another mandatory stop. Viewing platforms were set up at various locations to allow views into 'the other side' and private or organised day trips into East Berlin were also popular. The area along the side of the Wall facing West Berlin was extremely desolate, reflecting the policy of the FRG government of forbidding any structure which would stand in the way of a speedy rejoining of the two halves of the city (Elkin and Hofmeister, 1988).

Attractions in East Berlin

East Berlin, containing the central districts of the historical city, also contained the majority of the cultural institutions of the pre-war capital. The 1987 edition of the 'Berlin Programme' enumerated 20 museums, 16 special exhibitions and 19 smaller galleries (750 Years Berlin, 1987).

In keeping with the city's function as a cultural magnet for the nation and for foreign tourists, music and theatre in East Berlin received considerable government financial support. Demand for performances at the *Schauspielhaus*, the *Berlin Ensemble*, and the *Komische Oper*, for instance, was very high. Tickets were very hard to come by, most having been bought in advance by trade unions for their members and by western travel agencies, which offered them to tourists paying hard currency (Elkins and Hofmeister, 1988). The preference given to foreigners resulted in high prices (although low by international standards) and a low supply for GDR citizens (Bräuninger, 1986). The most renowned museums of the East stood together on the so-called Museum Island in the Spree River in central Berlin.

The function of East Berlin in the Cold War period as a showcase to the world justified the large sums spent on city-beautification measures as well as cultural and entertainment facilities and food and consumer goods in the capital city, as compared to other locations in the GDR. The GDR government recognised its inheritance of historical buildings as an important component of East Berlin's attractiveness, and spent heavily on restoration programmes, especially for the boulevard Unter den Linden and its immediate surroundings (Kerpel, 1990) such as the German State Opera and Schinkel's Schauspielhaus. The 18-metre red granite statue of Lenin on Leninallee and the huge memorial to the Soviet soldiers who fell in the siege of Berlin were two of the best-known monuments, which featured prominently in tourism promotion material and served as the focus for government-organised mass events.

The Berlin Television Tower (Fernsehturm) has been a notable landmark in Berlin since its construction in 1965–69 because of its striking form, its soaring height and its prominent position directly on Alexanderplatz at the centre of East Berlin. A ride to its observation platform was an essential component of a trip to Berlin and often figured in the itineraries of visiting heads of state and other luminaries. Domestic tourists and tour groups from other socialist countries accounted for most of the visitors (averaging 1.3 million a year) in the tower. Tourists from the West were rare (personal communication, 2001).

Attractions in post-reunification Berlin

The physical change in Berlin since Reunification has been at a rapidity and scale without equal in Europe. Many of the monuments, which formed the foci of the East Berlin urban geography have been removed and many streets renamed to purge references to communist figures. Demolition of the Palast der Republik, the Parliament building of East Germany, a locus for many tourism-relevant functions in East Berlin, was completed in 2008. Meanwhile, new districts are springing up on former wastelands, shifting the points of reference within the urban fabric for residents as well as tourists.

The combination of the cultural and entertainment facilities of the two quasi-cities into one has enriched the depth and variety of the city's offerings. At the same time, it has also led to a number of redundancies: functions or attractions which existed in similar or contradictory forms in East Berlin and West Berlin now competing for visitors, publicity and funding. Berlin's three opera houses illustrate this point. The State Opera and the Comic Opera in East Berlin and the German Opera in West Berlin, accustomed to the preferred status in the government funding policies of their respective former countries, are now facing the possibility of closure by a financially-strapped federal government which does not see the need for three state-funded opera houses in a single city. The same situation also applied to the two zoos, Zoologischer Garten in the West and Tierpark in the East, both of which have lost government subsidies (Frädrich, 2001).

With the fall of the Wall and Reunification, all contracts between the Television Tower and central tourism organisations became invalid, removing the source of almost 100% of the attraction's users. The demographics of the visitors to the Television Tower changed immediately with the removal of travel restrictions and the dissolution of the government monopolies. According to the manager, individual travellers and families accounted for 97% of all visits, with groups of more than 20 people making up only 3%.

New shopping and office buildings along Friedrichstraße by world-renowned architects have brought back some of the street's former consumerist flair. The *Hackesche Höfe*, a building complex with a series of interior courts (*Höfe*) previously famous for underground cultural events, has been commercialised and extensively renovated and now contain a collection of trendy shops, restaurants, galleries, cinemas and other uses and has become a popular spot for tourists.

Daimler Benz invested four billion marks, and Sony two billion, to build a new urban centre at Potsdamer Platz, on a site adjacent to the former path of the Berlin Wall that was nothing more than a desolate weed patch in 1990. With its office towers, cinema complex, restaurants and extensive shopping arcade, the new Potsdamer Platz is one of the main sightseeing attractions of the new Berlin.

The Berlin Wall – the defining structure of Berlin's urban fabric and one of its premier tourism sights, at least for Western tourists – was an early casualty of Reunification. The dismantling of the Wall began with the stretch between Friedrichstraße and the Brandenburg gate in March 1990, four months after the opening of the border. Initiatives for the preservation of parts of the inner-city wall as a reminder to future generations were outstripped by the sheer speed of progress of the demolition process. By the end of 1990, the Wall had disappeared, except for a 212-meter length between the residential districts of Wedding and Mitte and another, known as the 'East Side Gallery' which had been covered with mural paintings by famous and non-famous artists (Sälter, 2007: 11–17).

Conclusions

Since the immediate aftermath of the Second World War, Berlin has occupied a pivotal position in the political geography of Europe, and its fortunes have been a reflection in microcosm of the atmosphere of the continent as a whole. The divisions, controls, and mistrust of Cold War Europe were experienced by all visitors to East and West Berlin, just as a traveller coming to the German capital today encounters the growing-together of East and West and the rebirth of Germany at the middle of the new Europe.

The competition between Berlin and other cities for a share of tourism markets and a favoured position on the tourism map of the new Europe is also mirrored in the various locations and districts within Berlin itself. Competition between similar attractions and services in the two city-halves is fiercer and more direct now than before the German Reunification as noted above. It should be hoped that this competition will be met with inventive attempts to define niche markets and thereby enrich and diversity the city's offerings, rather than the demise of less competitive operators or attractions.

Although the distinction between 'East' and 'West' patterns is still useful and meaningful when speaking of patterns within the different facets of the tourism industry, the city as a whole is no longer divided into two separable markets and is characterised by complex relations of competition, co-operation and complementarity.

A central component of Berlin's attractiveness, before and since the fall of the Wall, has been the feeling of being in the place where the current situation of German and European history, policies, and society has been put on show and made tangible. The social freedoms associated with West Berlin and the socialist optimism for which East Berlin was a built advertisement were made more poignant by the Berlin Wall. The political changes of the late 20th century, accompanied by the symbolic removal of the physical barrier of the Wall, allowed the conversion of the static energy which existed in both city halves into the dynamic energy which is the defining factor of the fascination of Berlin at the present time. The return of the German federal government to Berlin, the proud presentation of new buildings and monuments as evidence of progress and the celebration of the centrality of the city as a symbol of the power and optimism with which the nation faces the world find no antecedents in pre-Reunification Berlin or the previous capital in Bonn.

Occurrences of the magnitude and consequence of the fall of the Berlin Wall and German Reunification cannot be expected to recur in Berlin in the near future, nor would one wish any further upheavals upon a city that has already survived more changes and traumas than most cities will ever have to face. The continued success of Berlin in the international tourism market will rely on the ability of the city to continue to capture the imagination of travellers in a global competitive free market.

References

Benthien, B. (2000) 'Tourism in Germany ten years after Reunification – problems and results of transformation', in Mayr, A. and Taubman, W. (eds), *Germany Ten Years after Reunification*, Leipzig: Institute für Länderkunde.

Bericht IHK 1981/82 Berlin (1982) Berlin: Industrie- und Handelskammer zu Berlin.

Bericht IHK 1984/85 Berlin (1985) Berlin: Industrie- und Handelskammer zu Berlin.

Bericht IHK 1985/86 Berlin (1986) Berlin: Industrie- und Handelskammer zu Berlin.

Bericht IHK 1990/91 Berlin (1991) Berlin: Industrie- und Handelskammer zu Berlin.

Bericht IHK 1991/92 Berlin (1992) Berlin: Industrie- und Handelskammer zu Berlin.

Berlin Tourismus, From: http://www.visitberlin.de/reiseindustrie/index.en.php?seite= ueberuns_btm (accessed 4 September 2009).

Berlin Tourismus: Press Information: 16/ 06/2009, From: http://www.visitberlin.de/ english/presse/download/e_pr_342_Aprilstatistik.pdf (accessed 4 September 2009)

Bräuninger, J. (1986) 'Development and organisation of the tourism in Berlin, capital of GDR', in Vetter, F. (ed.), *Big City Tourism*. Berlin: Dietrich Reimer, pp. 64–71.

Bundesministerium für innerdeutsche Beziehung (1985) *DDR Handbuch*, vol.1 A-L, Cologne: Wissenschaft und Politik.

Treuhandanstalt (1994) Dokumentation 1990-1994, Band 6 and 8, Berlin: Treuhandanstalt, pp.139–194, 980–993.

Elkins, T. and Hofmeister, B. (1988) *Berlin: The Spatial Structure of a Divided City*, London: Methuen.

Frädrich, H. (2001) 'Zoologischer Garten Berlin', in Bell, C. (ed.), *Encyclopedia of the World's Zoos*, Vol. 3, R-Z, London: Fitzroy Dearborn Publisher, pp. 1448–1452.

Godau, A. (1991) 'Tourism policy in the new Germany', *Tourism Management*, 12 (2), 145–149.

Heineberg, H. (1977) *Zentren in West- und Ost-Berlin: Untersuchungen zum Problem der Erfassung und Bewertung großstädtischer funktionaler Zentrenausstattungen in beiden Wirtschaft- und Gesellschaftssystemen Deutschlands*, Paderborn: Schöningh.

Hill, R. (1993) 'Tourism in Germany', in Pompl, W., and Larvery, P. (eds.), *Tourism in Europe: Structures and Developments*, Oxon: CAB International, pp. 219–241.

Kerpel, E. (1990) 'Tourism in Eastern Europe and the Soviet Union: prospects for growth and new market opportunities', *Economist Intelligence Unit, Special Report No. 2040*.

Mellor, R. (1991) 'Eastern Germany (The former German Democratic Republic)', in Hall, D. (ed.), *Tourism and Economic Development in Eastern Europe and the Soviet Union*, London: Belhaven, pp. 142–172.

Merritt, R. (1986) 'Postwar Berlin: Divided city', in Francisco, R.A. and Merritt, R.L. (eds), *Berlin between Two Worlds*, London: Westview, pp. 153–175.

Neues Deutschland, (East German Newspaper) (1989) November 10 and November 19.

Poock-Feller, U. (1996) "Berlin lebt–Berlin ruft". Die Frendenverkehr Werbung Ost- und West-Berlin, in der Nachkriegszeit, in Spode, H. (ed.), *Goldenstrand und Teutonengrill: Kultur- und Sozialgeschichte des Tourismus in Deutschland 1945 bis 1989*, Berlin: Verlag für Universitäre Kommunikation, pp. 105–116.

Sälter, G. (2007) Mauerreste in Berlin, Herausgegeben von Verein Berlin Mauer Berlin: Gedenkstätter und Dokumentationszentrum e.v.

Schloemp, U. (1994) 'Die Struktur der Berliner Beherbergungsgewebs am 1 Januar 1993', in *Berliner Statistik 12/94*, Berlin: Statistisches Landesamt Berlin.

Schnell, P. (1998) 'Germany: still a growing international deficit?' in William, A. and Shaw, G. (eds), *Tourism and Economic Development: European Experiences*, 3rd ed., London: John Wiley and Sons, pp. 269–300.

Ministerat der Deutschen Demokratischen Republik (1980, 1981, 1982, 1983, 1984, 1985, 1986, 1987, 1988) Staatliche Zentralverwaltung für Statistik, *Statistischer Jahresbericht über then Stand und die Entwicklung des Tourismus und Erholungswesen der DDR*, Berlin: Ministerat der Deutschen Demokratischen Republik.

Statistisches Landesamt Berlin (1990) *Tourismus in Berlin, Information der amtlichen Statistik*. Berlin: Statistisches Landesamt Berlin.

Statistisches Landesamt Berlin (2000) 'Zehn Jahre Berlin Einheit – Daten und Analysen zum Vereinigungsprozess' in *Statistisches Monatsschrift*, No. 1–6, Berlin: Statistisches Landesamt Berlin.

Treibel, W. (1992) *Die Deutsche Luftfahrt: Geschichte der Deutschen Verkerhsflughäfen*, Bonn: Bernard and Graefe.

Verkehr in Berlin (1990) Berlin: Senatsverwaltung für Arbeit, Verkehr und Betriebe.

Zahlen und Faken, 1990 *Statistisches Bundesamt der DDR*. Berlin: J.B.Metzler/ C.E.Poeschel.

750 Years Berlin 1987 Information (1987) Berlin: Presse- und Informationsamt des Landes Berlin.

4 The European Union: Between the Global and the National, and Between Neo-Liberalism and Interventionism

Allan M. Williams and Vladimir Baláž

Introduction

The figures relating to the role of tourism in the economy of the European Union (EU) bear strong testimony to its material significance in terms of production and consumption. The European Union is the most visited region of the World and six European countries ranked among the top ten tourist destinations in 2006 in terms of international tourist receipts (WTO 2007). Most tourism markets in Europe tend to be in the mature stages of development, and have relatively low rates, especially in the face of global competition. Tourism development, partly because of its socially-constructed spatial and temporal polarization, is also associated with a range of cultural and environmental challenges (Shaw and Williams 2002, Chapter 1). And while most tourism activity remains domestic, international tourism is an important component of the industry and most forms of tourism are shaped by the internationalization of capital and labour markets. In other words, tourism and tourism impacts cannot be thought of as bounded or contained by national spaces, so that there is a compelling logic for the EU to be considered a key site for regulation and intervention.

Despite overwhelming evidence of the material significance of tourism, at first sight it seems to be weakly represented in the institutions and policies of the EU. It is not mentioned specifically in the founding treaty of the European Economic Community (as it was then named), the Treaty of Rome. The first policy document which explicitly targeted tourism development was the 1982 'Initial Guidelines on a Community Policy on Tourism' (COM (82) 235). This was the '... first comprehensive attempt to take stock of tourism's importance to the Community and to situate it in the context of other related fields of policy' (Robinson 1993: 13). It addressed several important agendas which still resonate now: the seasonality of tourism, the development of alternatives to beach holidays, and support for social tourism. These issues largely duplicated the policy concerns of national tourism policies (regional development, the environment, consumer protection, seasonality) and did not make a compelling case for an enhanced and distinctive EU level policy. There were, however, two exceptions to this: the role of the EU in removing barriers to travel and freedom of movement amongst Member States, and the harmonisation of working conditions and provision of freedom of movement for tourism workers. These showed that the EU performed a significant role in shaping the operating environment for tourism, although through its general treaties rather than through tourism specific competences (Williams and Shaw 1998). Indeed, tourism has continued to teeter at the edge of the European agenda, compared to say agriculture, manufacturing or financial services. There is a brief reference to tourism in the Maastricht Treaty (1993), but the development of specific supranational tourist policies has been extremely modest (Anastasiadou 2008).

Although tourism has remained largely the preserve of national and sub-national policies, it has been shaped by the EU in a number of ways, especially in terms of broad regulatory frameworks as already indicated, but also via expenditures in support of tourism within the budgets of the structural, cohesion, cultural and other funds. The role of the EU in tourism has, therefore, been subject to the same tension between competing neo-liberal and interventionist visions of the EU (Lee 1990; Hudson and Williams 1999) as have other economic sectors. These tensions are explored here through a discussion of three main themes: the creation of a common mobility space, growth and competitiveness, and cohesion and interventionism.

A common mobility space: enacting a neo-liberal vision of the EU

Arguably, the fundaments of modern tourism in Europe were laid down in the era of political stabilisation and rapid economic development in the 1950s and 1960s. Tourist arrivals increased tenfold in Greece, fourfold in Germany, Austria, Portugal and Turkey, threefold in the Netherlands and twofold in the UK, Ireland and Italy between 1950 and 59 (OECD 1989: 15). This international tourism boom was backed by a framework of supportive policies at the national level such as removing barriers to travel (in the form of currency restrictions, visa requirements, etc.) rather than by specific tourism policy actions. In other words, national states took steps towards opening their economies to international mobility for a variety of purposes, including tourism. This was reinforced by state supported marketing campaigns specifically for tourism. Combined with increases in real per capita incomes and leisure time, this laid the foundations for mass tourism growth in Europe (Shaw and Williams 2002). The logic for these measures was mostly couched in terms of the exigencies of needing to generate foreign exchange earnings, but also constituted part of a neo-liberal vision of the European space, defined above by the removal of barriers, whether to trade or human mobility. The limits to this approach were exposed in the late 1960s and early 1970s, when rising unemployment and the first oil shock in 1973/74 sharply decreased international tourist flows. The oil shocks in 1973/74 and 1979/80 negatively impacted on balances of payments in Europe and led to temporary restrictions on foreign exchange availability for tourism purposes; for example, the French government imposed a 2000 franc maximum currency allowance on French citizens in 1983 (Airey 1983: 238). These restrictions were temporary and thereafter there was renewed commitment to the vision of a European mobility space. However, there was to be a more generalised policy shift with greater emphasis on local economic development priorities, and social and environmental issues, as well as on the quality of tourism provision, rather than simply on growth and exports.

The Treaty of Rome (1957), which brought into existence the European Economic Community, significantly advanced the freedom of travel, removing the right to impose visa or other obstacles to border crossing, and by creating rights of residence and property purchase (the latter was to be important in the growth of international second or holiday homes). While much of the regulation was generic, it was supplemented by tourism specific measures such as the 1968 Council Directive 68/367/EEC which regulated freedom of establishment and freedom to provide services in the hotel and restaurant sector. This was supplemented later by the Schengen agreement, which removed routine passport controls on mobility between members of this elective group of EU countries. The Treaty on European Union, which paved the way for the elective introduction of the euro in January 2002, can also be seen in terms of creating the freedom of mobility space among the initially 12 participating Member States, increasing to 16 by 2009. Other measures include reducing significantly the roaming fees for mobile communications in the EU, introducing a Europe-wide emergency telephone number, and implementing effective aviation safety standards. These measures have contributed, to varying degrees, to creating a single European mobility space, where market forces are played out over a vastly increased and relatively homogeneous economic space, rather than through a mosaic of fragmented national economic spaces.

Secondly, the creation of the EU was driven not only by economic goals, but also by the goal of creating a new political framework which would promote peace and collaboration in Europe. Over time the EU has become the bulwark of political, legal and social stability in Europe, creating an environment conducive to international travel and tourism. Thirdly, the EU has played a major role in the deregulation of international air travel in Europe. Air transport in the EU was liberalised in three stages between 1987 and 1997. The third package of measures, in July 1992, was the most radical: as of April 1997, all EU carriers have had open access to virtually all routes within the EU. Combined with favourable macro economic conditions, and organizational innovations, this has led to a rapid expansion of low- cost air carriers and shifts in the practices of legacy air carriers, significantly changing the geography of accessibility in Europe, while lowering the cost and convenience barriers to mobility in the continent in terms of labour migration, capital and knowledge flows, and tourism (Williams and Baláž 2009). This was further reinforced by EU funding support for transport infrastructures.

Many of the above measures, which are associated with the creation of a single market, represent selective forms of the 'deepening' of European integration. Alongside this there was a different EU agenda of 'widening' by admission of new Member States. The key moments were the Northwestern enlargement in 1972, the Southern enlargement in the 1980s, the Northern and Alpine enlargement in the 1990s, and the Eastern enlargement in the 2000s. Rapid international tourism growth in these countries had commenced prior to accession. For example, there was a tenfold growth in foreign tourist arrivals in Poland, threefold growth in the Czech Republic and Slovakia, and twofold expansion in Hungary between 1989 and 1996 (Baláž and Williams 2005). However, the role of the EU in the transformation of these economies after 1989, especially through the European Agreements and the prospect of future membership (Pridham 2005), was critical in the opening of their economies, and to increased international mobility.

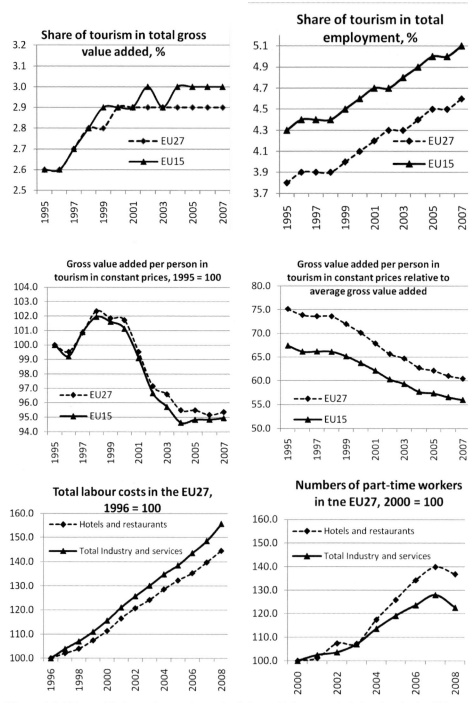

Figure 4.1: Value added, employment, productivity and labour costs in tourism in the EU, 1995-2007. Sources: authors' computations based on the Eurostat and National Accounts aggregates and employment by branch

Note: Tourism defined as Hotels and Restaurants only.

Growth and competitiveness: tourism at the centre of an ideological battleground

A recurrent theme within the EU has been the need to sustain or enhance its global competitiveness, and although this debate has mostly centred on issues relating to high technology or knowledge-intensive manufacturing and (more recently) producer services, many of the same issues are germane when considering tourism. Competitiveness is ultimately a key battleground for competing European economic and social models (Sapir 2006).

It is, perhaps, not surprising that tourism has largely been absent from EU-level discourses about European competitiveness. Tourism activities are generally labour-intensive, and characterised by above-average shares of low- and medium-skilled workers. Not surprisingly, therefore, the value added per worker is some 40% lower in tourism than the average value added per worker in the economy generally. The overall numbers mask considerable differences in tourism sub-sectors: gross value added per person varies from €17,000 in the restaurant and café sector, to €29,000 in the hotel sector and €56,000 in the tour operator and travel agent sector. The last of these figures surpassed the average productivity in market services in general, €41,000 (CEC 2007a), but the generally low levels of productivity have meant that tourism, unwisely, has rarely featured on the EU's competitiveness agenda.

The productivity, and therefore in part the competitiveness, of EU tourism is, however, more problematic than might appear from these static comparative data. Since 1995 the share of tourism in both total employment and gross value added has expanded (Figures 4.1 and 4.2). Growth in employment, however, has outpaced the growth in gross value added in tourism. Gross value added per person in constant prices fell by about 5% in both the old and new Member States. The decrease in the relative productivity of the tourism industry was even more pronounced. The gross value added per person in the hotel and restaurant sector was 75.1% of the average total value added per person in the EU27 and 67.4% in the EU15 in 1995 (Figure 4.2). However, by 2007 the gross value added per person in the hotel and restaurant sector was only about 60.5% of the EU27 average and 56.0% of the EU15 average. This relative decline in productivity can be explained because, while in the period 1995–2007 tourism benefited from technological and organisational innovations (e.g. the introduction of low-costs airlines, Internet booking), it did so to a lesser degree than many other industries. Tourism has played an important role in generating employment in recent years, so that many national and European initiatives to assist tourism have been rationalized in terms of job creation. The problem is that there have also been strategies aiming to increase the competitiveness of the industry, and these two targets have probably been contradictory, as increases in competitiveness can be accompanied by job losses or lower rates of employment growth. Productivity and competitiveness in tourism are unusually complex. Tourism has benefited from technological and organisational innovations, such as the rapid spread of Internet bookings of flights and accommodation services which have resulted in impressive increases in the numbers of tourists, nights spent and absolute volumes of value added generated in the hotel and restaurant sector.

In recent years, economists have increasingly focused on the need to understand relatively low, but internationally varied, productivity levels in consumer services (Broadberry and O'Mahoney 2004). This has meant that tourism, belatedly, has begun to be incorporated into discussions of productivity and competitiveness. For example, the 2001 Commission communication on tourism policies (COM (2001) 665 final) listed a lack of skilled manpower for certain jobs, service quality, and the adoption and the incorporation of new information and communication technologies amongst the challenges for the tourism sector. Since 2006 the European Commission has gone further and sought to integrate Community tourism policies into the Lisbon Strategy. A Commission communication in March 2006 on 'A renewed EU Tourism Policy – Towards a stronger partnership for European Tourism' (COM (2006) 134 final) indentified ' … changing demography, global competition, concern for sustainability and the demand for specific forms of tourism' as major challenges for European tourism development. A new tourism policy was required to meet the 'challenges facing this sector and fully exploit its potential'. The necessary actions for promoting sustainability and competitiveness of European tourism were summarised in the 'Agenda for a sustainable and competitive European tourism', approved by the Commission in October 2007 (COM (2007b) 621 final), and included:

♦   Mobilising actors to produce and share knowledge (conferences, research, formal and non-formal tourism education and training, platforms for exchanging knowledge on good and bad practices, improved statistical data);

♦   Promoting destinations of excellence (supporting destinations where tourism development is consistent with social, cultural and environmental sustainability);

♦   Mobilising EU financial instruments to support tourism, for example, the Cohesion Policy, European Agricultural Fund for Rural Development, European Fisheries Fund, and the 7th Framework Programme, 'Leonardo da Vinci' programme.

♦   Mainstreaming sustainability and competitiveness in Commission policies, especially environment, transport, employment and research policies.

Tourism has therefore been incorporated into the broader goals of the Lisbon Strategy, in terms of creating a more knowledge driven and globally competitive economy. Tourism is often portrayed in economic policy discourse as a relatively successful sector (at least in comparison with, say, traditional manufacturing) and that the way to maximize its growth is via continued relatively light touch regulation and interventionism, other than necessary actions to minimise its environmental and cultural impacts. But interventionists would contest this in terms of the need for the state to support the sector if it is to retain its global competitiveness. In reality, however, tourism remains at the margins of substantive EU actions and funding designed to bolster competitiveness, although as seen in the next section, this does overlap with spending in terms of the cohesion objectives.

Cohesion: EU interventionism in tourism by the back door

The neo-liberal vision for Europe has emphasised the role of the market in terms of promoting growth and welfare in the longer term. Little more than ten years ago, there was still a view that shocks only '...*temporarily* threaten regional and social cohesion'

(CEC 1996:51, emphasis added). However, there has long been a critique which argues that persistent social and spatial inequalities within the EU are inherent to, rather than temporary or 'just a 'by-product' of, capitalist development.

There is no space here to investigate systematically the contribution of tourism to regional convergence/divergence or any other dimension of social cohesion. However, we can note three significant features of the sector. First, as noted in the introduction, it accounts for a significant proportion of jobs and output in the EU. Secondly, its shares of output and employment have increased over time. For example, there was a 23.4% increase in the total number of bed places in hotels and similar establishments between 1994 and 2007, and a 37.3% increase in nights spent in hotels.

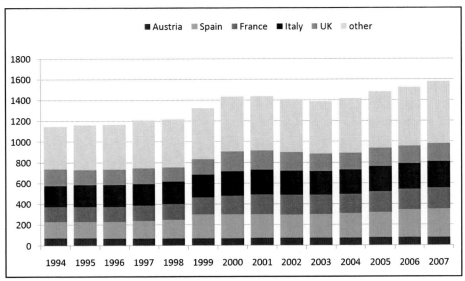

Figure 4.2: Nights spent in hotels and similar establishments in the EU 27, 1994-2007 (millions) Source: Eurostat

Third, the broad structure of accommodation capacities has remained fairly stable over time, perhaps reflecting the influence of sunk capital. The share of the five main providers (UK, Italy, France, Spain and Germany) in total hotel beds in the EU27 only decreased from 69.4% to 67.7% in this period, although there was an important shift from France (–3.8 percentage points) to Spain (+2.9 percentage points). Therefore, although most of the discussion around cohesion has focused on the manufacturing and business services sectors, tourism could not be entirely neglected, not least because international tourism constitutes an export sector and an important source of job growth.

The EU has no direct competence to intervene in tourism and – unlike in the case of agriculture – such competences remain firmly rooted at the national, regional and/or local levels. The 1960s and 1970s saw rapid growth of national scale interventionism in infrastructure supportive to tourism: e.g. motorways, mountain tunnels for rail/car transport, airports, and marinas. National states also co-financed construction of tourism facilities (hotels, restaurants), especially in Southern Europe. They also introduced new tourism policy instruments, namely land use planning, staggering holidays, and the education and training of tourism workers. Governments also intervened to regulate the quality and prices of tourism services, while other initiatives aimed to protect natural and historical heritage sites. These regulations encouraged shifts from targeting quantity to quality. An analysis of tourism policies in the six founding Member States of the EEC (based on a content analysis of the OECD annual reports, 1972–82) established the following ranking of tourism policies: 1. Regional development, 2. Seasonality, 3. Consumer protection, 4. Balance of payments, 5. Social Tourism, 6. Rural/green tourism, 7. Environmental protection (Airey 1983). The fact that these broadly concur with current national priorities – with the exception of addressing the ageing population of Europe – indicates the relative maturity of European tourism, and tourism policies.

Tourism policies also became better coordinated and involved a broader range of stakeholders (from the culture, environment, social affairs and other domains). A survey of tourism policies (Akehurst *et al.* 1993), for example, found that the most successful countries in promoting tourism in the 1980s (France, Portugal and Ireland) shared some common features. First, they had coherent central government strategies for developing tourism, and for co-ordinating tourism with other policies, particularly with respect to transport, the environment, cultural development, and regional policy. Second, there was increased diversification of tourism products towards rural and cultural tourism. And, third , they had higher direct investment in the tourism sector, including the use of EEC funds and fiscal incentives to the private sector.

Although the EU has no direct competence in respect of tourism, interventionism in the sector is achieved via other EU competencies. The 1982 guidelines, mentioned earlier, were an early indication of awareness of these indirect EU tourism competences. Over time, EU tourism policies have become more systematic. The Community Action Plan to assist tourism (published April 1991), for example, listed many policy areas that provided indirect support to tourism development, culture, heritage, environment protection policies plus several direct interventionist actions such as the directive on package holidays (1990) and The European Year of Tourism (1990).

There are several EU policy instruments which address issues of social and territorial convergence/divergence, that are relevant to tourism. Not least, tourism is identified as an important instrument for assisting economic development in the EU's less developed regions. Financial assistance to tourism development by the Community is provided under the 'Convergence', 'Regional Competitiveness and Employment' and 'Inter-regional Cooperation" objectives. Article 4 of the ERDF regulations (No 1080/2006) on the Convergence Objective specifies which tourism tourism-related projects can be supported:

> *Tourism, including promotion of natural and cultural assets as potential for the development of sustainable tourism, protection and enhancement of the cultural heritage in support of economic development, aid to improve the supply of tourism services through new higher value-added services.*

Similarly, Article 5 on the 'Regional competitiveness/Employment' Objective refers to the:

> *Protection and enhancement of the natural and cultural heritage in support of socio-economic development and the promotion of natural and cultural assets as potential for the development of sustainable tourism.*

The Territorial Cooperation Objective (Art. 6) identifies activities related to the environment:

'Actions may include protection and enhancement of the natural heritage in support of socio-economic development and sustainable tourism'.

The Strategic Guidelines for Cohesion (SGC) do not mention tourism under the three main priorities, but tourism is included in the territorial dimension of Cohesion Policy, namely in terms of the attractiveness of cities and the restructuring of rural areas.

Probably the single most important instrument in respect of tourism has been the European Regional Development Fund (ERDF), established in 1975. Although not specifically concerned with tourism, it became the first financial instrument to provide EU support for tourism infrastructure. Between 1986 and 1988 some 5 % of the ERDF was allocated to tourism-related projects. More recently, the ERDF allocated some €7.7bn to tourism in the period 2000–06. Most assistance addressed the competitiveness of the tourism industry and the quality of tourist services in laggard regions: (a) building tangible tourist infrastructure (accommodation facilities, tourist information centres, 65%), (b) supporting intangible investments (tourist services, 20%), and (c) improving effectiveness of the tourism industry (networking, trade fairs, 15%). In the planning period 2007–13, the competitiveness of the tourism industry and quality of tourist services remain the main targets for assistance, but significant support is also channelled to projects addressing tourism sustainability.

The overall budget for the entire Cohesion Policy (including other structural funds such as the Social Policy) is about €347 billion in 2007–13. Between 2007 and 2013, directly targeted EU support for tourism under Cohesion Policy amounting to more than €6 billion is planned, representing 1.8% of the total budget. €3.8 billion is allocated for the improvement of tourist services, €1.4 billion for the protection and development of the natural heritage, and €1.1 billion for the promotion of natural assets. In addition, support for tourism-related infrastructure and services is also provided under other headings, such as innovation, promotion of small and medium-sized enterprises, information technology applications and human capital.

In the period 2007–13, the largest assistance to tourism is planned in Poland (€979m), Italy (€894m), the Czech Republic (€692m), Spain (€468m) and Hungary (€448m), reflecting the overall aims of the cohesion strategy. In relative terms, tourism accounts for higher shares of total assistance under the Cohesion policy in Italy (3.2%), Finland (3.2%), Estonia (3.1%), Malta (2.9%) and the Czech Republic (2.6%), reflecting national specificities. Sustainability issues are prominently addressed in Lithuania, Denmark, Malta, Bulgaria and the UK, while competitiveness issues are prominent in Latvia, the Czech Republic, Poland, Austria and Estonia (Figure 4.3).

Support to tourism has also become better coordinated with more policies promoting regional development, competitiveness and cross-border cooperation in the 1990s. The cross-border cooperation programmes (INTERREG) in particular accounted for a large share of tourism-related projects. Whereas tourism interventions were more or less isolated actions in the first period (1990–93, INETERREG I), a more structured approach emerged in INTERREG II, 1994–99 (Moniz 2009).

While this chapter has focused mostly on the cohesion strategy and funds, the EU also has some competences in relation to tourism via some of its other common policies. For example, under the common environmental policy, directives aimed at the quality of bathing water (1976) and pollution in the Mediterranean and protection of

Europe's cultural heritage (1979) helped to create a framework supportive to tourism development. The European Commission also promotes cultural tourism as a means of underpinning 'unity in diversity' as part of its 'cultural policy'. Cultural tourism is seen as a way of stimulating job creation, as a growing market, as strengthening local and regional cultures, and as a means of reinforcing or projecting distinctive identities and images (OECD 2008: 19-20). This also reflects trends at the national scale, where some 25 countries in the developed world have combined their administrative structures for culture and tourism in some way, as for example within a single ministry or department (OECD 2008: 24). In summary, then, the EU has far greater competence in respect of tourism than appears at first sight.

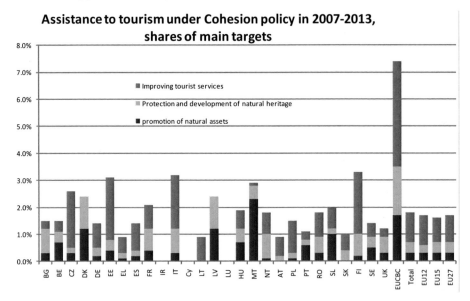

Figure 4.3: Assistance to tourism under Cohesion policy in 2007–13, shares of main targets. Source: DG REGIO.

Notes: Breakdown of data on Ireland, Cyprus and Luxembourg not available. EUCBC = European Cross-Border Cooperation; Total allocation to tourism = allocation by EU27 + EUCBC

Conclusion

The state, at whatever scale, is a contested ideological and policy battleground, and the engagement of the state with tourism is therefore necessarily shaped by (and to a limited extent shapes) this. We have sought to explore this argument in relationship to the EU in terms of three main themes: the creation of a single European mobility space, growth and competition agendas, and social cohesion and interventionism. Although the ideological and policy contest has ebbed and flowed over time, we contend that the neo-liberal agenda has been dominant in shaping the EU's engagement with tourism, albeit there are some important, if often indirect, outcomes related to interventionism. Ultimately, however, EU interventionism is constrained not just by a dominant neo-liberalist discourse, but also by the EU budget and the evolution of the EU as a cross between intergovernmentalism and cooperative federalism (Kirchner 1992), whereby the national remains the dominant but not the only site of regulation. Of course, the

EU engagement with tourism does not occur in a vacuum, and is often enfolded with activities at the national and the local scales, in other words demanding a multi-level governance perspective when pursuing more detailed studies than we have had scope for here. This process of enfoldment can occur in a number of ways, varying from joint funding and management of particular projects, to the incorporation of EU directives or best practices, into national legislation. Tourism also has to be considered in terms of its relationships with other sectors, whether agriculture or urban regeneration, another theme which has lain outside the scope of this contribution.

Looking to the future, there are clearly a number of key issues that will pose challenges for the EU, as well as for national and regional states. These include dealing with the consequences of population ageing on both demand for tourism and the supply of labour, sustainability issues in the face of technological and climate changes, new forms of risk management, and global competitiveness as the centres of economic and political power are redefined in the course of the first half of the twenty-first century. Despite the enormity of these challenges, there is little evidence to suggest that the EU competence in respect of tourism will shift significantly at least in the short and medium term. However, at the time of writing, the question of whether the economic crisis of the late 2000s leads to a reframing of the contestation between neo-liberalism and interventionism remains unresolved.

References

Airey, D. (1983) 'European government approaches to tourism', *Tourism Management*, 4, 234–44.

Akehurst, G., Bland, N. and Nevin, M. (1993) 'Tourism policies in the European Community member states', *International Journal of Hospitality Management* **12**, 33–66.

Anastasiadou, C. (2008) 'Tourism interest groups in the EU policy arena: characteristics, relationships and challenges', *Current Issues in Tourism*, **11**, 24–63.

Baláž, V. and Williams, A.M. (2005) 'International tourism as bricolage: an analysis of Central Europe on the brink of European Union Membership', *International Journal of Tourism Research*, 7, 79–93.

Broadberry, S. and M. O'Mahony (2004) 'Britain's productivity gap with the United States and Europe: a historical perspective', *National Institute Economic Review*, **189**, 72–85.

CEC, Commission of the European Communities (1968) Council Directive 68/367/EEC of 15 October 1968 laying down detailed provision concerning transitional measures in respect of activities of self-employed persons in the personal services sector. OJL 260, 22 Oct 1968.

CEC, Commission of the European Communities (1996) *Employment in Europe*, Luxembourg: Commission of the European Communities.

CEC, Commission of the European Communities (2001) *Working Together for the Future of European Tourism*, COM (2001) 665 final, Brussels, 13 Nov 2001.

CEC, Commission of the European Communities (2006) *A Renewed EU Tourism Policy - Towards a Stronger Partnership for European Tourism*, Brussels 17 March 2006.

CEC, Commission of the European Communities (2007a) *The European Tourism Industry in the Enlarged Community, Gaps are Potentials and Opportunities*, Brussels.

CEC, Commission of the European Communities (2007b) *Agenda for a sustainable and competitive European tourism*, COM(2007) 621 final, Brussels, 19 Oct 2007.

CEC, Commission of the European Communities (2008) Cohesion Policy 2007–2013: Tourism, DG REGIO, EU Cohesion Policy – The Thematic Pages, from http://ec.europa.eu/regional_policy/themes/index_en.htm (Accessed 3 August 2009)

Eurostat (2009) Main Tables and Database, from http://epp.eurostat.ec.europa.eu/portal/page/portal/eurostat/home (Accessed 3 August 2009)

Hudson, R. and Williams, A. M. (1999) 'Re-shaping Europe: the challenge of new divisions within a homogenized political-economic space', in R. Hudson and A. M. Williams (eds), *Divided Europe: Society and Territory*, London: Sage.

Kirchner, E. J. (1992) *Decision Making in the European Community: the Council Presidency and European Integration*, Manchester: Manchester University Press.

Lee, R. (1990) 'Making Europe: towards a geography of European integration', in M.Chisholm and D. M. Smith (eds), *Shared Space Divided Space: Essays on Conflict and Territorial Organization*, London: Unwin Hyman.

OECD (1989) *Tourism Policy and International Tourism in OECD Member Countries*, Paris: OECD.

OECD (2008) *Tourism in OECD Countries 2008: Trends and Policies*, Paris: OECD.

Pridham, G. (2005) *Designing Democracy: EU Enlargement and Regime Change in Post-Communist Europe*, Basingstoke: Palgrave Macmillan.

Robinson, G. (1993) 'Tourism and tourism policy in the European Community: an overview international', *Journal of Hospitality Management*, **12**, 7–20.

Sapir, A. (2006) 'Globalization and the reform of European social models', *Journal of Common Market Studies* **44**, 369–90.

Shaw, G. and Williams, A. M. (2002) *Critical Issues in Tourism: Geographical Perspectives*, Oxford: Blackwell.

Shaw, G. and Williams, A. M. (2004) *Tourism and Tourism Spaces*, London: Sage.

Williams, A.M. and Baláž, V. (2009), 'Low cost carriers, economies of flows, and regional externalities, *Regional Studies* **43**: 677–91.

Williams, A.M. and Shaw, G. (1998) Tourism policies in a changing economic environment, in A.M. Williams and G. Shaw (eds), *Tourism and Economic Development: European Experiences*, Chichester: Wiley, pp.375–91.

WTO, World Tourism Organisation (2007) *UNWTO World Tourism Barometer*, 5 (2).

5 The Implications and Effects of the Handover of Colonies – Macau

Glenn McCartney

Background to Macau's development

A 'Handover' of a city or destination implies that it is being returned or given back to its original nation, perhaps through political process, economic necessity, or re-position of power. History has shown the colonisation (or administration) of many destinations, both West and East, by European nations through their advanced naval and military positions. The Portuguese were one of the first naval powers to begin this global journey of establishing settlements on other continents. Through this process, Macau became one of the first ports (over 450 years ago) to act as a trading post between East and West. Macau has journeyed through a series of political and administrative changes during this time. Initially established in 1557 as an overseas settlement of Portugal, from 1582 the isthmus at the southern tip of China was run under a leasehold agreement with China. Unlike Hong Kong which was to be formed three centuries later, Macau was not conquered or established as a result of war but was through trade and merchants and the efforts of Portuguese maritime adventurers rather than a strategy of colonisation designed in Lisbon (Pons, 1999). While today Macau and Hong Kong are both Special Administrative Regions within the People's Republic of China and though their beginnings are based on different reasons, their course of history and development are intrinsically linked.

British involvement and settlement in Macau for what would be a relationship lasting over 200 years through trade and commerce would later lead to the establishment of Hong Kong. The British arrived in Macau in 1637 under orders from King Charles I. It was through their business dealings in Macau that two Scotsmen, William Jardine and James Matheson, would meet. With interests and dealing in the opium trade, Jardine, Matheson and Company was formed in 1832, and is still one of Hong Kong's most significant and influential trading companies to this day. It was also through the opium trade that the British had to move from Macau to Hong Kong Island. This island was later ceded 'forever' to the British under the signing of the Treaty of Nanking in 1842 which had followed British forces advancing as far as Nanking and the Chinese suing for peace (Coates, 1988).

It was only in 1887 that sovereignty of Macau actually changed hands to the Portuguese from the Chinese agreeing that 'Portugal will forever administer Macau' (Cheng, 1999: 1).

Cheng (1999: 26) also writes 'It seemed that the Portuguese never paid attention to the issue of sovereign rights over Macau until the British officially acquired these over Hong Kong…It was only then realized that while Hong Kong was held by right, Macau was held on sufferance'. Again the British influence, acting from a position of power in the region, was a major factor, as was the trade of opium. This administrative agreement for Macau was placed as a point of protocol in a treaty of amity and commerce between Portugal and China (Coates, 1978). It was also to be the last time the British would influence Macau governance.

This period, with the Portuguese assuming sovereign power in the 1887 treaty was viewed differently to the three centuries previously when China could execute sovereign power over Macau. 'This was undoubtedly an unequal treaty that a foreign power forced on China. It not only violated the international law but also ran counter to the concept of equal treatment and ran counter to the general people's desires' (Ieong and Ieong, 2004: 138–139). It was thus felt that this amounted to illegal occupation of Chinese territory. Yet history was to show that these assertions of perpetual occupation of Macau and Hong Kong would not stand the changing landscape of both the political sentiment back in Portugal and the United Kingdom as well as developments resulting from the post-Cultural Revolution China. Within 150 years both Hong Kong and Macau would be handed back to China with the establishment of two SARs (Special Administrative Regions) within the People's Republic of China.

By 1979, China and Portugal had already agreed on 'Macau as a Chinese territory under Portuguese administration' (Cheng, 1999: 1) and that on Macau's return to Chinese rule on 20 December 1999, it would be created a Special Administrative Region. This would be a second such region, with Hong Kong's handover set for two years earlier. In 1974, after Portugal's own revolution, there had been an unsuccessful attempt to return Macau to China, and a new Macau constitution written by Lisbon ended direct elections in Macau, dividing power between the Governor and Macau legislators, in essence, giving more control to the Chinese. A secret agreement was signed in Paris in 1979 and made public in 1987. This recognised Macau sovereignty as belonging to the PRC (People's Republic of China) with the Handover, with conditions to be discussed at a later stage. This was later achieved with the Joint Declaration on the Question of Macau signed by the Prime Ministers of Portugal and China (Afonso and Pereira, 1991).

Impact of Portuguese administration

Under Portuguese rule, Macau was characterized as a 'minimally-integrated social political system' (Lam, 1991: 323). After 400 years, the only official language was Portuguese and the Governor was appointed by the President of Portugal to whom the Governor needed to report. Executive positions such as undersecretaries and other senior levels of the Macau Government were staffed by political colleagues of either the President or Governor. Language alone acted as a barrier to interaction and engagement with Chinese society or in business or politics. With very few formal channels to communicate and interact between Chinese society and Portuguese bureaucrats, a general distrust could be found among Macau Chinese residents (Lam, 1991). Limited participation and decision making prior to the Macau handover meant that local Chinese suddenly found themselves suddenly in highly elevated government posts with critical decisions needing to be made on Macau's future. Issues had been left unresolved under the previous Portuguese administration. Leading the agenda after the Macau handover was to be social stability and security which was directly connected to the casino industry.

The Handover of Hong Kong in 1999 was an event laden with pomp and ceremony, which attracted global television viewing. Macau's image in contrast had suffered from bloody triad turf wars from 1996 up until 1999, with assassinations in broad daylight. The international media reported Macau rather negatively. 'Macau is no Hong Kong, for sure. Where Hong Kong is a kaleidoscope of trade, finance and high-profit services, Macau is a shadowy blur of blackjack, roulette, poker and prostitution' (Speth, 1999). This author mentions that Macau could not be more dissimilar to Hong Kong, the latter viewed as a well run and largely uncorrupt colony which encouraged democratic reforms a decade before Handover. In contrast Macau was criticised for lack of democratic reform, the prevalence of corruption, particularly in the police and civil service, an antiquated judiciary, and self-censoring press.

The exodus of top Portuguese civil servants near to and on the actual day of Macau's handover left previously lower ranked local Chinese civil servants now filling key government posts. Macau's post-handover Court of Final Appeal team of judges was claimed as one of the youngest of any supreme court in the world with the three judges having an average age of 37, while that of their Hong Kong equivalents was around 60 years (Bruning, 1999). There were concerns about the inexperience of those filling key government positions, especiallywith critical decisions having to be made on Macau's future development post-handover.

Casino liberalisation policy

Several commercial, policy and administrative issues were left unanswered, reflecting a lack of decisive action and political will by the previous Portuguese administration. During Portuguese administration, Macau was a city of monopoly consortia. This was not only within the casino industry but stretched throughout the public utilities, including water supply and treatment, rubbish collection and disposal, power generation, and telecommunications. Upon the establishment of the Macau SAR Government, a liberalisation policy and strategy for these monopoly entities began almost immediately. The first action was in telecommunications liberalisation, with a 'Provisional Licensing Process for Public Mobile Telecommunications' in 2000, awarding two further GSM licences in 2001. The Government also reviewed the Investment Residency Law (1995), modifying the administrative procedures to make Macau more attractive for international investment which subsequently saw a large increase in numbers of applications including those for tourism facilities. A new Commission of Audit was set up to deal with monitoring government spending and use of government resources. Leading the agenda was a review of the casino monopoly. A monopoly casino concession had been awarded in 1962 to STDM (Sociedade de Turismo e Diversões de Macau, in English 'Society for Tourism and Entertainment in Macau') a company managed by Stanley Ho. This had remained unchanged up until the Handover (see McCartney (2010) for a fuller discussion of the role of Stanley Ho in the development of tourism in Macau).

The casino concession had remained as a monopoly concession for most of the 20th century, although gambling legalisation in Macau can be tracked back to the 1850s.

Due to growing triad violence and dominance in the gaming industry, particularly in the highly lucrative VIP rooms, stagnating visitor numbers, and a destination only appealing to the gaming centric visitor, the new Macau SAR Government passed one of its most significant and ambitious regulations. The introduction of Law No. 16/2001 (Gaming Industry Framework) looked to enhance and reform the casino industry, transforming it into a world class operation, removing criminal influences, and bringing economic diversity and social stability to Macau (Commission for the First Public Tender to Grant Concessions to Operate Casino Games of Chance of the Macau SAR, 2001).

Table 5.1: Macau visitor arrivals and gross gaming revenues (in Macau Patacas (MOP), 1US$ = 8 MOP)

	Visitor arrivals [a] (millions)	Gaming revenues [b] (millions)
1997	7.00	17,784
1998	6.94	14,566
1999	7.44	13,037
2000	9.16	15,878
2001	10.28	18,109
2002	11.53	21,546
2003	11.89	27,849
2004	16.67	41,511
2005	18.71	46,047
2006	21.00	56,623
2007	27.00	83,022
2008	30.19	108,772

a Macau Statistics and Census Department (2009)
b Commission for the First Public Tender to Grant Concessions to Operate Casino Games of Chance of the Macau Special Administrative Region (2001); Macau Gaming Control Board (2009)

The liberalisation process could be judged to be an economic success from the outset. Gaming revenues had decreased in 1998 and 1999 due to the ongoing violence. However, ten years after the Handover (2009), gross gaming revenues have climbed from MOP13,037 million to MOP108,772 million, and 40% of this is taxed for government coffers. Visitor arrivals have also dramatically increased from 7.44 million in 1999 to over 30 million in 2008 (Table 5.1).

Yet the success and the rapid expansion of the gaming industry in Macau has been a two-edged sword. The Government is now grappling with several planning and management issues and the impacts now being felt by such rapid expansion in a total landmass of less than 30 sq km. These range from human resource management and development issues, and managing environmental and social impacts, as well as providing physical infrastructure in line with the building of several casino mega structures in the course of less than five years. The casino expansion has also made the government increasingly dependent on gambling as a single primary source of revenue.

China's 'one country, two systems' policy

The Basic Law of both the Hong Kong SAR and Macau SAR stated that the previous capitalist system and way of life would remain unchanged for 50 years. It was pointed out by Deng Xiaoping (of PRC) who formulated the concept of 'One country, two systems' that 50 years was arbitrary and had been chosen as a time period to give stability to both SARs. 'As a matter of fact, 50 years is only a vivid way of putting it. Even after 50 years our policy will not change either. That is, for the first 50 years it cannot be changed, and for the second there will be no need to change it' (Ieong and Ieong, 2004:247, citing Deng Xiaoping (1994:2 62)).

The principle of 'One country, two systems' has meant that the liberalisation and development of the Macau's gaming industry could continue, even with support from the Chinese Government. It was stated by the Chinese leadership that the liberalisation of the gaming industry was an internal affair for Macau and that the Chinese Government would not intervene. However, the Chinese Government prohibited any mainland funded organisation from bidding for a casino licence with a penalty of facing disciplinary action for doing so (Government Information Bureau of the Macau SAR, 2002).

The Macau casino industry had developed through its own historical, social and political circumstances and by the Handover was the main revenue provider. Macau's economic survival depended on gaming continuing. The 'One country, two systems' scenario permits this to carry on without overt interference from China.

Macau (as Hong Kong) has kept its close connections to Europe. Macau SAR passport holders have been granted visa-free access to the European Union since 2000. Macau also extended visa-free tourist entry for all EU citizens from the previous 30 days to 90 days. Macau has maintained its link with Portugal, using the Portuguese-speaking platform and historical legacy to cooperate with other Portuguese-speaking nations. This has been through the signing after the Handover of various economic and trade, culture, education and sports protocols. These actions have also been taken to attract international tourists to Macau.

Challenges in developing Macau as an international tourism destination

Macau's recent tourism slogan was 'a world of difference, the difference is Macau', leveraging Macau's historical and cultural heritage. In terms of arrival numbers and casino revenues Macau is succeeding, yet Macau's tourism success is based largely on casino tourism and a 'no choice' scenario on having a border-location strategy feeding off the China and Hong Kong travel markets, origins in which casino gambling is strictly prohibited (McCartney 2005a).

Lo (2008: 19) has also been critical of this dependency on casino policy and administration stating that the 'weaknesses of the politico-administrative state in Macau, including the absence of institutional checks and balances, the frail civil society and the relatively docile mass media, have magnified the negative impacts of casino capitalism on Macau'. This became particularly apparent with the Mr Ao Man Long scandal, the Secretary for

Public Works in the post-handover government, who was found to have taken millions of dollars in bribes on land and construction deals. He is now serving a lengthy jail sentence.

A new Chief Executive was appointed uncontested in 2009 (with the previous Chief Executive having served the maximum two terms of five years in succession) and is tasked with resolving outstanding issues and dealing with fresh challenges as the casino industry grows, and subsequent effects of the Handover 10 years previously are still felt.

Language

Prior to the Handover most legislative, government or policy making documents were in Portuguese. The Portuguese language and cultural legacy can act as an important feature in offering Macau distinct destination attraction attributes within Asia. It also acts as a platform between Portuguese-speaking countries for exchange, trade and tourism. However this should not be as a restrictive bureaucratic hurdle in dealing with international audiences using an English platform both in terms of trade investment and tourism development. Language policy within government is fragmented, with varying usage of English (which formally had no legal standing). In recent years, English language print and broadcast media have emerged which provide useful reference and analysis on Macau.

Policy and regislation

Notwithstanding the complexity of language, although translation of all enacted laws into Chinese was made compulsory in 1989 (Alfonso and Pereira, 1991), there can still be confusion between what the meaning is in Chinese written in character form and that in the Portuguese expression. The legal framework in Macau is mostly based on Portuguese law.

Macau's political development has been slow. One factor has been the presence of governing and social elites, including gambling tycoons which 'tends to exclude the general public from participating in the decision-making process…Nevertheless, persistent bottom-up pressure will, in the long-run, force the (Macau) government to be open and accountable to the people' (Yee, 2001: 143). Compared to Hong Kong, Macau has a weaker pro-democracy force. As such, both the central government in Beijing and its office in Macau (Liaison Office) have been less prominent and interventionist compared to their counterparts in Hong Kong (Lo, 2001). The outcome of this interaction between residents and political elite, and demand for greater transparency will be factors in the success of Macau's future development.

There have been key advancements. Since the Handover the Macau Government has emphasized the importance of better governance. This has been seen by the appearance of performance pledges in Macau Government departments, an annual policy address by the Chief Executive, and a new operating style of Macau's anti-corruption agency, the Macau Commission Against Corruption. This display of procedural fairness started to show with the invitation of casino concession tenders in 2001 (Lo, 2001) which has had a major impact on subsequent tourism development and growth.

Education

A large proportion of Macau's citizens are under-educated compared to those in Hong Kong. In 1999, only 27.4% of Macau's employed population had completed a secondary school or higher level education although by 2007 this had increased to 45.5%. With Hong Kong having only around 30% of their employed population with less than secondary education level, the number of those educated in Macau needs to increase (Gu and Siu, 2009). Macau also does not have any common exam system and a laissez-faire approach to secondary school examination format. The post-handover Government recently took a protectionist stance on employment. Laws were created that only local residents could be casino dealers and work permits for foreign nationals were cut or not renewed. The Government has been accused of indiscriminately cutting work permits, disregarding qualifications, and artificially filling jobs with residents (Azevedo, 2009). Dealer salaries have grown due to lack of supply, attracting many of Macau's youth to enter the casino industry. Imported skilled labour is also leaving Macau. Failure to reform education and assessing human resource needs could have major implications for the health of Macau's tourism industry in the future.

China cooperation

From the outset as an SAR, Macau promoted cooperation and exchanges with provinces in China, particularly within the Pearl River Delta Region. Agreements such as the Pan-PRD (Pearl River Delta) or '9+2' (being the nine provinces in southern China and the two SARs) and CEPA (Closer Economic Partnership Arrangement) provided frameworks for better closer collaboration between China and the two SARs, which included trade and tourism.

The PRC has also shown its support for both SARs by relaxing the travel restrictions on its citizens to visit there. Hong Kong and Macau were the first destinations to receive China outbound tourism in the 1980s and later led the way in being given the title of 'Approved Destination Status (ADS)'. Most PRC outbound tourism is still to Hong Kong and Macau. In 1998 PRC visitors to Macau were almost 12% of total visitor arrivals. By 2008 this had reached around 60%, with Hong Kong visitors almost 30% (Statistics and Census Service Macau SAR Government, 2009). Due to Macau's close proximity to Hong Kong, Macau could be viewed as a neighbour rather than a separate 'tourism destination'. Throughout the years, numbers of visitors from Hong Kong have been fairly consistent.

Macau, rather than being an international destination in terms of arrivals, chiefly relies on China for tourism. China, however, has the ability to control travel over its borders by restricting visas, which are still needed for travel to Macau and Hong Kong. This has already been done on occasions when it was felt that the gaming industry was overheating. However, as part of China, it is highly unlikely that any future Chinese travel restrictions would be used as a strategy aimed at damaging either the Hong Kong or Macau economies.

Reliance on gaming

Prior to the liberalization of the gaming industry in 2001, gambling activities (mostly by non-locals) generated approximately 60% of Macau's GDP. By 2008, gambling represented around 80% of economic activity in Macau. From an initial tax base set at three million patacas in 1962, this increased to 10.8% of casino gross revenue in 1976. Incremental increases through the years have meant that taxation contributions to the Macau Government by casinos totalled around 40% under the liberalization terms (McCartney, 2005b). Macau's manufacturing industry slowed eroded and moved to China due to lower operating costs. While the new government of Macau has focused on the expansion of the casino industry after Handover, these actions acted as a catalyst for the economy to become evenmore focused on a sole industry, namely casino tourism.

The Chief Executive's address in 2002 acknowledged that Macau's economy would be structured with the gaming sector as its 'head' and the service industry as its 'body' (Government Information Bureau of the Macau SAR, 2002). There have been attempts to broaden tourism into other fields such as culture, sports and MICE (meetings, incentive travel, conventions, exhibitions), but the allure of gambling continues to increase in dominance due to the huge economic awards. Macau's gaming industry remains largely divorced from the need for MICE tourism as its gaming revenues continue to grow compared to the Las Vegas model which later looked to the high yield convention model as its development strategy (McCartney, 2008).

Macau invested substantial resources in hosting three major events from 2005 to 2008; the 4th East Asian Games, 1st Sino-Portuguese Games and 2nd Indoor Asian Games. In the hope of encouraging cultural tourism, Macau upgraded several historical sites. Its 'Historic Centre' a group of 12 historic buildings received inclusion on the World Heritage Site list in 2004. Although also of benefit of the local community, event and cultural tourism remains a low primary motive for the average Macau tourist. The path of gaming liberalization after the Handover placed Macau on a path which will be difficult to reverse. In hindsight, a post-Handover tourism development strategy which included not only planning and management objectives but also mechanisms to effectively monitor developments and enforce corrective actions would have been useful. The new Government now must create an equitable balance between a gaming industry that has invested vast amounts of finance in Macau, and at the same time developing other tourism and leisure markets.

A future Las Vegas of the east?

Macau is one of the oldest colonial jurisdictions that existed in the East. The rise and fall of Portugal as a maritime power was also mirrored by developments in Macau and the influences of other emerging powers such as the British. Frequently termed for many years before 1999 as the 'Las Vegas of the East' the fact was that prior to the Handover gaming dominance was less than it is now. The physical face of Macau in the 21st century has changed drastically with large casino properties now part of the skyline. Macau's population mix has also changed. Around half of Macau's population is made up of migrants settling in Macau ten or 15 years prior to the Handover. Their awareness of Macau's cultural legacy and the importance they place on its preservation will be less than in the case of the traditional residents.

With an increasing dominance of the casino industry and the China travel market, Macau and its casinos rely heavily on the growing affluence of the Chinese traveller. Beijing would like to see Macau diversify beyond gaming and has mentioned this on several occasions. While supporting Macau's legitimacy to develop itself, and one that has led to greater dependency on gaming, future Beijing intervention could be felt from across the border in the future.

The casino liberalization policy with good intentions opened Macau for the first time to large and highly business astute international conglomerates which included Wynn, The Venetian and MGM Grand (all established major operators in Las Vegas). The casino development was perhaps too rapid for the new post-Handover government to cope with, given the less than adequate pre-Handover legislation and lack of policies in place to handle such accelerated developments.

From the Handover onwards, Macau has been in the almost unique position of not being limited by financial resources, having large fiscal reserves and a constant stream of liquidity from gaming taxation. The post-handover government inherited a system and culture of governance from the Portuguese administration. However the pace of change in Macau has been dramatic. Due to the increasing needs of the casino industry, international investors and growing community, this system and culture are increasingly challenged to cope. Policies aimed at regulating the growth have at times resulted as a reaction to the development and been merely short-term fixes. With a new government now being installed, this is an apt moment to assess issues that have remained unresolved since the Handover and to establish a long-term perspective towards legislation and policy creation. This should not be at the detriment of the legacy of the Portuguese heritage and culture in Macau. Rather it should look to elevate and strengthen Macau's planning and managing process to work in parallel and give strategic input to the tourism industry to help Macau compete at an international level in the years to come.

References

Afonso, R., and Pereira, F. G. (1991) 'The constitution and legal system', in R. D. Cremer (ed.), *Macau: City of Commerce and Culture: Continuity and Change*, 2nd edn, API Press, pp. 283–297.

Azevedo, P. (2009) 'ID blackmail', *Macaubusiness*, October, pp.11.

Bruning, H. (1999) 'Average age of 37 for top Macau judges', *South China Morning Post*, 8 October.

Cheng, C. M. B. (1999) *Macau: A Cultural Janus*, Hong Kong: Hong Kong University Press.

Coates, A. (1978) *A Macau Narrative*, Hong Kong: Oxford University Press.

Coates, A. (1988) *Macau and the British 1637–1842*, Hong Kong: Oxford University Press.

Government Information Bureau of the Macau SAR (2002) *Macau Yearbook*, Macau: Government Printing Bureau of the Macau SAR.

Gu, Z., and Siu, R.C.S. (2009) *Macau Gaming Human Resources Issues and Solutions*, Macau: Macau Association of Economic Sciences.

Ieong, W.C. and Ieong, S.L. (2004) *'One Country, Two Systems' and the Macau SAR*, Macau: Centre of Macau Studies, University of Macau.

Lam, T.C. (1991) 'Administration and public service system in Macau', in R. D. Cremer (ed.), *Macau: City of Commerce and Culture: Continuity and Change*, 2nd edn, API Press, pp. 323–351.

Lo, S. (2001) 'Constitutional conventions and political development in Macau', in *Proceedings of Macau on the Threshold of the Third Millennium*, Macau Ricci Institute, 14-15 December, Hong Kong, pp. 93–100.

Lo, S. (2008) 'Casino capitalism and its legitimacy impact on the politico-administrative state in Macau', *Journal of Current Chinese Affairs*, **38** (1), 19–47.

Macau Gaming Control Board (2009) Gaming statistics, from:http://www.dicj.gov.mo/web/en/information/DadosEstat/2009/content.html#n1(accessed 10 March 2010)

Macau SAR Government (2001) 'Commission for the first public tender to grant concession to operate casino games of chance of the Macau SAR', Information Memorandum, Macau: Macau SAR Government.

McCartney, G. (2005a) 'Casinos as a tourism redevelopment strategy – the case of Macau', *Journal of Macau Gaming Research Association*, Issue **2**, 40–54.

McCartney, G. (2005b) 'Casino gambling in Macau: through legalization to liberalization, in C.H.C. Hsu (ed.), *Casino Industry in Asia Pacific*, Haworth Press Inc, pp. 37–58.

McCartney, G. (2010) Stanley Ho Hung-sun: The 'King of Gambling' in Butler, R.W. and Russell, R. (eds) *Giants of Tourism*, Walllingford: CABI.

Pons, P (1999) *Macau*, Hong Kong: University Press.

Speth, A. (1999) 'Macau's big gamble', *Time Magazine*, 154 (24), from: www.time.com/time/asia/magazine/99/1220/macau.handover.html (accessed 10 March 2010)

Statistics and Census Service, Macau SAR Government (2009) Visitor Arrivals, from: www.dsec.gov.mo/Statistic/TourismAndServices/VisitorArrivals.aspx (accessed 10 March 2010)

Yee, H.S. (2001) 'Mass political culture and political development in post-1999 Macau', in *Proceedings of Macau on the Threshold of the Third Millennium*, Macau Ricci Institute, 14-15 December, Hong Kong, 127–149.

Part II
Increasing
Autonomy

6 Devolution – Towards Independence: Tourism in Scotland in the 21st Century

Rory MacLellan

Introduction

Scotland has a distinct identity within the UK to the extent that internationally it has a higher recognition factor than many nation states. In spite of greater devolution of powers in the past decade, however, Scotland remains a region rather than an independent country. How the move towards greater autonomy and the difference between international image and political reality has affected tourism in Scotland is the focus of this chapter. The chapter describes the context within which political changes have taken place in Scotland and focuses on public policy and support structures for tourism pre and post re-establishment of the Scottish Parliament in 1999.

The thorny issue of where tourism fits into the political process has been identified by several authors (Hall, 2000; Lennon and Seaton, 1998; MacLellan and Smith, 1998) and this has vexed tourism policy makers in Scotland for decades. The need for a central organisation for tourism, such as an National Tourism Organization (NTO), has now been accepted throughout the world (Pearce, 1992; Jeffries, 2001) and destinations with national aspirations such as Scotland have embraced the NTO model in spite of there being a British Tourist Authority representing the nation state (UK).

Historical context and political structures

Scotland constitutes around one third of the area of the UK but has only 9% of its population (5.1 million). Located to the north of England, it is peripheral in both European and UK terms resulting in accessibility and transportation challenges. However the combination of relatively low population density and remoteness affords Scotland advantages in the quality and variety of its natural environment. The tourism identity of Scotland has traded on images of romantic scenery, mountains, glens and lochs, interspersed with castles and rural villages, although in reality, most tourism takes place in the major cities of Scotland. The Greater Glasgow conurbation represents one of the UK's large urban agglomerations with around 1.65 million people and has become a successful business and retail tourism destination in its own right. The capital city Edinburgh has a population of only 530,000 but as the historic centre of government arts and culture has established itself as one of the most successful arts festival cities in the world.

According to an official government briefing document (Dewer, 2007) tourism is important to Scotland for primarily economic reasons: spending by tourists in Scotland amounts to over £4bn annually; the spending supports around 200,000 jobs; a disproportionate number of these jobs are located in rural areas where employment opportunities are limited.

Table 6.1: Tourist visits to Scotland 2008. Source: VisitScotland 2008

Origin	Trips 2008 (m)	Nights 2008 (m)	Spend 2008 (£m)
Scotland	5.84	19.19	927
England	5.74	23.14	1682
Northern Ireland	0.36	1.16	127
Wales	0.21	0.70	76
Total UK tourism	12.15	44.19	2812
Total overseas tourism	2.48	19.34	1235
Total	**14.63**	**63.53**	**4047**

In 2008, around 15 million tourists took overnight trips to Scotland and the annual spend was over £4.0 billion. Scottish tourism contributes 11% of the Scottish service sector economy compared to 9% for the UK as a whole. The UK as a whole accounts for 83% of tourism trips to Scotland with overseas tourism accounting for the remaining 17%.

Although the European Union is the largest overseas market with six of the top ten inbound markets sharing the single European currency, the USA remains the biggest single national market with 21% of overseas spend.

Scotland's identity has been created, shaped and branded in conjunction with the development of tourism. Scottish tourism marketing has been described as capturing the essence of its brand from its history (Yeoman *et al.*, 2005); history has created the sense of place, (Durie *et al.*, 2005) critical to promoting Scotland. A conscious effort has been made to create a national image, 'a collective and united way of describing Scotland to the world' (McCrone *et al.*, 1995). From the re-imaging of Scotland by Sir Walter Scott and in particular the visit of the reigning monarch George IV in the 1800s (Butler, 1985), the branding of Scotland has sought to play down the less attractive characteristics attributed to Scotland and the Scots and place the emphasis more on the changed, reformed nature of a rapidly changing country, both economically, politically and socially; but at the same time without losing the dramatic, romantic, wild imagery of the primarily Highland natural landscape. The process of image creation may be far from an accurate or authentic representation of Scotland and many have criticised the 'tartanising' of Scottish culture (Butler, 1998). However the re-imaging, started in the early 19th century by Scott and others has been successful to the extent that most Scots today find it hard to separate fact from fiction in their reflections on themselves and Scotland. Recent Hollywood interpretations of Scotland through films like *Highlander* and *Braveheart* have reinforced this romantic, but less than accurate, portrayal. The result is that Scotland has a largely positive international recognition factor that gives it a competitive advantage in an increasingly crowded tourism marketplace.

Political changes pre-1999 devolution and the implications for tourism

Scottish tourism changed significantly in the last quarter of the twentieth century, in terms of product offering and visitor markets. Whilst trips to Scotland by overseas visitors increased from 620,000 in 1970 to over two million in 1998, trips by UK visitors declined over the same period from 12.3 million in 1970 to 9.8 million in 1998. This reflects the virtual disappearance of the main UK holiday market, only partially compensated for by the rise in short-break tourism.

In terms of product, there were significant shifts in the volume and quality of accommodation stock, with the number of hotels increasing from just over 2000 in 1970 to 2500 in 1998. An indication of the upgrading of facilities is shown in the number of hotel bedrooms with en-suite facilities, increasing from 35% in 1970 to 87% in 1998. The changes in the visitor attraction sector have been almost as dramatic with substantial increases in the number and range over the same period and vast improvements in the quality of visitor facilities and interpretation. Employment in tourism related industries is estimated to have increased from 112,000 in 1970 to 177,000 in 1998.

Therefore the recent history of Scotland's tourism industry has been one of almost steady progress and improvement, despite inconsistent periods in the late 1980s and late 1990s. These improvements may be attributed to a variety of factors from the public sector support systems to innovations of individual businesses. A review of the tourism industry in Scotland by Barrie (1999) lists some key factors contributing to the improvements in the 1990s including the renaissance of Glasgow and investment of £120 million in Edinburgh and Glasgow airports. Despite these improvements, several intractable factors remained as impediments to growth and prosperity through tourism including seasonality; lack of direct air access; service attitudes; price; and the ineffectiveness of the public agencies, in particular the Scottish Tourist Board (STB).

It is worth describing the public sector support mechanisms prior to Devolution (1999) as it is here that changes in policy would have their most immediate effect. It might be assumed that the advent of the Scottish Parliament would herald a greater degree of devolution in policy-making for tourism, however, by the late 1990s, most power had already moved north from Westminster, to Edinburgh (Day and MacLellan, 2000), although some responsibility for tourism promotion of Scotland remained with the British Tourist Authority. In almost every other respect, the public agencies involved in tourism in Scotland took orders from the Scottish Office in Edinburgh.

By the 1990s, the core responsibility for tourism rested with the national tourism organisation, the Scottish Tourist Board and the economic development agencies, Scottish Enterprise and Highlands and Islands Enterprise, although other important organisations had achieved a greater level of input to tourism policy-making (for example: Scottish Natural Heritage, Historic Scotland, Scottish Sports Council, Scottish Museums Council, Convention of Scottish Local Authorities). Tensions still existed regarding the division of responsibility for promoting tourism, although these had been largely resolved through measures taken at national and local levels. The Scottish Tourist Board gained the right to market itself overseas in 1993 in conjunction with the British Tourist Authority and locally the rationalisation in 1996 of the Area Tourist Board network, from an unwieldy 34 to a more manageable 14, had led to more cohesive and marketable tourist destinations.

The Scottish Tourist Board was viewed as the lead agency, however the Scottish Enterprise Network had the budget to make a difference, creating some tensions. The establishment in 1992 of the Scottish Tourism Co-ordinating Group by the Scottish Office, to oversee tourism policy implementation, went some way to resolve these. An important achievement of this agency was the development of the Strategic Plan for Scottish Tourism in 1994 to bring a more integrated approach to tourism support activities of the public agencies (Smith, 1998). It is important to re-emphasise that responsibility for addressing the problems of Scottish tourism was largely in the hands of Scottish agencies. Attempting to find unique Scottish tourism solutions to the unique Scottish problems is not new, however the advent of the Scottish Parliament in 1999 provided an ideal opportunity to take advantage of increased devolution.

The moment of devolution: the Scottish Parliament

The establishment of the Scottish Parliament in 1999 followed a lengthy period of debate on constitutional change in Scotland and a whirlwind period of action after the Labour UK election victory in 1997. As Hay (2007) points out, this gave Scotland the chance to rebrand Scottish Agencies to emphasise their Scottish roots: SportScotland, EventScotland, Creative Scotland and eventually VisitScotland.

Scotland was described as 'one of the most centrally controlled (Scottish Office) polities in Europe' (Fairley, 1999: 17). There was a requirement to redistribute powers in the hands of government agencies by recentralising policy expertise from quasi-autonomous non-governmental organisations (quangos) to the new Scottish Parliament committees. In addition, constitutional change was needed to devolve powers from Edinburgh to local authorities, placing more policy-making in local hands.

The broad political objectives for devolution and the establishment of the Scottish Parliament were twofold: first to create a new style of politics based on consensus and more representative of Scottish public opinion, (exemplified by the first government being a coalition); second, to enhance subsidiarity, devolution and decentralisation within Scotland. Power should flow from Westminster to the Scottish Parliament, then to local authorities, then to local communities. The committee system of the Parliament was intended as a device for holding the Executive to account, building policy expertise and overseeing procedures in parliament. The place of tourism in this structure provides some insight into how policy-making for tourism may be directed. Rather than a separate Department or Committee, with a separate Minister for Tourism, responsibility for tourism was placed within an already packed portfolio in the Department of Enterprise and Lifelong Learning (DELL).

Perhaps the greatest concern over tourism in Scotland was policy fragmentation at committee level, where tourism related policy areas were spread across a range of committees such as transport, considered remote from tourism. Cross-committee communication has improved but the administrative structure remains illogical and confusing and has not led to a concentration of policy expertise. A separate Minister for Tourism may not be necessary but the problem of dispersed decision making in tourism has been exacerbated by its position in the Scottish Parliament. Rather than gaining a strong, unified voice for tourism, the past decade has seen contradictory policy-making, for example, transport policy acting as a barrier to visitors to rural areas, rural policies focusing on traditional primary industrial sectors, whilst tourism policies attempted to spread benefits into peripheral locations (MacLellan, 1999).

The post-devolution period has certainly seen tourism come under close scrutiny by successive ministers and administrations. Strategies have evolved and been refined depending on the prevailing policy mood and jargon: Tourism Framework For Action 2000 was followed by Tourism Framework for Action 2002-2005 and then Scottish Tourism: the Next Decade – a Tourism Framework For Change (Scottish Executive, 2006). Although a logical progression can be perceived in these documents, much of the subtext of the tourism strategies was the buck passing of responsibility. The public agencies recognised the need to pass the lead role to the private sector but challenges remained in forming a united industry view and tourism continues to rely on public sector support (Kerr, 2003).

Initially, inclusion of tourism matters in debates in the Scottish Parliament, before the publication of the New Strategy for Scottish Tourism February 2000 (Scottish Executive, 2000) broadly reflected the concerns of industry documented as part of the consultation exercise in 1999: the funding of Area Tourist Boards (ATB); high cost of fuel; Scotland being too expensive; lack of direct links (air and sea) to Scotland; opportunities of e-commerce. The subjects raised give an insight into opposition party views on tourism. Views expressed by opposition parties on support mechanisms for tourism range from moderate calls to streamline structures, gain independence from the BTA, fund ATBs direct from the STB, to more radical changes such as having one separate Minister for Tourism and taking powers from the STB and passing them to the Scottish Enterprise Network (Kerr and Wood 1999).

A key concern in the post-devolution period has been the principal promotional agency, the STB. Lennon and Hay (2003) undertook a benchmarking study highlighting the core functions of a successful NTO but to many in the tourism industry in Scotland, the STB was a tainted organisation and an independent review of the STB was undertaken by PriceWaterhouseCoopers on behalf of the Scottish Executive and the STB. The results painted a picture of an organisation with tired staff, inadequate budgets, poor leadership and unclear objectives (Hay 2007). The Scottish Executive, seeing the need for changes in the political management of tourism, took the decision to restructure not only the STB but also the ATB structure and merge all ATBs into one organisation. In 2001 the name was changed from STB to VisitScotland, and in April 2005 became a single, country-wide comprehensive organisation managing all 120 Tourism Information Centres (TIC) in Scotland, with 14 regional offices and its own offices in London, Edinburgh and Inverness. It is now probably the world's first fully integrated tourist board, providing a single contact point for all tourists and tourism businesses (Hay, 2007).

The publication of <u>Scottish Tourism 'The Next Decade – A Tourism Framework for Change'</u> (Scottish Executive, 2006) was another attempt to take a fresh look at tourism markets both globally and in Scotland, and possible market changes over the next decade. It built on previous post-devolution strategies and set out what tourism and hospitality businesses, related sectors like transport and retail, and the public sector agencies which support them, needed to do to keep Scottish tourism growing sustainably.

In the introduction, the challenges that faced the industry in 2005 were highlighted. Patricia Ferguson, Minister responsible for tourism stated: 'A document like this can't predict exactly what Scottish Tourism will look like in 10 years' time.... We want Scotland to be one of the world's foremost tourism destinations by 2015' (Scottish Executive, 2006: 3).

A key element of the revised strategy was the overarching ambition to grow tourism revenues to Scotland by 50% in the ten years to 2015 and make the country one of the world's foremost tourism destinations. This reflected greater recognition of tourism as an economic engine in Scotland and confidence in tourism growth, but the specific 50% target was not based on rigorous research or specific visitor number projections, but on focus group hype. Nevertheless the framework marks a shift in policy leadership, placing the ball firmly in the private sector court with emphasis placed on the need for business to take the lead and the importance of entrepreneurial attitudes to improve product development and innovation and to match customer needs (Scottish Executive, 2006).

The strategy also acknowledges priorities in the public sector domain: the critical importance of access to and around Scotland; the need for an integrated marketing effort; and a sustainable approach to tourism development– economically, socially and environmentally. However the framework makes it clear that it is the industry that needs to make these changes with the public sector agencies, such as VisitScotland, playing a supporting role. This was agreed, in part, by industry, although the Scottish Tourism Forum (STF), the lead private sector umbrella organisation, notes this is more a partnership:

> 'The TFFC was developed as a vehicle to remove barriers, build successful strategies and partnerships and to provide a focus for the industry to work in partnership with the public sector', and they recognise the critical importance and difficulties they face in bringing all their members on board '...there is an industry driven desire to bring together a wide and sometimes apparently divided sector into a united industry working together to unlock the huge economic potential that clearly exists within tourism in Scotland.'
>
> *(Herbert, 2009: 1).*

In spite of the inter-sectoral tensions it is clear that tourism policy-making in Scotland had entered a more mature phase where stakeholders acknowledge the value of their partners and the need to compromise and get on with the job rather than reverting to old habits of a blame culture. The devolved powers focused attention within the policy-making arena of Scotland, on Edinburgh rather than London and in a relatively small country where organisations and personalities brush shoulders regularly in close proximity. The number and quality of debates on tourism in the Scottish Parliament reflect the gradual improvement in understanding of the key issues and a more pragmatic attitude to policy-making (Scottish Parliament, 2007; 2008).

One might expect the election of a minority administration led by the Scottish National Party (SNP) to place greater emphasis on political independence rather than matters such as tourism, however, the new administration recognised that tourism was a core concern of the Scottish people, one that had already received a lot of attention and a policy area where they might gain some positive publicity. Another review of tourism was quickly initiated whereby the new Minister, Jim Mather gave his resounding support to the sector:

> *There is a new realisation that tourism is economically important in providing jobs and revenue, in maintaining and broadcasting the brand and in attracting people to Scotland who will invest, return and buy Scottish goods and services. Indeed, there is a new awareness that we are all in the tourism business.*
>
> *(Scottish Parliament, 2007: 1).*

A subsequent government document further clarified the important position of tourism within Scotland, where it was listed as one of the six main priority industries identified by the Scottish Government's enterprise agencies as key growth sectors. A central component of the strategy repeats that the Scottish Government and the tourism industry should adopt an 'ambition' of increasing gross tourism revenues by 50% (in real terms) by 2015, using the revenue figures for 2005 as the baseline (Scottish Parliament, 2008: 1).

One might expect an administration led by a party with independence for Scotland as its raison d'être to place greater emphasis on nationalistic promotions such as the recent 'Year of Homecoming' event throughout 2009. A counter argument points to the sensitivities involved in an overly Scottish nationalistic image: one must be careful not to alienate neighbours in a United Kingdom, particularly as they constitute the main visitor market for the Scottish tourism product. Nonetheless most new SNP initiatives related to tourism have been minor and innocuous, such as the proposed slogan 'Welcome to Scotland'and the branding of partnership working towards a unified approach to selling Scotland as 'Team Scotland'. On the one hand, critics suggest the SNP have run out of ideas, on the other, why fix what is not broken: tourism policy-making in Scotland had already received more attention in the previous decade than ever before and tourism support organisations had undergone extensive restructuring without the opportunity to 'bed in'.

Discussion: the place of tourism in political changes — issues and controversies

Post devolution, tourism in Scotland has certainly been given an elevated position in public policy if the number of enquiries, benchmarking studies and strategy documents produced is any indicator. Although there is evidence of partial success the jury is still out regarding whether over the last 10 years, Scottish administrations have resolved decades-old barriers to tourism development or met core targets (the ambitious 50% growth aspiration). The same issues, seemingly examined in some depth in 2000, still seem to be key concerns in political debate and there is still a lack of understanding of the fundamentals of tourism and repeated lists of action points with little real evidence of change.

However, in spite of recent concerns regarding failure to reach tourism growth targets it would be unfair to be too critical of progress in tourism policy-making and development in the post-devolution era. It is inevitable that progress will not all be smooth and that there will be battles fought and differences in opinion in the new political scene. If anything, a key criticism might be an over-confidence and ambition in the power of tourism to transform Scotland's economy, something that was clearly not evident before 1999. One might conclude that this reflects the maturing of tourism policy-making and the recognition of its value to Scotland, not only in a narrow economic sense but also in terms of giving justification in the minds of Scots to valuing their culture, natural and built environment. Pride in Scotland has gradually shifted from celebrating their ability to make things and trade, (industry and commerce) to pride in the beauty, scenery and historic interests of Scotland.

The maturing process over the past decade has also affected stakeholder relationships in tourism. The culture has shifted from blame to co-operation and recognition of the need for public and private sectors to form partnerships. Although there are still elements of distrust and misunderstandings, the public sector no longer acts as 'big brother' dictating tourism strategies from above and the private sector, strongly encouraged by government, has begun to take the lead in tourism development. At last a more cohesive voice can be heard with organisations like STF providing a balanced positive way forward.

The effect of devolving powers from London to Edinburgh has made some differences in tourism policy-making, generally without undermining the positive relationship between the key British tourism agency, VisitBritain, and the key Scottish tourism promotion organisation, VisitScotland. As mentioned earlier, Scotland relies heavily on visitors from England so Scottish nationalistic rhetoric must not reduce the strong brand position of Scotland in UK and overseas markets. On balance, evidence suggests that the marketing of Scotland has benefited since 1999, although perhaps not to the extent envisaged in the heady days of the new Scottish Parliament in 2000. The greatly improved tourism promotion budget has probably had a greater impact on growth in visitor numbers rather than any raising of profile attributable to devolution.

The restructuring of tourism support arrangements within Scotland has been less harmonious, in particular the reorganisation of the ATB network experiencing greater control from VisitScotland. There will always be tensions between national, regional and local organisations and there is evidence to suggest Scotland has some way to go in the evolution of tourism support structures. The growth in prominence of the private sector has been more than matched by the strengthening powers and confidence of the leading cities in Scotland, notably Edinburgh and Glasgow. Their autonomy in promoting themselves as places not only to visit but also to work, live, study and invest cannot be over-ruled by VisitScotland. Their brands as destinations are arguably more cohesive and as strong if not stronger than Scotland as a whole. New hybrid organisations have emerged in 2009 to lead the cities, for example Destination Edinburgh Marketing Alliance, that explores new working mechanisms and challenges 'top down' national tourism strategies. The concern over public sources of funds for tourism development is another thorny issue that has yet to be resolved. Heated debates over options for national and local tourism taxes continue without a clear way forward emerging.

There has also been a number of independent Destination Management Organisations (DMOs) formed in rural areas, acting independently of VisitScotland and the reorganised tourism network. Ironically these have been encouraged and supported by VisitScotland's public sector partner, the economic development agency, Scottish Enterprise, through its promotion of a DMO toolkit. This is further evidence of the anomaly of separating tourism development from tourism promotion and illustrates the type of mixed message emanating from government agencies. The small scale of some of these emergent rural DMOs calls into question their viability. However, they are popular in their local areas and fill a vacuum in post-devolution reorganisation, giving a channel for independent local thinking and autonomy. Tourism organisational structures continue to evolve and, although the current situation may not be neat and tidy, it perhaps reflects the increased voice of private sector companies and local views, which is something encouraged as a key goal of devolution.

The need to persuade key public sector bodies to work closer together has already been mentioned. In particular, a closer alignment of the strategies and operating plans of the national tourist board, the two enterprise agencies and Scottish Development International is to be encouraged. There is still evidence of institutional reluctance to change and, on occasion, in-fighting between public bodies, all to the disadvantage of improving support to the tourism industry. Changing entrenched working practices, vested interests and departmental autonomies takes time but must be achieved if tourism in Scotland is to achieve its potential.

There is still a danger of fragmented policy-making with regard to the roles of different public bodies, for example in relation to skills and training. Related to providing an educated tourism workforce is the need for improved research and market information in tourism yet in both educational and research terms there is a lack of synergy between tourism organisations and the higher education sector specialising in tourism. Attempts to build tourism research networks have so far failed to achieve success and provision of tourism related degree courses have, if anything, been diminished with the demise of the longest established institution (formerly The Scottish Hotel School) in 2009.

Conclusions: lessons learned and implications for the future

Scotland has undergone considerable changes in the past decade and, while it may not always be obvious, the political changes have had a major effect on tourism policy-making and structures. Even if many closely involved in tourism focus on the difficulties, especially during the current economic recession, on the whole the post-devolution changes have been positive and reflect improved communications and a maturing of relationships amongst key stakeholders.

The nation is blessed with an exceptional 'tourist product' and, compared to some nations, Scotland has an identity and a brand second-to-none. Many of these products have been refined and niche markets identified and exploited to diversify the range of visitors. The current recession may ironically provide an opportunity to build on these developments as a weak currency makes Scotland a more attractive 'value for money' destination to key international markets.

There is still a need for rationalisation of public sector functions in tourism and a need for clarification of structures and hierarchies between national, regional and local level tourism organisations. There also remains concern, particularly within the private sector, about remaining duplication of effort, wasted resources, the plethora of initiatives and the increasing 'mission creep' whereby certain bodies are now acting in a fashion beyond that originally intended. However there have always been overlapping initiatives operated by different public bodies in Scotland. The point here is that the duplication and confusion have arguably been diminishing since devolution.

One area of concern remains, that of tourism skills training and education where the current structure is patently failing to deliver. Industry continues to complain about the problems they face in recruitment and retention, the mismatch between the skills they need and those offered by the graduates and the confused state of affairs in terms of what is provided overall. They argue for a need to rationalise the provision of education, skills and training in the sector and reprioritise the resources towards a system that is demand-led, enjoys the support of the industry. This, of course, takes policy-making beyond that traditionally covered within the tourism umbrella and it is perhaps this expansion into wider policy areas such as education, which should be the next step for a devolved Scottish government.

The profile of Scotland is high and on the whole positive, in spite of some mixed messages regarding who leads and who follows in promotion, city or nation, public sector or industry. However the evidence indicates a healthy, more transparent debate on this and many other important issues for tourism after devolution. The increased autonomy has acted as a catalyst for more open dialogue and has accelerated change, hopefully in the long run, towards a more successful inclusive tourism sector in Scotland.

References

Barrie, N. (1999) 'Scotland country report', *Travel and Tourism Analyst*, 1, 43–65.

Butler, R.W. (1985) 'Evolution of tourism in the Scottish Highlands', *Annals of Tourism Research* 12, 371–91.

Butler, R. W. (1998) 'Tartan mythology, the traditional tourist image of Scotland', in Ringer, G. (ed.), *Cultural Landscapes of Tourism*, London: Routledge.

Day G. and MacLellan L.R. (2000) 'The Scottish Parliament and tourism', in Robinson, M., Evans, N, Long, P, Sharpley, R and Swarbrooke, J. (eds), *Management, Marketing and the Political Economy of Travel and Tourism*, London: Business Education Publishers

Dewer, J. (2007) Tourism in Scotland – Subject Profile, SPICe Briefing 07/34, Edinburgh: The Scottish Parliament.

Durie, A.J. Yeoman, I.S. and McMahon-Beatie, U. (2005) 'How the history of Scotland creates a sense of place', *Place Branding*, 2(1), 43–52.

Fairley, J. (1999) 'Scotland's new democracy – new opportunities for rural Scotland?' paper presented at the conference The Scottish Parliament and Rural Policy: What Room for Manoeuvre?'3 November, University of Aberdeen, Department of Agriculture.

Hall, C.M. (2000) *Tourism Planning: Policies, Processes and Relationships*, Harlow: Prentice Hall.

Hay, B. (2007) 'Lessons for the future: the history and development of the Scottish Tourist Board', in Middleton, V.T.C. (ed.) *British Tourism: The Remarkable Story of Growth*, London: Butterworth-Heinemann.

Herbert, I, (2009) *Tourism Framework for Change Scottish Tourism: Making a Step Change*. Review and Recommendations from the Scottish Tourism Forum; Edinburgh: Scottish Tourism Forum.

Jefferies, D. (2001) *Governments and Tourism*, Oxford: Butterworth-Heinemann.

Kerr, W. R. and Wood, R C (1999) 'Scottish tourism after devolution?' *Hospitality Review*, April: 16–23.

Kerr, W.R. (2003) *Tourism Public Policy, and the Strategic Management of Failure*, Oxford: Elsevier.

Lennon, J.J and Hay, B. (2003) *Benchmarking Scotland*, Edinburgh: VisitScotland.

Lennon, J.J. and Seaton, A.V. (1998) 'Pathways to success: contrasting roles in public sector business development for the tourism industry – a comparison of Glasgow and Dublin', *International Journal of Public Sector Management*, **11** (213), 139–153.

MacLellan, R. and Smith, R. (1998) *Tourism in Scotland,* London: International Thomson Business Press.

MacLellan, L.R. (1999) 'The Scottish Parliament and rural policy: where tourism fits in?' paper presented at the conference The Scottish Parliament and Rural Policy: What Room for Manoeuvre?'3 November, University of Aberdeen, Department of Agriculture.

McCrone, D., Morris, A. and Kelly, R. (1995) *Scotland the Brand: The Making of Scottish Heritage*, Edinburgh: Edinburgh University Press.

Pearce, D. (1992) *Tourist Organisations*, London: Longman.

Scottish Executive (2000) *A New Strategy for Scottish Tourism*, Edinburgh: The Stationary Office.

Scottish Executive (2006) *Scottish Tourism: the Next Decade – a Tourism Framework for Change*, Edinburgh: The Stationary Office.

Scottish Parliament (2007) Official report on the First Parliamentary Debate on Tourism under the New SNP Administration, 29 November, Edinburgh: Scottish Parliamentary Corporate Body Publications.

Scottish Parliament (2008) Economy, Energy and Tourism Committee 6th Report, (session 3) Growing Pains – Can We Achieve 50% Growth in Tourist Revenue by 2015?, Edinburgh: Scottish Parliamentary Corporate Body Publications.

Smith, R. (1998) 'Public policy for tourism in Scotland', in MacLellan, L.R. and Smith, R. (eds) *Tourism in Scotland*, London: International Thomson Business Press.

VisitScotland (2008) *Tourism in Scotland 2008*, Strategic Research Department Edinburgh: VisitScotland.

Yeoman, I.S., Durie, A.J., McMahon-Beatie, U. and Palmer, A. (2005) 'Capturing the essence of a brand from its history: the case of Scottish tourism marketing', *Brand Management*, **13** (2), 134–147.

7 Political Change and Tourism in Arctic Canada

Emma J. Stewart and Dianne Draper

Introduction

I was walking to the airport with my host in Pond Inlet and I was curious to learn more about a conversation we'd started the previous evening. During that conversation I had asked her why I had experienced a sense of resignation toward tourism among some of the people I had been interviewing that week. She drew a parallel to welfare programs where she said Inuit had become "passive recipients" rather than "active participants" in the system. This was a consequence, she said, "thrust upon Inuit" and which had become a "learnt response" over the generations since the tuberculosis/influenza outbreaks prompted the movement of Inuit into settlements. On our walk to the airport I quizzed her on what it felt like, as a people, to be passive recipients. Her response was: "dehumanizing". She went on to say that there seems to be an opportunity to make a shift from this condition, that the new generation has the power to change things so that Inuit become active participants, or at least have the "choice to do so".

(Stewart, field journal, Pond Inlet, June 2007)

In-gathering of Inuit into settlements occurred across the Canadian Arctic in the 1950s, a period known as the settlement era (Damas, 2002). The switch from a traditional transitory to a largely community-based lifestyle has been extraordinarily rapid in Arctic Canada. The inter-generational shock of this transitional period has manifested itself in many ways with socio-economic problems lingering in communities of Arctic Canada (Einarsson *et al.*, 2004). But out of social, economic and spiritual changes to Inuit culture during the settlement era came a realization by the 1960s that Inuit were no longer willing to defer to *qallunaat* (the Inuit term for non-Inuit) and instead were "finding strong voices of their own" (Tester and Kulchyski, 1994: 204). Testament to this realization was the 1993 signing of the Nunavut Land Claims Agreement (NLCA) which gave the Inuit of Nunavut rights of ownership and use of land (van Dam, 2005). The final agreement paved the way for the creation of a new Inuit-led political machine, the territory of Nunavut on 1st April 1999 (Bone, 2003) (see Figure 7.1).

Political change can affect many aspects of indigenous tourism (Butler and Hinch, 2007) such as the structure of public agencies responsible for indigenous tourism development, management, marketing and promotion, policy formulation and implementation and the development of tourism resources (Hall, 2007). To understand these aspects of indigenous tourism, it is vital to understand the political processes from which they emerged (Hall, 2007). Nowhere is this more important than in Arctic Canada where a key concern for researchers and communities is to understand how individuals, families, culture, environment, and livelihoods might be affected by current political and economic development and wider global changes (Caine *et al.*, 2009).

The current attention given to the Canadian Arctic is unprecedented; issues such as climate change, sovereignty, contaminants, species depletion, natural resource development, and aboriginal well-being, are receiving broad media coverage (Fenge and Penikett, 2009; Shadian, 2009). However, within this wider milieu of change, tourism is rarely mentioned (Maher and Stewart, 2007), and even less is known about the linkages between tourism and political change following Nunavut's creation. This chapter provides a context for understanding how tourism developed in Nunavut during the lead up to partition, and how tourism has fared since the founding of Nunavut, at the regional and local scale. The chapter utilizes case study material from two Nunavut communities, Pond Inlet on Baffin Island and Cambridge Bay on Victoria Island drawn from a wider study of resident attitudes toward tourism development (see: Stewart, 2009).

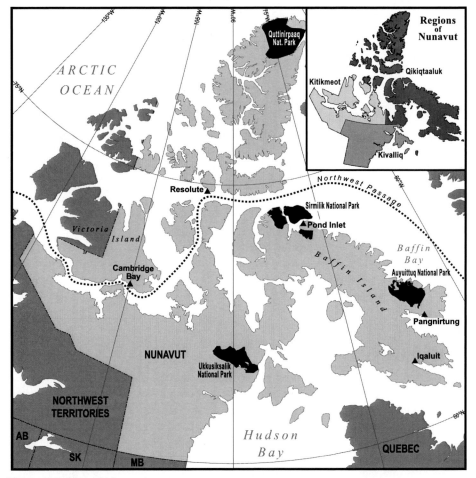

Figure 7.1: Map of Nunavut.

Political change in Arctic Candada

In the early 1970s, the Supreme Court of Canada recognized the existence of Aboriginal title, which paved the way for the signing of treaties or 'comprehensive agreements', which make explicit the nature of the arrangement between Aboriginal groups and the government of Canada under areas such as self-governing powers, control over social services, compensation payments, environmental assessment, land use regulations and the management of lands and resources (Berkes and Fast, 2005). The James Bay and Northern Quebec agreement was the first to be signed in 1975. The 1993 Nunavut Land Claims Agreement (NLCA) was the largest aboriginal land claim agreement in Canada's history in terms of financial compensation and land (an area approximately one-fifth of Canada's land mass) (Merritt, 1993; van Dam, 2005). It provided the terms and conditions of c$1.173 billion in federal payments over 15 years (ending in 2007) and established land right uses specific to Inuit as beneficiaries of the agreement. In return Inuit surrendered their Aboriginal title and certain claims to lands and waters (Gregoire, 2009, Merritt (1993)). The signing of the agreement was a landmark for all indigenous peoples in Canada and changed the northern political landscape immeasurably (Merritt, 1993). The NLCA provided a new organizational structure including Nunavut Tunngavik Incorporated (NTI) to administer, manage and invest the compensation funds on behalf of Inuit beneficiaries. Territorial and regional economic development organizations were charged with spreading wealth from the NLCA to Inuit (Gregoire, 2009).

The territory of Nunavut, meaning 'our land' or 'Inuit homeland' was established with the passing of the Nunavut Act on 1st April 1999. Carved out of the Northwest Territories (NWT), Nunavut's jurisdiction extends over 2.1 million square kilometres, consisting of three regions (Kitikmeot, Kivalliq and Quikiqtaaluk) (see Figure 7.1). The Aboriginal population of these three regions is 29,325, representing approximately 95 percent of Nunavut's total population (Statistics Canada, 2009). The young and rapidly growing population is one of the most prominent features of Nunavut's demographic profile, with 80 per cent of the population aged between 20-29 years (Simeone, 2008). The youthful characteristic of Nunavut presents significant policy implications such as the challenge to find meaningful employment opportunities (Simeone, 2008). Tourism, with opportunities to showcase the northern environment and culture, as well as the potential to stimulate economic activity in remote areas, has long been regarded as an important source of supplementary income for residents of northern Canada, particularly for Nunavut's youth (Hinch and Swinnerton, 1993).

Tourism before partition

In the 1980s, before the partition of Nunavut, tourism consisted mainly of remote fishing and hunting camps, and adventure tourism operations, largely owned and operated by non-Inuit (Robbins, 2007). The first Canadian Arctic cruise took place in 1984, when the MS *Explorer* made the first successful passenger transit of the Northwest Passage (Stewart *et al.*, 2007). The success of community-based tourism planning activities in Pangnirtung (Baffin Island) confirmed the Government of Northwest Territories' (GNWT) commitment to tourism as an important form of community economic development and resulted in increased numbers of licensed outfitters and the establishment of Inuit-owned and operated tourism businesses throughout Arctic Canada (Robbins, 2007). Community tourism plans, akin to the prototype developed in Pangnirtung, were written for many of the other Inuit communities in the 1980s (Robbins, 2007). The intention was to develop an industry that was substantially planned, owned and operated by Inuit which reflected aspirations of local residents (Hinch and Swinnerton, 1993) diversifying local economic development and reducing economic dependence on the GNWT (Reimer, 1994; Corliss, 1999). Tourism was a centrepiece of the GNWT's economic development policy in the 1980s, supported by millions of dollars from the Canada NWT economic development agreements (Milne, 2006).

However, in the early 1990s as division of the territories approached, the flow of funding from GNWT to tourism operators and agencies in the proposed Nunavut territory began to dry up (Milne, 2006; Robbins, 2007), just as many Inuit-owned businesses in particular were becoming viable and successful. Nunavut Tourism, founded in 1996, is a small arm's length industry organization created out of the Northwest Territories Tourism Industry Association, with wide-ranging responsibility for marketing, product development and training. The organization is funded by industry members and contributions from government to the tune of c$2 million (Robbins, 2007). By comparison, the GNWT and Yukon government funded their respective tourism associations at c$11 and c$19 million. Tourism in Nunavut also receives federal funding from Indian and Northern Affairs (INAC), Aboriginal Business Canada, Canadian Tourism Commission, Canadian Tourism Human Resource Council, Canadian Heritage and Parks Canada. However, as pointed out by the Standing Senate Committee on Aboriginal Peoples (2006), accessing this myriad of funding is complex and the funding channels (based on southern Canadian models) may not reflect the needs of Nunavut (Standing Committee on Aboriginal Peoples, 2006).

In Nunavut, virtually all tourism is long haul, all transportation is expensive, and accommodation is limited, both in variety and quality. With persistent low levels of funding, promotional activities became Nunavut Tourism's priority, while product development, education, training and licensing received less attention. As a result of tourism largely being neglected by the GNWT through the 1990s, there were huge expectations that tourism would reclaim political support and interest from the new government of Nunavut (GN), because 'the Inuit of Nunavut would be able to take charge of their own destiny' (Milne, 2006: 90).

Tourism in the New Territorial Government

At the time of the landmark signing of the Nunavut Act, tourism was estimated to be worth approximately c$30 million annually to the new jurisdiction. The Conference Board of Canada identified tourism as one of Nunavut's three growth pillars alongside mining and fishing (Vail and Clinton, 2002). In Nunavut, although tourism falls under the remit of the Department of Economic Development and Transportation (EDT), the tourism sector includes a complex array of multi-level stakeholder groups. At the local level, hamlet councils, hunting and trapper organizations (HTO) and cooperatives all have varying levels of association with the tourism sector. Similarly, at the regional scale, the GN, Nunavut Tourism (NT), Nunavut Planning Commission (NPC), and Regional Inuit Associations (RIAs), who represent and support the interests of the Inuit politically and through economic development opportunities (via development corporations) have interests in tourism development matters. At a national scale, the Department of Indian and Northern Affairs (INAC), the Canadian Coast Guard, Parks Canada (PC), and many others, are involved with the management of tourism in Arctic Canada, making the governance of tourism in Nunavut multi-layered and complex.

Recognizing the complexity of managing tourism, as well as the unique circumstances of Nunavut's tourism products, the NLCA included a provision to re-examine the Travel and Tourism Act that had been grandfathered across from NWT as this Act did not reflect the particular circumstances of tourism in Nunavut such as Inuit rights and the roles and responsibilities of designated Inuit organizations (DIOs), and institutions of public government (IPGs) that were established under the NLCA. Redrafting the Act has started but the revisions to the Travel and Tourism Act have not been completed. The NLCA also contained several other articles of direct interest to tourism including wildlife, parks and archeological sites, including the establishment of three new national parks. Sirmilik National Park, in the northern Baffin Island region was created in 1999 and in 2000, Ellesmere Island National Park Reserve was renamed Quttinirpaaq ('top of the world') National Park. In 2003, Ukkusiksalik National Park became the fourth national park within Nunavut's boundaries (Auyuittuq National Park had been designated in 1976). The NLCA required the undertaking of Inuit Impact Benefit Agreements (IIBAs) for Nunavut's protected natural areas, a process completed in 2008. The obligations pertinent to tourism include: cultural resources inventories (where traditional knowledge will be used in interpretive materials for each protected area); creation of an Inuit tourism provider's fund; and training for Inuit from communities adjacent to new National Wildlife Areas on effective conduct of ecotourism businesses in the protected areas, and assistance in developing and marketing those businesses.

Many of Nunavut's protected natural areas, particularly the territory's four national parks, have become important tourism attractions in their own right, and áre ports of call for an increasing number of cruise ship visits (Stewart et al., 2008). In the lead up to partition, Parks Canada reported a surge in visitor numbers, particularly to Auyuittuq National Park, from only 355 visitors in 1998, to 1,191 in 1999. Although short-lived, the concentrated media attention on Nunavut appeared to increase visitor numbers (Stewart et al., 2008).

A 2006 survey revealed that approximately 9300 tourists visited the territory between June and October 2006, including around 2100 on cruise vessels. In 2006, the majority of visitors were male (62 percent), with an average age of 37.5 years, and mostly from Canada (79 percent). One-half of the visitors came for business purposes, one-third for a vacation and the remainder either were visiting friends or family (VFF) or participating in an educational trip. Visitors from the USA were most likely to be vacationers, and vacation travel was highest in the Baffin region, while VFF was highest in the Kivalliq region. Iqaluit, the territory's capital, attracted the most visitors (30 per cent), due to the prevalence of business tourism there. The 2006 report suggested that the summer tourism industry accounted for nearly c\$4.4 million dollars to Nunavut; over half of which was spent in the Baffin region. Of this total, cruise tourism was estimated to have generated c\$2.1 million dollars (Datapath, 2006).

The following two case studies illustrate how tourism has fared at the community scale since the inception of Nunavut, and sheds light on how decisions in Iqaluit, Nunavut's territorial capital, have had an impact on local tourism development.

Cambridge Bay

Cambridge Bay is situated in the Kitikmeot region on the southern shores of Victoria Island overlooking the Northwest Passage (see Figure 7.1). With the advent of Nunavut, Cambridge Bay became a key transport and supply centre, and it remains so with the community now established as the regional centre for Kitikmeot. According to the last Canadian census the hamlet had a population of 1477; 83 per cent of residents self-identified as having aboriginal status (Statistics Canada, 2008c), 95 per cent of whom were Inuit (Statistics Canada, 2008a). Stewart's (2009) study found that Cambridge Bay residents overwhelmingly supported the tourism industry despite the fact that tourism directly generates employment for only a small sector of the population (carvers, guides and outfitters). Support for the industry was expressed because tourism connects young guides to the land, and tourism provides an important opportunity to meet new people and educate visitors about life in the north.

Sport hunting has been one of the community's tourism success stories. The community has hosted sport hunters on a regular basis since the 1980s; according to the Hunters' and Trappers' Organization (HTO) up to 150 sport hunters come each year to hunt muskoxen, caribou, sheep, and polar bear. The community also hosts accompanied bird watching, nature tours and sport fishing.

Cambridge Bay is is a service centre for three nearby wilderness lodges and a key port of call for Northwest Passage travellers, being a featured stop on itineraries of most cruise ships sailing the Passage (see Figure 7.2). Since 1984, cruise ships increasingly have

Figure 7.2: *Kapitan Khlebnikov* on a Northwest Passage tour, near Cambridge Bay (photograph by Emma J. Stewart)

docked in Cambridge Bay, and the six planned visits during the 2009 season represent the most cruise ships this community has hosted. However, managing cruise visits is still a work-in-progress, as one Cambridge Bay stakeholder indicated in Stewart's (2009: 187) study:

> *Cruise ships in Nunavut are a joke, although they are incredibly beneficial in the east [referring to the Baffin Region], they are not here. We are now in a position of subsidizing the costs of people's vacations, because cruise operators are not willing to meet the costs of a community visit. Even when we charge them out of pocket expenses, they say it's too expensive....So ships come in and ask for the sun, the moon and the sky, but when you calculate the benefits to the community (e.g. sales at the souvenir shops) it is very low.*

Cambridge Bay represents a late phase of exploration and an early phase of involvement according to Butler's (1980) TALC model. This is because overall visitor numbers are low and, in line with the involvement stage, visitor patterns are developing some regularity in the case of cruise tourists, sport hunters, and retreat and conference guests. Facilities such as hotels and home stay accommodation have been provided explicitly for tourists (although Cambridge Bay is an important regional government centre so business travelers have been accommodated for some years). Tourists are attracted by unique natural and cultural features, contact with locals is high (especially for sport hunters where guides are almost always local residents) and overall activities of tourists are of little significance to the social and economic lives of most permanent residents. Stakeholders in Cambridge Bay confirm observations made earlier in the chapter that:

> *when Nunavut and the Northwest Territories were one, we had quite a developed tourism industry, but that was because the Northwest Territories were committed, but here in Nunavut we were not. We were way behind and that became obvious when we split...*
>
> *(Stewart, 2009: 182)*

As elsewhere in Nunavut, tourism was not regarded as a priority for residents in Cambridge Bay, evidenced by research undertaken for the community's 15-year development plan: 'In the visioning exercise, tourism came up as an important factor, but not as an immediate priority, community wellness came up far beyond anything else' (Stewart, 2009: 203). Stakeholders identified a number of barriers to tourism that would need to be addressed: physical infrastructure, product development, exorbitant travel costs and the confusion created by overlaps in agency roles and responsibilities (Stewart, 2009). In particular, tourism stakeholders stressed the need for direction from the GN, for example:

> *We have assisted a couple of start up projects; it's been dribs and drabs elsewhere, very informal. It's a bottom up approach, but direction is needed from the government. But there doesn't seem to be a concerted effort in government to give this direction. We are pushing for an economic development strategy for this region, and tourism should be included in that. But in Nunavut effort has been slow.*
>
> *(Stewart, 2009: 203)*

Pond Inlet

Pond Inlet is located to the east of Cambridge Bay in the northern Baffin region overlooking Eclipse Sound (see Figure 7.1). In 1999, with the establishment of Nunavut, Pond Inlet, like Cambridge Bay, became a regional centre (Sawtell, 2005). In 2006, it had a population of 1315, with Inuit status identified by 92 per cent of community members (Statistics Canada, 2008b). Among Pond Inlet residents, tourism garners a high level of support, mainly because residents associate tourism with economic gain and believe tourism provides an opportunity to promote cross-cultural awareness (Grekin, 1994; Stewart, 2009). However, 'Greenpeace' tourists (a label given to visitors perceived to have an animal rights persuasion) are unwelcome as 'they have the potential to jeopardize the freedom of locals to hunt' (Grekin and Milne, 1996: 89). As Hinch (1998) comments, a common strategy among northern residents is to keep tourists away from indigenous hunting. This strategy is utilized in Pond Inlet, where residents appear to have an unwritten rule to conceal hunting from tourists (Stewart *et al.*, in press).

Figure 7.3: Bylot Island from Pond Inlet (photograph by Emma J Stewart).

Currently, tourism activities in Pond Inlet include sport hunting, hiking, whale-watching, accompanied visits to the floe-edge to see narwhal, polar bears and birds, and other outdoor adventure activities such as kayaking and mountaineering. Pond Inlet is also an important service centre for tourism activities in the nearby newly-established (1999) Sirmilik National Park. There was much anticipation that the proposed National Park would bring in "hundreds of thousands of dollars in local wages and northern expenditures" (Myers and Forrest, 2000: 139–140), but visitor numbers to date have been low, only 230 park visitors were recorded in 2005 and 216 in 2006, the majority being cruise passengers. Among Canadian Arctic communities, Pond Inlet is one that cruise ships visit most frequently. For each of the summer seasons from 2006 to 2008, between nine and twelve ships disembarked approximately 100 passengers per ship over a relatively short 40 day period (Stewart *et al.*, 2008). At the start of the 2008 cruise season, however, a local Inuit resident mounted a one-man protest regarding the European Union ban on seal skin imports against European visitors from the *Hanseatic* cruise ship (see Figure 7.4). (CBC news, 2008). An unfortunate consequence of the protest is that the *Hanseatic* does not plan to return to Pond Inlet in 2009.

Figure 7.4: *Hanseatic* in Pond Inlet (2007) (photograph by Dianne Draper).

Pond Inlet represents a late phase of involvement and an early phase of the development stage of Butler's (1980) TALC model. In the late phase of involvement, it can be expected that a market area and tourist season has emerged which, in Pond Inlet, is defined largely by the arrival of cruise ships between the end of July and mid-September. In turn, cruise ship arrivals mean adjustments will be made in the social patterns of at least those residents involved in providing services to the tourism industry, contact between hosts and guest likely will remain generally high and, assistance in terms of travel arrangements has been made, to help facilitate access to nearby Sirmilik National Park.

However, there is a perennial issue of recruiting staff into the tourism industry in Pond Inlet. As one stakeholder suggested in Stewart's (2009: 201) study:

> *We've had various visitor centre managers but now we are at an all time low. We need a local person doing the job, but they don't necessarily have all the skills that this position demands. One person might be good at organizing the cultural demonstrations but terrible with accounting or product development ... It's hard because it's only 30 hours per week and then there is the summer crunch. And since the GN provides better employment conditions I can see why people would want to work there.*

The two community case studies indicate that although tourism was regarded as a main pillar of the new administration's economic development strategy, at the local level partition appeared to have had only a negligible impact on the provision and development of tourism. Ten years on, as Stewart's (2009) study reveals, tourism stakeholders are increasingly concerned about the lack of direction from the GN, for example:

It's the Department of Economic Development and Transport (GN) that needs the strategic view. Nunavut Tourism has no enforcement powers. Tourism needs to be supported much more by government if it is going to succeed. There is no interest in the larger picture.

(Stewart, 2009: 203–204)

Discussion

Apart from the redrafting of the Travel and Tourism Act and provisions relating to protected natural areas, wildlife and archaeological sites, the NLCA did not address tourism in its totality. Nunavut Tourism is a GN entity but with non-Inuit status. The result is that Nunavut Tourism does not have access to funds beyond those of its members and the GN; both status and funding may have been the reason for the lack of political interest in tourism, at least in the first ten years of Nunavut's administration. With a sometimes turbulent relationship between Nunavut Tourism and the GN, tourism has not been fully supported by the administration. Despite important foundations laid in the 1980s, the GN has not and does not place great importance on tourism. Priorities appear to lie with other sectors such as fishing and mining, as well as pressing concerns relating to healthcare, education and housing, all of which warrant urgent attention from the GN (Robbins, 2007). In Pond Inlet, for example, the development of an iron mine at Mary River has overshadowed other perhaps less significant economic opportunities. Unfortunately tourism development has suffered from a lack of input from the hamlet (Stewart, 2009); an indication of the low priority tourism is afforded over other development activities.

Despite numerous consultation reports on the potential for tourism growth in Nunavut there is a lack of a clearly defined process and appropriate tools to guide the tourism industry in the territory. Previous tourism strategies commissioned by the GN have not been implemented or politically championed, resulting in an ad hoc, piecemeal approach to the tourism sector (Nunavut Tourism Renewal Study, 2007), partly due to the multiplicity of agencies involved in tourism and their overlapping roles and responsibilities. Layered regulatory systems are common in resource development sectors in Nunavut, and although tourism was not mentioned explicitly, the restructuring, streamlining and improving of this type of layered system was the focus of a 2008 government of Canada report called *Road to Improvement* (Indian and Northern Affairs Canada, 2008).

In the context of cruise tourism, there are complex interactions of stakeholders at all levels of governance. At a local level, Parks Canada, Environment Canada, Canadian Wildlife Service and hamlets are involved in providing tourists with permits for shore visits, and at a regional level Nunavut Tourism, the Government of Nunavut, Customs Canada, Transport Canada, Department of Fisheries and Oceans and the Coast Guard are all active in overseeing the development and safety of the industry as well as being responsible for implementation and monitoring of various levels of existing shipping regulations. On the international level the Arctic Council works to ensure that voluntary codes of practice are adhered to (Stewart and Draper, 2006) (Editors' note, for comparison with arrangements in Antarctica, see chapter by Bauer this volume). This labyrinth of regulation is complex and unnecessary in the tourism sector (Marquez and Eagles, 2007). However, dialogue between these different layers of governance may be improving with the creation of the Nunavut Tourism Task Force, which brought together a variety of tourism stakeholders in Nunavut (representatives from the arts and crafts sector, NTI, Parks Canada, Nunavut Tourism, GN, Chamber of Commerce and the Francophone Association). Despite having no mandate and no budget, this informal consortium of interest groups is engaging in dialogue about many of the critical issues facing tourism in Nunavut.

An overall lack of data undermines collective knowledge about tourism issues in Nunavut. It was not until 2006 that the GN commissioned the first Nunavut-wide visitor exit survey, and the survey has not been repeated since. Clearly, more resources are required to maintain accurate data collection, since it is not advisable to manage tourism without knowing the scale and scope of the phenomenon. With growth in Nunavut's cruise sector, there is a pressing need for a knowledge base which can underpin the development of this sector so that cruising is safe and sustainable.

Conclusion

Indigenous people are becoming increasingly politically aware and active, with many groups such as the Inuit of Nunavut securing land claim agreements, financial gain and resource management responsibilities (Butler and Hinch, 2007). In Nunavut, the journey toward these 'responsibilities' can be traced to the end of the settlement era, when Inuit participation in community affairs was highlighted (Damas, 2002). Since the 1970s Inuit have made much progress in reasserting autonomy over their homelands, and there was a heightened sense of expectation of further change when Nunavut was created. But ten years into the GN's administration, it is clear that tourism, once regarded as an important vehicle for diversifying Nunavut's economy, has struggled to gain necessary political support. More recently, the Tourism Task Force has precipitated a much better working relationship with the GN than has been the case in the past. This bodes well for the future of tourism in Nunavut and may bring much needed government involvement, particularly in the redrafting of the Travel and Tourism Act.

Despite an overall lack of political interest, some sectors of tourism (such as cruising) have grown since Nunavut was created, but other sectors such as land-based and adventure-based tourism activities have declined. This situation may have arisen because development has been largely industry-led. The fledgling administration has been slow to recognize, and act on, the potential of tourism to provide sustainable economic development opportunities (Robbins, 2007). The time has come for overarching policy direction from the GN. Residents clearly support further development of the tourism industry (Stewart, 2009), particularly to capitalize on the burgeoning cruise industry, but if ambitions are to be realized, political will is necessary to ensure the evolution of new governance structures and regulatory regimes, that will enable the Inuit of Nunavut to become 'active participants' in future tourism development (Simeone, 2008).

Acknowledgement

The Pierre Elliot Trudeau Foundation is thanked for their generous funding in support of Emma Stewart's doctoral research in Arctic Canada. In preparation of this book chapter, we would like to extend our thanks to numerous stakeholders in Nunavut for their insight. We would also like to thank Robin Poitras, cartographer in the Department of Geography at the University of Calgary for creating the map used in this chapter.

References

Berkes, F. and Fast, H. (2005) 'Introduction', in Berkes, F., Huebert, R., Fast, H., Manseau, M. and Diduck, A. (eds) *Breaking Ice: Renewable Resources and Ocean Management in the Canadian Arctic*, University of Calgary Press, pp. 1–19.

Bone, R. M. (2003) *The Geography of the Canadian North: Issues and Challenges*, 2nd edn, Oxford University Press.

Butler, R., and Hinch, T. (eds), (2007) *Tourism and Indigenous Peoples: Issues and Implications*, 2nd edn, Oxford: Butterworth-Heinemann.

Caine, K., Davidson, C., and Stewart, E. J. (2009) 'Preliminary field-work: methodological reflections from northern Canadian research', *Qualitative Research*, 9(4) 489–513.

Cambridge Bay Hamlet (2008) Welcome to Cambridge Bay, from: http://www.cambridgebay.ca/ (14 June 2008).

CBC news (2008) Nunavut Officials in Damage Control over Cruise Ship Incident, from: http://www.cbc.ca/canada/north/story/2008/08/14/pond-cruise.html (1 February 2009).

Corliss, G. (1999) *Community-based Tourism Planning and Policy: The Case of the Baffin Region, Nunavut*, Montreal: McGill University.

Damas, D. (2002) *Arctic Migrants/Arctic Villagers: The Transformation of Inuit Settlement in the Central Arctic*, Montreal: McGill-Queen's University Press.

Datapath (2006) Nunavut Exit Survey.

Einarsson, N., Larsen, J. N., Nilsson, A. and Young, O. R. (eds), (2004) *Arctic Human Development Report*, Akureyri: Stefansson Arctic Institute.

Fenge, T., and Penikett, T. (2009) 'The Arctic vacuum in Canada's foreign policy', *Policy Options*, April, 65-70.

Gregoire, L. (2009) 'Nunavut – territory of unrequited dreams', *Canadian Geographic Magazine*, January/February, 1–5.

Grekin, J. (1994) *Understanding the community level impacts of tourism development: The case of Pond Inlet, NWT*. Unpublished Masters thesis,McGill University, Montreal.

Grekin, J., and Milne, S. (1996) 'Towards sustainable tourism development: The case of Pond Inlet, NWT', in Butler, R W and Hinch, T D (eds), *Tourism and Indigenous Peoples*, London: International Thomson Press, pp. 76-106.

Hall, C. M. (2007) 'Politics, power and indigenous tourism', in Butler, R W and Hinch, T D. (eds.), *Tourism and Indigenous Peoples: Issues and Implications*, Oxford: Butterworth-Heinemann, pp. 305–318.

Hinch, T. D. (1998) 'Ecotourists and indigenous hosts: Diverging views on their relationship with nature', *Current Issues in Tourism*, 1 (1), 120–124.

Hinch, T. D. and Swinnerton, G. S. (1993) 'Tourism and Canada's Northwest Territories: issues and prospects', *Tourism Recreation Research*, **18** (2), 23–31.

Indian and Northern Affairs Canada (2008) *The Road to Improvement*, Ottawa: Government of Canada.

Indian and Northern Affairs Canada (2009) Nunavut Land Claims Agreement, from: http://www.ainc-inac.gc.ca/al/ldc/ccl/fagr/nuna/nla/nunav-eng.asp (24 March 2009).

Maher, P. T., and Stewart, E. J. (2007) 'Polar tourism: Research directions for current realities and future possibilities', *Tourism in Marine Environments*, 4(2-3), 65–68.

Marquez, J. and Eagles, P. (2007) 'Working towards policy creation for cruise ship tourism in parks and protected areas of Nunavut', *Tourism in Marine Environments*, **4** (2–3), 85-96.

Merritt, J. (1993) 'Nunavut: Canada turns a new page in the Arctic', *Canadian Parliamentary Review*, **16** (2), online.

Milne, S (2006) 'Baffin Island, Nunavut, Canada', in Baldacchino, G. (ed.), *Extreme Tourism: Lessons from the World's Cold Water Islands*, London: Elsevier, pp. 88–99.

Myers, H., and Forrest, S. (2000) 'Making change: economic development in Pond Inlet, 1987-1997', *Arctic*, 53 (2), 134–145.

Nunavut Tourism Renewal Study (2007) *Sivuliuqatigiitut Pularatulirinirmut: Taking Leadership for Tourism*, Iqaluit: Submitted to Government of Nunavut.

Reimer, G. (1994) *Community Participation in Pangnirtung*, Hamilton: McMaster University.

Robbins, M. (2007) 'Development of tourism in Arctic Canada', in Snyder, J M and Stonehouse, B. (eds). *Prospects for Polar Tourism*, Wallingford: CABI, pp. 84–101.

Sawtell, S. (2005) 'Pond Inlet', in Nuttall, M. (ed.), *Encyclopedia of the Arctic*, London: Routledge, p. 1682.

Shadian, J. (2009) 'Building bridges (and boats) where there was once ice: adopting a circumpolar approach in the Arctic', *Policy Options*, April, 71–75.

Simeone, T. (2008) The Arctic: Northern Aboriginal Peoples, from: http://www.parl.gc.ca/information/library/PRBpubs/prb0810-e.htm (30 March 2009).

Standing Committee on Aboriginal Peoples (2006) Standing Committee on Aboriginal Peoples. Issue 12 – Evidence – Meeting of November 28, 2006, from: http://www.parl.gc.ca/39/1/parlbus/commbus/senate (30 March 2009).

Statistics Canada (2008a) Aboriginal Population Profile, 2006 census (Cambridge Bay), from: http://www12.statcan.ca/english/census06/data/profiles/aboriginal/Details (3 June 2008).

Statistics Canada (2008b) Aboriginal Population Profile, 2006 Census (Pond Inlet), from: http://www12.statcan.ca/english/census06/data/profiles/aboriginal/Details (3 June 2008).

Statistics Canada (2008c) Community highlights for Cambridge Bay, from: http://www12.statcan.ca/english/census06/data/profiles/community/Details (16 March 2008).

Statistics Canada (2009) Population by Year, by Province, by Territory, Available: http://www40.statcan.gc.ca/l01/cst01/demo02a-eng.htm (30 March 2009).

Stewart, E. J. (2009) Resident attitudes toward tourism: community-based cases from Arctic Canada, unpublished PhD, University of Calgary.

Stewart, E. J. and Draper, D. (2006) 'Sustainable cruise tourism in Arctic Canada: an integrated coastal management approach', *Tourism in Marine Environments*, **3** (2), 77–88.

Stewart, E. J., Draper, D. L. and Dawson, J. D. (in press) 'Coping with change and vulnerability: a case study of resident attitudes toward tourism in Cambridge Bay and Pond Inlet, Nunavut, Canada', in Maher, P.T., Stewart, E.J. and Luck, M. (eds), *Polar Tourism: Environmental, Political and Social Dimensions*, London: Cognizant Communications.

Stewart, E. J., Howell, S., Draper, D., Yackel, J. and Tivy, A. (2008) 'Cruise tourism in a warming Arctic: implications for northern National Parks', Paper presented at the Parks for Tomorrow Conference, University of Calgary, Canada, 8–13 May.

Stewart, E. J., Howell, S. E. L., Draper, D., Yackel, J. and Tivy, A. (2007) 'Sea ice in Canada's Arctic: Implications for cruise tourism', *Arctic*, **60** (4), 370–380.

Tester, J. and Kulchyski, P. (1994) *Tammarnit (Mistakes): Inuit Relocation in the Eastern Arctic, 1939–63*, Vancouver: University of British Columbia Press.

Vail, S. and Clinton, G. (2002) *Nunavut Economic Outlook May 2001: An Examination of the Nunavut Economy*, Ottawa: the Conference Board of Canada.

van Dam, K.I.M. (2005) 'A place called Nunavut: Building on Inuit past', in Ashworth, G.J. and Graham, B. (eds), *Senses of Place: Senses of Time*, Farnham: Ashgate, pp. 105–117.

8 Central and Eastern Europe: the End of the Soviet Union and its Satellites

Derek Hall

Introduction

This chapter evaluates the relationships between tourism and political change in the former state socialist countries of Central and Eastern Europe (CEE), particularly in relation to the fall of communism in 1989–91, the disintegration of Yugoslavia during the 1990s, and EU accession of ten states in 2004/2007. Its major objectives are: (a) to describe the 'region' its tourism and political structure; (b) to describe and analyse the political changes over the last 25 years and their implications for tourism; and (c) to assess future implications and lessons to be learned.

The societies considered in this chapter include the now European Union (EU) member states of Czech Republic, Estonia, Hungary, Latvia, Lithuania, Poland, Slovakia and Slovenia (members since 2004), Bulgaria and Romania (since 2007), together with Albania, Belarus, Bosnia-Herzegovina, Croatia, (FYR) Macedonia, Moldova, Montenegro, (European) Russia (including the Kaliningrad exclave), Serbia, Ukraine. This list testifies to two significant characteristics.

First, although embracing former state socialist societies in Europe, it does not correspond with what used to be referred to as the Soviet bloc, but includes Albania, which effectively left the Soviet bloc in 1961, It also includes the states of former Yugoslavia, which was expelled from the bloc in 1948 and subsequently followed its own 'third' way – developing 'market socialism' in the 1960s – until destroyed by fragmentation and conflict in the 1990s. This litany of states, second, emphasizes the political and cultural (and environmental) diversity of CEE, and the importance of the role of the EU and other supranational bodies in bringing some coherence to post-communist fragmentation and consequent development processes, including tourism (e.g. Anastasiadou, 2006; Hall and Roberts, 2004).

Employing a crude evolutionary framework, general trends in the relationship between patterns of tourism development and political environment, prior to the disintegration of state socialism in the region, were identified (Hall, 1991: 79–115):

(a) Early state socialism: the 'Stalinist' period saw heavy industrialization taking precedence over all other economic sectors. Inbound and outbound tourism was severely constrained for ideological reasons, but facilities were developed for subsidised, group-oriented domestic leisure and recreation;

(b) Middle state socialism: in the years following Stalin's death in 1953 there slowly developed collective intra-bloc international tourism and the consolidation of facilities for domestic tourism. Exceptionally, Yugoslavia began attracting Western market mass tourism in the 1950s, and by the mid-1960s was receiving greater numbers of such international tourists than the rest of state socialist CEE combined;

(c) Later state socialism: most Soviet bloc economies moved to an emphasis on attracting Western tourists in order to gain hard currency to help upgrade seriously outdated technology that was undermining their economic capacities. This programme had limited results because of inadequate infrastructure, service quality and capacity, coupled to an inflexible centralised organizational structure. Domestic tourism became more sophisticated with rising levels of car and second-home ownership in the more advanced economies (East Germany, Czechoslovakia, Hungary, Poland). Intra-bloc international flows became more complex, including VFR travel.

Tourism and 'transition'

Fundamental to evaluations of the relationship between tourism and political change in CEE are two key terms - 'post-communism' (or 'post-socialism') and 'transition':

(a) Post-communism: Czepczynski (2008, 3–4) distinguishes two perspectives. The first, particularly for researchers from CEE, views the concept of 'post-communism' as relating directly to the burden of the social, economic, environmental and cultural inheritance of the state socialist regimes. It has strong pejorative (and experiential) connotations. Second, for the majority of Western analysts, 'post-communism' acts largely as a shorthand term for the general political, economic, social and cultural environment of CEE (and beyond) since the period of state socialist implosion (1989–91).

(b) 'Transition' entails movement between two specific points, the end point in the case of CEE being integration into the world (capitalist) economy and Western ('democratic') institutions, notably the EU (Agnew, 2000). But this political economy agenda has tended to marginalize social, cultural and wider environmental considerations (Marangos, 2003; Hall, 2004b, 2004c). 'Transformation' can be employed as an alternative concept. It can accommodate structural change, is less concerned with an end state, and acknowledges the substantial (converging and diverging) differences between individual countries.

Path dependency analyses can illuminate such differences by emphasizing that specific variables ('path contingencies': Johnson, 2001) play a critical role in creating and constraining each country's development path (Williams and Baláž, 2000; Saarinen and Kask, 2008). Thus 'transition' processes may perpetuate, reinforce or rejuvenate core–periphery, urban–rural, class, ethnic, gender and regional inequalities (Petrovic, 2008). For example, early post-communist privatization of power was often characterized by vertical and horizontal networks of reciprocity – 'survival networks' (Kewell, 2002) – which, with roots in the communist period, could support or impede restructuring processes, such as the privatization of hotels and other tourism assets and infrastructure. They could also ensure that individuals already in managerial and technocratic positions within tourism and tourism-related industries under state socialism were well placed to benefit from such processes while excluding others (e.g. Koulov, 1996).

Significance of political change for tourism in CEE

Two elements of the demise of state socialism were central and immediately significant for the further structural and spatial development of tourism: (1) the removal of physical mobility restrictions, both domestically and internationally; and (2) the restructuring and decentralisation of political economies, such that tourism was decoupled from the heavy and inflexible hand of centralised state bureaucracy.

First, the easing of entry, exit and currency restrictions to, within, and from countries of the region, while permitting incoming international tourists relatively free access to the region, was tempered by varying degrees of difficulty for CEE citizens to gain access to convertible currencies for the purposes of travelling abroad and notably to be able to purchase often costly Western entry visas. For some, the 'Iron Curtain' was replaced by the 'Dollar Curtain'.

Second, economic restructuring processes, emphasizing privatization, devolution and local initiative and innovation, also exposed domestic economies to the global market, bringing immediate issues of unemployment, loss of local skills and individuality with the influx of Western multinational corporations and high pressure marketing. New social costs of tourism arose from the promotion of foreign investment opportunities. Media publicity highlighting low property and land prices led to an increased awareness among western Europeans of potential second homes in selected locations and regions (Vágner and Fialová, 2004). One consequence of this has been that local residents find themselves priced out of their own local housing markets, whether in desirable urban sectors, rural regions or coastal locations.

Foreign direct investment in major infrastructure, accommodation and attraction projects has been important in raising quality standards and diversifying product availability (see Chapter 12 of this volume by Suntikul), but may also leave smaller states vulnerable to the power of transnational corporations and the vagaries of global market conditions (Behringer and Kiss, 2004; Bachvarov, 2006). Tourism can assist labour market adjustment, but it may also remain one of the lowest paid sectors (although real earnings and benefits may be significantly greater than those officially recorded). In Hungary, although during the 1990s new entrants to tourism employment transferred from a variety of occupations, Szivas and Riley (2002) detected a relatively low level of spatial mobility, i.e workers tended to stay in the same geographical area. This characteristic has been modified with EU accession.

The increasing diversity of both tourists and workers in the tourism industry and the growing competitiveness of destinations and businesses has required internationally transferable skills that can enhance employability (Aitken and Hall, 2000), including the need to embed 'new mentalities' (e.g. Cottrell and Cutumisu, 2006) to eradicate low quality service, information, and market research. Third, as a result of both the first two major processes, gaps widened between those from the region able to afford holidays and those unable to do so, a cleavage exacerbated by the privatization of previously subsidized domestic enterprise and trade union vacation facilities. A tourism 'underclass' has persisted.

Fourth, later pre-accession processes and the EU entry of ten of the region's countries has, theoretically, seen 'transition' run its course, such that one might speak of a 'post-postcommunist' period for those states at least. One notable knock-on, though not dependent, effect of EU accession (Smith and Hall, 2006a) has been the introduction and growth in operations of low-cost airlines (LCAs) to (often secondary or tertiary level) airports in CEE as a significant factor for intra-European mobilities, not least through spatially diffusing international arrival points. The market for air transport users has been substantially deepened and widened by the LCAs' business model of stripped down costs, relatively low fares and exploitation of personal information technology (Dobruszkes, 2006). This has included facilitating low-cost regular travel to second homes and wider international student mobility (Richards, 2006). 'Open skies' agreements within Europe are now being supplemented by EU – United States agreements adding further dimensions to this mobility influence (Button, 2009), while also raising issues of sustainability and climate change impacts.

Resulting patterns of tourism flows

An overall increase in growth of international arrivals numbers, reflecting hitherto low absolute levels, was experienced in CEE during the 1990s and into the 2000s (Table 8.1). This overall picture was modified by enormous immediate growth in cross-border movements from east to west with the removal of physical constraints, and from west to east as a result of pent-up curiosity. Both processes were relatively short-lived, in the first case because of the prohibitive expense of travelling to and in the West, and in the latter case because facilities and service quality in the East were initially generally poor and did not encourage return visitation in the short term.

Regional cross-border mobility has been a significant by-product of post-communist restructuring (e.g. Baláž, 2006; Baláž and Williams, 2005). It reflects forces both of integration – tourism, labour migration, shopping – and of disintegration, or at least dis-location – refugee flight and continued demand for informal petty trading and exchange (e.g. Aidis, 2003; Egbert, 2006).

A longer term growth in international, regional and domestic visitor numbers and diffusion of spread has taken place as infrastructures, service levels, regional image and information have been improved through financial assistance, (re-)building programmes and the provision of better quality training related to standards of Western expectations. Still enormous variations remain between countries, although the preparations for EU accession in 2004 and 2007 have brought some degree of consistency to the tourism development processes of the ten CEE accession countries. It has also imposed new constraints on old markets. For example, Poland's joining the Schengen scheme (see Chapter 4 of this volume by Williams and Baláž) in January 2008 meant that travellers to that country from Russia, Ukraine, and Belarus now need visas for the first time. This has impacted negatively on demand from such important source markets. By contrast, Turkey has a favourable exchange rate and relaxed visa regime facilitating travel from Russia, the CIS countries and the Middle East.

The EU's newest members were revealing contrasting experiences prior to the current (2009) economic recession: international arrivals to Bulgaria increased 17% in the first half of 2008, while those to Romania decreased by 4%. Both countries claimed to be making great efforts to improve their quality of services to compete with Mediterranean destinations, with Bulgaria reporting improvements in infrastructure and investments in resorts, holiday villages and new products in such high-value niche sectors as golf, spas and wellness, and nature and cultural tours (UNWTO, 2008b).

Table 8.1: CEE international tourist arrivals, 1990-2007.

	Series	International tourist arrivals (in millions)					Average annual growth %
		1990	1995	2000	2006	2007(c)	1990-2007(c)
Albania	THS	0.03	0.04	n.a.	n.a.	n.a.	n.a.
Belarus	TF	n.a.	0.16	n.a.	n.a.	n.a.	n.a.
Bosnia –Herzegovina	TF/TCE(a)	n.a.	0.04	0.11	0.26	0.31	(a)
Bulgaria	TF	1.59	3.47	2.79	5.16	5.15	12.4
Croatia	TCE	7.05	1.49	5.83	8.66	9.31	1.7
Czech Republic	TCE	7.28	3.38	5.70	6.44	6.68	-0.4
Estonia	TF	n.a.	0.53	1.10	1.94	1.90	19.9(d)
Georgia	TF	n.a.	0.09	n.a.	n.a.	n.a.	n.a.
Hungary	VF/TF(a)	20.51	19.62	15.57	9.26	8.64	(a)
Latvia	TF	n.a.	0.52	na	1.54	1.65	14.2(d)
Lithuania	TF	n.a.	0.65	1.23	2.18	na	18.3(e)
Macedonia, FYR	TCE	0.56	0.15	0.22	0.20	0.23	-3.3
Moldova	TF	n.a.	0.03	0.02	n.a.	n.a.	n.a.
Montenegro	TCE	1.19(b)	0.23(b)	n.a.(b)	0.38	0.98	n.a.
Poland	TF	3.40	19.22	17.40	15.67	14.98	18.9
Romania	TF/TCE(a)	3.01	2.76	3.27	1.38	1.55	(a)
Russia	VF/TF(a)	n.a.	10.29	21.17	20.20	n.a.	(a)
Serbia	TCE	1.19(b)	0.23(b)	n.a.(b)	0.47	0.70	n.a.
Slovakia	TCE	0.82	0.90	1.05	1.61	1.69	5.9
Slovenia	TCE	0.65	0.73	1.09	1.62	1.75	9.4
Ukraine	TF	n.a.	3.72	n.a.	18.94	23.12	40.1(d)

Notes:

TCE:	tourist arrivals at all accommodation establishments
TF:	tourist arrivals at frontiers
THS:	tourist arrivals at hotels
VF:	visitor arrivals at frontiers
n.a.:	data not available
(a):	change of accounting method during the period covered by this table
(b):	combined figures for Serbia-Montenegro
(c):	2007 figures are provisional
(d):	figures for 1995–2007
(e):	figures for 1995–2006

Sources: UNWTO, 2008a, 2008b; WTO, 2002a, 2002b; author's calculations

In terms of international tourism receipts (Table 8.2), the UNWTO's CEE region (which excludes the former Yugoslavia and Albania) continues to return the lowest levels of income per arrival of any world region, at just $510 per arrival (compared to $940 for Southern and Mediterranean Europe), with 5.6% of the world share of international tourism receipts). Iin 2007 Ukraine received the 8th highest number of international arrivals of any country – comparable with Turkey – with 4.8% of the world share, but with only 1.1% share of international receipts (compared to Turkey's 4.3%) (UNWTO, 2008a). A characteristic since communist times, this low per capita receipt level reflects a combination of often interrelated factors: significant proportions of low-spending visitors from within the region, limited high quality goods and services, relatively low (but rapidly rising) costs, significant proportions of short stays, and the inclusion of various cross-border non-tourism activities within the statistics.

Table 8.2: CEE international tourism receipts, 1990-2007

	International tourism receipts (in US$mn)					Average annual growth %
	1990	**1995**	**2000**	**2006**	**2007** (b)	**1990-2007** (b)
Albania	4	65	389	1010	1372	1900
Belarus	n.a.	23	93	278	306	94.6 (c)
Bosnia-Herzegovina	n.a.	7	233	604	728	792.3 (c)
Bulgaria	320	473	1076	2588	3130	50.2
Croatia	1704	1349	2782	7902	9254	23.9
Czech Republic	419	2875	2972	5520	6618	84.8
Estonia	n.a.	353	508	1024	1035	14.9 (c)
Georgia	n.a.	n.a.	97	313	384	37.0 (d)
Hungary	824	2640	3757	4233	4728	26.3
Latvia	n.a.	20	131	480	671	250.4+
Lithuania	n.a.	77	391	1038	1153	107.5 (c)
Macedonia, FYR	45	19	38	129	185	17.3
Moldova	n.a.	4	39	112	164	307.7 (c)
Montenegro	419(a)	42(a)	n.a.(a)	362	630	n.a.
Poland	358	6614	5677	7239	10627	159.4
Romania	106	590	359	1298	1464	71.2
Russia	n.a.	4312	3429	7628	9607	9.4 (c)
Serbia	419(a)	42(a)	n.a.(a)	398	531	n.a.
Slovakia	70	620	433	1513	2013	154.2
Slovenia	721	1084	965	1953	2483	13.6
Ukraine	n.a.	3865	394	3485	4597	1.45 (c)

Notes:

n.a.:	data not available
(a):	combined figures for Serbia-Montenegro
(b):	2007 figures are provisional
(c):	figures for 1995-2007
(d):	figures for 2000-07

Sources: UNWTO, 2008a, 2008b; WTO, 2002a, 2002b; author's calculations

Tourism products, marketing and re-imaging

An important element for most CEE tourism industries was to establish a clear post-communist identity for their products and activities, emphasizing a 'Europeanness' to attract new markets and a disassociation from the ideologies and instability of the recent past (e.g. Croatia). International tourism and marketing imagery have acted as vehicles through which distinctive national (and local) identity has been able to seek expression (Hall, 2001, 2002, 2004a; Light, 2006). Emphasizing the diversity and uniqueness of cultural and natural resources (e.g. Hall, 2003; Light, 2006; Puczkó and Rátz, 2006b), re-imaging became a crucial part of the escape strategy from the past.

The promotion of urban 'cultural' destinations has often employed imaging strategies emphasizing (again potentially paradoxically) 'European' heritage and progress, to appeal both to tourism and wider economic investment markets (e.g. Hungary, see Rátz *et al.*, 2008). Many rural areas have been re-imaged (Hall, 2004d) by the promotion of traditional, 'idyllic' portrayals of sustainability alongside the development of eco- and nature tourism, gastronomy, heritage trails and activity/adventure holidays.

But negative, or at least conflicting destination images can easily be generated. For example, the Romanian government has worked hard to prevent the development of a Dracula theme park and the potential pejorative and discordant connotations such a destination attraction might project for the country's image (Tanasescu, 2006; Light, 2007). Based on low-cost flights, the development of short-break attractions, and notably 'stag' and 'hen' weekend packages, has attracted much negative publicity. In the case of Riga, for example, city and state authorities have needed to act to reduce advertising of sex-related tourism products in order to avoid the city gaining an unsavoury reputation (Druva-Druvaskalne *et al.*, 2006).

Conclusions

Lessons learned

There are always winners and losers (e.g. see Hall, 2005; Shanks, 2009). In the case of tourism in CEE, this has had both spatial and structural dimensions, with the role of initial advantage playing an important part. Spatially, certain regions have been long familiar with tourism development (often from before the communist period), while others have had the resource potential to encourage relatively rapid tourism given the appropriate political-economic circumstances. Other regions had no such experience or potential resource base (e.g. see Bobirca and Cristureanu, 2008). Structurally, those persons already in managerial and technocratic positions within tourism and tourism-related industries under state socialism were well placed to benefit from the privatization of assets and relaxation of centralised regulations in post-communist tourism development.

Future implications

First, issues of market positioning, image and identity reveal several paradoxes concerning the relationships between the search for national identity, re-awakening of ethnic particularism, images of authenticity, the domestic need for modernisation, and the roles of tourism in facilitating, articulating or compromising such sometimes conflicting aspirations. Commodification of the past and present for the purposes of visitor entertainment can create a dissonance that reveals trenchant and rancorous opposition to tourism development and, as a result, to tourism and to tourists themselves.

Adoption of 'heritage' as both a leisure resource and cultural symbol of identity highlights the irony of employing the (often distant) past as an element of restructuring for the future, particularly for those states wanting to forget the immediate past decades. A positive way forward would appear to be promoting the cultures of ethnic minority groups who previously may have been persecuted or marginalized (Jews, Roma).

Interrelated issues as heritage interpretation, authenticity and the cultural and entrepreneurial roles of ethnic groups, are highlighted in tensions between the indigenous majority ethnic groups of Estonia, Latvia and Lithuania and significant Russian minorities in those countries, and those between Croats and the Serb and Moslem minorities in Croatia. In the latter case, Goulding and Domic (2009) have pointed to a rewriting of cultural history and a 'cleansing' of heritage.

Visiting friends and relatives (VFR) tourism may become particularly important with the rejuvenation of diasporas through labour migration (Smith and Hall, 2006b). Crucial for Yugoslavia in the 1960s–80s period, such flows now appear to be particularly important for Poland, the Baltic states, south-eastern Europe, and, increasingly, Russia.

During the1990s there was a notable decline in the local consumption of 'high' culture within the region with declining domestic incomes and the loss of state subsidies for the arts (Richards, 2001). International markets – Western Europe, North America, Japan and latterly China – have helped to keep this sector buoyant. There is a requirement for institutions to respond more readily to the opportunities of dynamism and the possible threats of uncertainty in transformation. This includes practical issues of human resource training and institutional capacity building for tourism development and less tangible issues of political will and priority setting.

The roles of aid, assistance, structural funding, consultants and training as catalysts for culturally sensitive, truly sustainable tourism development continue to require close scrutiny and critical evaluation. Throughout the past 20 years, transfers of know-how and technology (predominantly from the EU and the USA) have 'supported' economic, social, civil and political restructuring processes despite relatively little debate and analysis concerning the suitability and sustainability of such processes (see Simpson and Roberts, 2000). By contrast, the potential synergies of partnerships and networks at local, regional and national levels, to help shape the path of tourism development (e.g. Roberts, 2004), still need to be fully realized.

Tensions will continue to arise concerning the interface between, and compatibility of, political imperatives and market requirements (e.g. Popesku and Hall, 2004, in the context of Serbia), which reflect the loosening role of the state, the need to meet international quality standards, and the nature and consequences of exposing economies, societies and cultures to (not always positive) global market forces. In this context, tourism development and its impacts may both reflect and be a component of relationships between political and socio-economic structures and processes. For example, the role and priorities attributed to the local and the global can emphasize the significance and differential local impacts on tourism development of such diverse global processes as foreign direct investment (e.g. Behringer and Kiss, 2004; Chidlow et al., 2009) and the conferment of World Heritage Site status (Puczkó and Rátz, 2006a).

Business travel and tourism is likely to increase as European integration strengthens. The (often discordant) aspiration of all tourism authorities to maximise income while minimising the adverse impacts of tourism will pose increasing dilemmas. Few CEE destination countries have managed to raise their per capita level of international receipts. Several reveal an unstable trend while others exhibit notable decreases. The continuing challenge to tourism policy makers is to develop a portfolio of products and services whose sustainability translates into cultural and financial wellbeing for both host and visitor, supporting environmental protection and enhancement, and political stability.

References

Agnew, J. (2000) 'How many Europes?' in D. Hall, and D. Danta (eds) *Europe Goes East: EU Enlargement, Diversity and Uncertainty*, London: Stationery Office, pp. 45–54.

Aidis, R. (2003) 'Officially despised yet tolerated: open-air markets and entrepreneurship in post-socialist countries', *Post-Communist Economies*, **15** (3), 461–473.

Aitken, C. and Hall, C.M. (2000) 'Migrant and foreign skills and their relevance to the tourism industry', *Tourism Geographies*, **2** (1), 66–86.

Anastasiadou, C. (2006) 'Tourism and the European Union', in D. Hall, M. Smith and B. Marciszewska (eds.), *Tourism in the New Europe: the Challenges and Opportunities of EU Enlargement*, Wallingford: CABI, pp. 20–31.

Bachvarov, M. (2006) 'Tourism in Bulgaria', in D. Hall, M. Smith and B. Marciszewska (eds.), *Tourism in the New Europe: the Challenges and Opportunities of EU Enlargement*, Wallingford: CABI, pp. 241–255.

Baláž, V. (2006) 'Slovakia: EU accession and cross-border travel', in D. Hall, M. Smith and B. Marciszewska (eds), *Tourism in the New Europe: the Challenges and Opportunities of EU Enlargement*, Wallingford: CABI, pp. 92–103.

Baláž, V. and Williams, A.M. (2005) 'International tourism as bricolage: an analysis of Central Europe on the brink of European Union membership', *International Journal of Tourism Research*, 7(2), 79–93.

Behringer, Z. and Kiss, K. (2004) 'The role of foreign direct investment in the development of tourism in post-communist Hungary', in D. Hall (ed.), *Tourism and Transition: Governance, Transformation and Development*, Wallingford: CABI, pp. 73–81.

Bobirca, A. and Cristureanu, C. (2008) 'Analyzing Romania's competitiveness as a tourism destination', *Advances in Hospitality and Leisure*, 4, 75–99.

Button, K. (2009) 'The impact of US–EU "Open Skies" agreement on airline market structures and airline networks', *Journal of Air Transport Management*, 15(2), 59–71.

Chidlow, A., Salciuviene, L. and Young, S. (2009) 'Regional determinants of inward FDI distribution in Poland', *International Business Review*, 18(2), 119–133.

Cottrell, S. and Cutumisu, N. (2006) 'Sustainable tourism development strategy in WWF pan parks: case of a Swedish and Romanian national park', *Scandinavian Journal of Hospitality and Tourism*, 6 (2), 150–167.

Czepczynski, M. (2008) *Cultural Landscapes of Post-Socialist Cities: Representation of Powers and Needs*, Farnham: Ashgate.

Dobruszkes, F. (2006) 'An analysis of European low-cost airlines and their networks', *Journal of Transport Geography* 14 (4), 249–264.

Druva-Druvaskalne, I., Ãbols, I. and Šĺara, A. (2006) 'Latvia tourism: decisive factors and tourism development', in D. Hall, M. Smith and B. Marciszewska (eds) *Tourism in the New Europe: the Challenges and Opportunities of EU Enlargement*, Wallingford: CABI, pp. 170–182.

Egbert, H. (2006) 'Cross-border small-scale trading in South-Eastern Europe: do embeddedness and social capital explain enough?' *International Journal of Urban and Regional Research*, **30** (2), 346–361.

Goulding, C. and Domic, D. (2009) 'Heritage, identity and ideological manipulation: the case of Croatia', *Annals of Tourism Research*, **36** (1), 85–102.

Hall, D.R. (ed.), (1991) *Tourism and Economic Development in Eastern Europe and the Soviet Union*, London: Belhaven Press, New York: Halsted Press.

Hall, D.R. (2001) 'Tourism and development in communist and post-communist societies', in D. Harrison (ed.), *Tourism and the Less Developed World: Issues and Case Studies*, Wallingford: CABI, pp. 91–107.

Hall, D. (2002) 'Brand development, tourism and national identity: the re-imaging of former Yugoslavia', *Journal of Brand Management*, **9** (4-5), 323–334.

Hall, D. (2003) 'Rejuvenation, diversification and imagery: sustainability conflicts for tourism policy in the eastern Adriatic', *Journal of Sustainable Tourism*, **11** (2/3), 280–294.

Hall, D. (2004a) 'Branding and national identity: the case of Central and Eastern Europe', in N. Morgan, A. Pritchard and R. Pride (eds), *Destination Branding: Creating the Unique Destination Proposition*, 2nd edn, Oxford: Elsevier, pp. 111–127.

Hall, D. (2004b) 'Introduction', in D. Hall (ed.), *Tourism and Transition: Governance, Transformation and Development*, Wallingford: CABI, pp. 1–24.

Hall, D. (2004c) 'Key themes and frameworks', in D. Hall (ed.), *Tourism and Transition: Governance, Transformation and Development*. Wallingford: CABI, pp. 25–51.

Hall, D. (2004d) 'Rural tourism development in South-eastern Europe: transition and the search for sustainability', *International Journal of Tourism Research*, **6** (2), 165–176.

Hall, D. (2005) 'Sustainable rural tourism and rural change', in D. Schmied (ed.), *Winning and Losing: the Changing Geography of Europe's Rural Areas*, Farnham: Ashgate, pp. 72–89.

Hall, D. and Roberts, L. (2004) 'Conclusions and future agenda', in D. Hall (ed.) *Tourism and Transition: Governance, Transformation and Development*, Wallingford: CABI, pp. 217–226.

Johnson, J. (2001) 'Path contingency in postcommunist transformations', *Comparative Politics*, **33** (3), 253–274.

Kewell, B. (2002) 'Hidden drivers of organisational transformation in Poland: survival networks amongst state owned and privatised firms in the early 1990s', *Journal for East European Management Studies*, **7** (4), 373–392.

Konečnik, M. (2006) 'Slovenia: new challenges in enhancing the value of the destination brand', in D. Hall, M. Smith and B. Marciszewska (eds.), *Tourism in the New Europe: the Challenges and Opportunities of EU Enlargement*, Wallingford: CABI, pp. 81–91.

Koulov, B. (1996) 'Market reforms and environmental protection in the Bulgarian tourism industry', in D. Hall and D. Danta (eds), *Reconstructing the Balkans*, Chichester: John Wiley and Sons, pp. 187–196.

Light, D. (2006) 'Romania: national identity, tourism promotion and European integration', in D. Hall, M. Smith and B. Marciszewska (eds), *Tourism in the New Europe: the Challenges and Opportunities of EU Enlargement*, Wallingford: CABI, pp. 256–269.

Light, D. (2007) 'Dracula tourism in Romania: cultural identity and the state', *Annals of Tourism Research*, **34** (3), 746–765.

Logar, I. (2009) 'Sustainable tourism management in Crikvenica, Croatia: an assessment of policy instruments', *Tourism Management*, in press.

Marangos, J. (2003) 'Global transition strategies in Eastern Europe: moving to market relations', *Development*, **46** (1), 112–117.

Petrovic, M. (2008) 'The role of geography and history in determining the slower progress of post-communist transition in the Balkans', *Communist and Post-Communist Studies*, **41**, 123–145.

Popesku, J. and Hall, D. (2004) 'Sustainability as the basis for future tourism development in Serbia', in D. Hall (ed.), *Tourism and Transition: Governance, Transformation and Development*, Wallingford: CABI, pp. 95–103.

Puczkó, L. and Rátz, T. (2006a) 'Managing an urban world heritage site: the development of the Cultural Avenue project in Budapest', in A. Leask and A. Fyall (eds), *Managing World Heritage Sites*, Oxford: Butterworth-Heinemann, pp. 215–225.

Puczkó, L. and Rátz, T. (2006b) 'Product development and diversification in Hungary', in D. Hall, M. Smith and B. Marciszewska (eds.), *Tourism in the New Europe: the Challenges and Opportunities of EU Enlargement*, Wallingford: CABI, pp. 116–126.

Rátz, T., Smith, M. and Michalkó, G. (2008) 'New places in old spaces: mapping tourism and regeneration in Budpest', *Tourism Geographies*, **10**(4), 429–451.

Richards, G. (ed.) (2001) *Cultural Attractions and European Tourism*, Wallingford: CABI.

Richards, G. (2006) 'Tourism education in the new Europe', in D. Hall, M. Smith and B. Marciszewska (eds.), *Tourism in the New Europe: the Challenges and Opportunities of EU Enlargement*, Wallingford: CABI, pp. 52–64.

Roberts, L. (2004) 'Capital accumulation – tourism and development processes in Central and Eastern Europe', in D. Hall (ed.), *Tourism and Transition: Governance, Transformation and Development*, CABI, pp. 53–63.

Saarinen, J. and Kask, T. (2008) 'Transforming tourism spaces in changing socio-political contexts: the case of Pärnu, Estonia, as a tourist destination', *Tourism Geographies*, **10** (4), 452–473.

Shanks, C. (2009) 'The global compact: the conservative politics of international tourism', *Futures*, **41**(6), 360–366.

Simpson, F. and Roberts, L. (2000) 'Help or hindrance? Sustainable approaches to tourism consultancy in Central and Eastern Europe', *Journal of Sustainable Tourism*, **8** (6), 491–509.

Smith, M. and Hall, D. (2006a) 'Enlargement implications for European tourism', in D. Hall, M. Smith and B. Marciszewska (eds.), *Tourism in the New Europe: the Challenges and Opportunities of EU Enlargement*, Wallingford: CABI, pp. 32–44.

Smith, M. and Hall, D. (2006b) 'Summary and conclusions', in D. Hall, M. Smith and B. Marciszewska (eds). *Tourism in the New Europe: the Challenges and Opportunities of EU Enlargement*, Wallingford: CABI, pp. 305–311.

Szivas, E. and Riley, M. (2002) 'Labour mobility and tourism in the post 1989 transition in Hungary', in C.M. Hall and A.M. Williams (eds), *Tourism and Migration*, pp. 53–72.

Tanasescu, A. (2006) 'Tourism, nationalism and post-communist Romania: the life and death of Dracula Park', *Journal of Tourism and Cultural Change* 4 (3), 159–176.

UNWTO (United Nations World Tourism Organization) (2008a) *Tourism Highlights*, 2008 Edition, UNWTO.

UNWTO (United Nations World Tourism Organization) (2008b) *World Tourism Barometer* Volume 6, No. 3, UNWTO.

Vágner, J. and Fialová, D. (eds) (2004) Regionální Differenciace Druhého Bydlení v Česku. Prague: Karlova University, Dept of Social Geography and Regional Development.

Williams, A.M. and Baláž, V. (2000) *Tourism in Transition*, I.B. London: Tauris.

WTO (World Tourism Organization) (2002a) *Compendium of Tourism Statistics* 1996-2000, WTO.

WTO (World Tourism Organization) (2002b) *Tourism Highlights 2002*, WTO, from: http://www.world-tourism.org (4 June 2004)

Part III
Normalisation/
Opening

9 Tourism as an Instrument of Foreign Policy: the US Trade Embargo on Cuba

Tom Hinch

Introduction

Tourism occurs in complex and dynamic environments, and it is impacted by and, in turn, impacts upon these environments. One goal of tourism research is to develop an understanding of this relationship and ultimately to articulate ways of influencing it. This chapter considers the US foreign policy environment in relation to tourism in Cuba.

At its core, the relationship between the US and Cuba has been characterized by fear, distrust and animosity since the Cuban revolution led by Fidel Castro in 1959. At the forefront of the US government's overt responses to these events was the 1962 economic embargo that restricted US citizens' right to trade with, invest in, or travel to Cuba. The embargo is still in place, 47 years after its original imposition and despite several rigorous critiques of its merits.

At the time of writing this chapter, expectations are high that the embargo is ripe for significant moderation, if not an outright removal, based on two developments. First, recently-elected US President Obama publicly stated that he was prepared to modify the US's strategy of isolating Cuba by relaxing the economic embargo. He has since tempered his statements but still seems committed to moving in this direction. The second major factor is that Fidel Castro has suffered health problems over the past few years and recently relinquished his post as President of Cuba to his brother Raul. Given the apparent personal nature of the animosity that exists between the two countries, the US is likely to be more willing to work with new leaders in Cuba. The direct impact of removing the US imposed travel restrictions, even in the absence of the removal of other aspects of the embargo, would be significant for tourism in Cuba and throughout the Caribbean. In the absence of the US travel restrictions, Padilla and McElroy (2007) estimate that in five years, annual visits by Americans would grow to 2.3 million, with up to two-thirds of these being diverted from other destinations and one in four being Cuban Americans. Similarly, in a working paper published by the International Monetary Fund, Romeu (2008) estimated that 3 to 3.5 million Americans would soon be visiting Cuba each year. The overwhelming consensus of these and other estimates is that Americans will flood to Cuba upon removal of the US travel restrictions with significant implications in terms of economic, social and physical impacts on Cuba and throughout the Caribbean.

The focus of this chapter is to develop an understanding of why this policy of confrontation and isolation has persisted for almost half a century and how Cuban tourism has managed to survive in the face such political changes. It is divided into three main parts. The first provides an overview of international tourism in Cuba by highlighting distinct periods of development before and after the 1959 revolution. The second section outlines the nature of the US embargo along with major modifications over the past 47 years. Finally, the third section presents a political economic analysis of the embargo.

Four eras of Cuban tourism

Tourism development in Cuba has been dramatically influenced by external as well as internal events and forces. Its path of development contrasts markedly with its Caribbean neighbours and other tourism destinations in general. While observers of Cuban tourism vary in their interpretation of the details, there is widespread consistency in their view of the overall pattern of development. A basic grasp of these phases provides an important context for appreciating the relevance of US policy aimed at isolating Cuba (Figure 9.1).

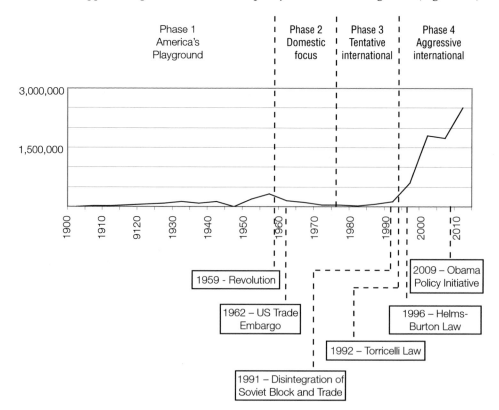

Figure 9.1: International visitors, phases of Cuban tourism and highlights of US foreign policy. Source: International visitor statistics adapted from Elliott and Neirotti (2008)

Pre-revolution (1900 to 1959) – America's playground

Soon after independence was won from Spain in 1898, Cuba began its climb as one of the leading tourism destinations in the Caribbean. By the 1920s, tourism had become Cuba's second 'cash crop' after sugar, and like the sugar industry, the tourism industry was closely tied to US investment and patronage (Schwartz, 1997; Elliott and Neirotti, 2008). In addition to its tropical climate and close geographical proximity to the US (90 miles off the Florida coast), Cuba was attractive to Americans who wanted to escape prohibition laws that were being instituted throughout the US (Khrushchev *et al.*, 2007). Visitor numbers dropped dramatically after the Stock Market Crash of 1929 and the concurrent economic and civil unrest in Cuba. When Batista seized power in 1933, tourism development resumed on pace. Initially this development emphasized Cuba's culture and heritage, but by 1937, casino tourism had become a major attraction and revenue generator. Batista responded by taking control of these casinos and bringing in American mobster, Meyer Lanksy, to manage these operations (Schwartz, 1997; Jaywardena, 2003; Elliott and Neirotti, 2009). After decreased visitation during WWII, tourism development resumed with prostitution and gambling the mainstays of the industry. In 1957, 272,000 international visitors arrived, 87% of whom were from the USA, Cuba had become what was widely characterized as a rather sordid playground dominated by American tourists and investors (Hinch, 1990). In their classic critique of international tourism, Turner and Ash (1975) suggest that while the Castro revolution was largely a response to American imperialism in the form of agricultural enterprises like United Fruit, '…at least part of the popular support for his struggle against Batista stemmed from revulsion against the excesses of the tourism industry – this latter-day, far more shadowy form of imperialism' (p. 103). This phase of Cuban tourism came to an abrupt end with the 1959 Communist revolution.

Post-revolution – (1960 to 1975) domestic focus

While the Castro led regime was quick to destroy Havana's casinos in the aftermath of the revolution, contrary to popular belief, the regime did not necessarily want to shut down international tourism completely. In fact Jayawardena (2003) reports that immediately following the nationalization of the leading hotels, Castro promoted Cuba as an international destination at the annual conference of the American Society of Travel Agents hosted in Havana in 1959. In addition to emphasizing Cuban hospitality, he highlighted cultural tourism and initiated a 1960 promotional campaign targeting black Americans.

Other events, however, such as the unsuccessful Bay of Pigs invasion by US government backed Cuban expatriates and heightened geopolitical issues associated with Cuba's collaboration with the Soviet bloc, soon overtook these tentative forays into international tourism. These events combined to drive down tourist demand with the coup de grâce being the US imposition of the 1962 economic embargo, including a travel ban on US citizens visiting Cuba. The combined effect of these events was that international visitation to Cuba dropped to 3000 to 6000 foreign visitors per year in the early 1960s, with most visitors being invited by the authorities based on their friendship and solidarity with the revolutionary cause (Hinch, 1990). For the next ten to 15 years, foreign visitation remained low but it should be noted that in keeping with the socialist ideals of the Cuban government, domestic tourism was encouraged and continued to develop. By the mid-1970s, it was estimated that over 3 million Cubans used official accommodation on an annual basis compared to 60,000 foreigners (Ward, 1978).

Post-revolution (1976 to 1991) – tentative international

Cuba had returned to the international tourism market in a significant way by the mid-1970s. This return was due in part to internal pressure in Cuba to address 'hard currency' shortages and to its vulnerability on sugar cane markets. In terms of demand, the relative stabilization of the post-revolution, post-Cuban Missile Crisis events led many international tourists to judge Cuba as a safe and attractive destination. The introduction of package tours from Canada in the early 1970s was soon followed by similar initiatives in the European and South American markets. Cuba began to develop a reputation as a low-cost sea, sun and sand destination in which foreign tourists did not have to compete with American tourists. By 1987, Cuba was reported to have 310,000 international tourist arrivals indicating a rapid increase in numbers (Hinch, 1990). While the goal of this phase was to internalize the benefits and mitigate tourism's formerly high social costs, these tourists were noticeably wealthier than locals and were given special privileges. To expand infrastructure, joint partnerships with foreign investors from Canada, Europe and South America were initiated, with majority ownership being held by the Cuban Government (Avella and Mills, 1996) (see Chapter 12 of this volume by Suntikul).

Post Soviet (1992 to 2009) – aggressive international

Jayawardena (2003) described this period as a tourism revolution in Cuba, but if it was a revolution, it was one borne of economic necessity caused by external political change. Prior to the dissolution of the Soviet bloc in 1991, almost 85% of Cuba's trade was with Soviet and Eastern bloc countries (Jayawardena, 2003; Elliott and Neirotti, 2009). Not surprisingly, therefore, the disbanding of the Soviet Union caused a financial crisis in Cuba as its international trade and financial subsidies disappeared. The hard currency gained through tourism was no longer simply an important supplement to the financial support provided by trade with former communist countries, it was now critical to Cuba's very survival (Sanchez, 2006). To address this financial crisis, Castro initiated a 'five-year "Special Period in Time of Peace" which enacted strict economic measures as a means to transition out of Soviet economic dependence and revive Cuba's crippled economy' (Elliott and Neirotti, 2009, p. 383). In addition to expanded tourism development and marketing activities, a variety of economic reforms was initiated including the legalization of hard currency holdings and the sanctioning of 'cuentapropias' or private micro-enterprises. Further initiatives were undertaken to increase foreign partnerships in new tourism developments. These initiatives have enjoyed considerable success with yearly international visitors surpassing 2 million in 2004. Cuba's share of Caribbean international arrivals increased from 3% during the 1985–89 period to 10% during the 2000–04 period (Padilla and McElroy, 2007). The country is positioned for cost-conscious travellers looking for sun, surf and sand. Rapid expansion has been accompanied by service issues and increased social issues related to income distribution and growing levels of prostitution. While it appears that the revenues associated with tourism have played an important role in the financial survival of Cuba after the fall of the Soviet bloc, it also appears to have been accompanied by echoes of past tourism excesses.

US foreign policy on Cuba

The USA has had an active interest in Cuba ever since its involvement in Cuba's struggle for independence from Spain in 1898 and has developed foreign policy as a way of protecting that interest. While the US military withdrew from Cuba after its independence from Spain was secured, its business and political interests developed rapidly. Sugden (2007) suggests that 'In the Platt Amendment of 1901, the US granted itself the right to interfere in Cuba's internal affairs should events occur there that were considered to be detrimental to US interests' (p. 244). It is within this context that the US policy response to the 1959 revolution was developed; a response characterized by confrontation and isolation. The policy was meant to remove Castro from power and to restore a democracy or at the very least, replace Castro's regime with a less threatening one. The underlying foundation of this policy was the Trading with the Enemy Act – better known as the Trade Embargo initiated by President Eisenhower in 1961 and implemented by President Kennedy in 1962.

The 1962 trade embargo – Trading With The Enemy Act

In essence, the trade embargo bans trade, investment and travel by US residents or corporations in Cuba. At the time of its inception, the rationale for the embargo was a response to Cuba's perceived internationalist agenda, repressive policies toward its own people, confiscation of property, and most importantly, its ties to the Soviet Union (Fisk, 2000, Peters, 2000). Fundamentally, the USA felt that its security was compromised by having a communist neighbour in close proximity. Perez (2002) surmised that:

> The presence of Soviet missiles in Cuba shattered the terms around which the USA had fashioned a sense of its well-being since early in the nineteenth century. The missiles in 1962, and the subsequent deployment of Soviet combat troops, the establishment of intelligence-gathering facilities, and the maintenance of a Soviet submarine base on the south coast of Cuba challenged some of the central assumptions upon which US strategic planning had rested. In a security culture so very much shaped by notions of 'balance of power' and 'spheres of influence', the presence of the Soviet Union at a distance of a mere ninety miles wrought havoc on some of the most fundamental premises of US strategic thinking. (p. 232).

The shock of this change in the geo-political environment of the Americas, along with the Bay of Pigs fiasco (a failed proxy invasion by Cuban exiles), help to explain the visceral nature of the US policy response. In hindsight, it is apparent that US policy was based more on emotion than logic. McKenna (2004) has argued that this hostile mindset was cemented in the Washington bureaucracy at this point and has influenced the US foreign policy on Cuba ever since.

The economic objective of the embargo was to block hard currency flows, including those associated with tourism, that could benefit the Cuban government (Khrushchev, *et al.*, 2007). It was designed to create economic disarray, thereby, debilitating the Cuban government and making the Soviet maintenance of this satellite very expensive. While military intervention was not advisable during the time of the Cold War given the threat of retaliation from the Soviet bloc, economic sanctions were seen as a feasible way of fuelling domestic discontent and opposition to Castro.

Resilence and retrenchment

There has been a variety of minor modifications and interpretations of 1962 Trade Embargo through eleven successive US Presidential administrations. However, relaxation of the embargo has been rare and fleeting while the strengthening of the embargo has been much more common. The two major adjustments to the embargo followed the dissolution of the Soviet bloc in 1991. Both were intended to topple the Castro regime at a time of vulnerability (Perez, 2002).

In 1992, the Cuban Democracy Act or Torricelli Law was passed by a Democratic-controlled Congress. On the one hand it permitted humanitarian donations, including food and medicines but on the other hand it increased economic pressure on Cuba by prohibiting US subsidiaries from trading with Cuba. It also prohibited any vessel from entering a US port for a period of 180 days after handling freight going to or coming from Cuba (Fisk, 2001). These changes had implications for the cruise ship industry and for US hospitality companies that may have entertained thoughts of circumventing the investment embargo through a non-US subsidiary. The Cuban Liberty and Democratic Solidarity (LIBERTAD) Act, better known as the Helms-Burton Law was passed four years later by a Republican-controlled Congress that was afraid that Democratic President Clinton would relax the embargo. It also added a controversial third element by expanding the target of possible sanctions against parties from outside the USA (Fisk, 2001; Lowenfeld, 1996; Peters, 2000). The intent of this legislation was to reverse the growing trend toward joint ventures, including those in the tourism industry, between Cuba and companies from other sovereign states. It was specifically designed to deter nationals of third-party countries from doing business with Cuba and as such it raised fundamental questions about sovereignty.

President Clinton originally indicated that he would veto the bill, but just prior to doing so, the downing of the US civilian planes, dubbed 'Brothers to the Rescue', in Cuban air space created a domestic and international uproar. The incident was likely a deciding factor in Clinton's decision to sign off on the bill on 12 March 1996.

Policy effectiveness and relevance

The fact that Cuba is still functioning as an independent state under Castro's regime despite the hardship that the embargo has caused, is an indication of US policy failure. On an international stage at the United Nations, Cuban motions of censure for the US embargo have been widely supported (Roque, 2005). Prior to the modifications in the mid-1990s, the embargo effectively prohibited 'the sale of food and medicine, in violation of the Fourth Geneva Convention of 1949' (Smith, 1996, p. 111). Even Pope John Paul II, in Cuba in 1998 appealed to Cuba to open itself to the world, and to the world to open itself to Cuba (Fisk, 2001).

The travel ban in particular has been unsuccessful, with a reported 200,000 Americans risking a $7000 fine in 2006 by entering Cuba via countries such as Canada and Mexico without a special permit. Reportedly, only 21 people were penalized for this breach of American law in 2006 (ETN, 2009). More fundamentally, the travel restriction is contradictory to basic American constitutional freedoms and counter-productive in terms of convincing Cuban citizens of the merits of democracy. While the embargo may have isolated Americans from Cuba, it has not isolated Cuba from tourists from other parts of the world as reflected by the growth in international tourist visits (Figure 9.1). International tourist visits to Cuba have increased dramatically in the past 20 years. Recently, revenues earned from these visitors have served as the key source of hard currency and have been instrumental in helping Cuba to survive the US embargo. Not only has the embargo failed to achieve its original objectives, but the fundamental security based rationale for the embargo was lost in 1991 with the dissolution of the Soviet bloc (Peters, 2000) and the cessation of Cuba's promotion of similar revolutions in other parts of the globe.

The resilency of Cuba tourism

Losing the US market, which represented 87% of the tourists visiting Cuba, as a result of the US imposed travel ban in 1962, was a major blow to international tourism in Cuba. It was not, however, a death blow. After a virtual hiatus from international tourism of about 15 years, international tourism has grown dramatically even though the US travel ban has remained (Figure 9.1). Similarly, the Cuban economy is still functioning despite the trade embargo of 1962 and the loss of Soviet trade and support in 1991.

First, from a government perspective, Fidel Castro has provided charismatic and consistent, if dictatorial, leadership throughout his 48-year tenure in Cuba. He has consistently espoused the socialist principles that were at the heart of the revolution and has proven to be very savvy in terms of strategically positioning Cuba within a dynamic geo-political landscape. Castro has gained popular support in Cuba by positioning himself as a Cuban patriot fighting for the independence of his people and his country (Peters, 2000). His revolution has improved the quality of life of Cubans who were living in rural areas or who were poor at the time of the revolution Even upon Castro's eventually death, his influence is likely to remain as his socialist principles are deeply ingrained in not only the government but throughout many areas of Cuban society (Padilla and McElroy, 2007). Castro has been successful at diverting the blame for the county's economic woes and for the hardships that its citizens face onto the very US policy of confrontation and isolation that was intended to undermine his popular support. These arguments have proved effective on the international stage as well as on the domestic one (e.g. Roque, 2005). Resiliency at a national level in Cuba is, at least in part, derived from the genuine loyalty of its citizens (Jayawardena, 2003). The reality is that for the majority of Cubans, quality of life has improved under Castro and that the economic suffering that they experience is often attributed to external factors such as the US trade embargo and the dissolution of the Soviet bloc.

Beyond popular support for the Castro regime, the second major factor in supporting the resiliency in the face of US foreign policy was the Cuban government's decision to encourage joint ventures between foreign investors and the Cuban government (Avella and Mills, 1996). This initiative introduced new capital for investment and development – much of this aimed at the tourism industry. It allowed Cuba to replace decaying tourism infrastructure and to expand its capacity in keeping with its aggressive expansion targets.

Finally, there were a series of economic reforms introduced in 1992 and 1993 that helped Cuba to address its financial crisis particularly by positioning the tourism industry more competitively within the Caribbean. These included:

♦ Liberalization of currency regulations to allow Cuban nationals to make transactions in and hold hard currencies;

♦ Authorization of licensed self-employment so that individual Cubans could operate private repair shops, laundries, restaurants and other small businesses;

♦ Re-establishment of farmers' markets designed to overcome food shortages and handicraft markets catering to tourists;

♦ Reduction of subsidies on luxury items such as cigarettes, alcoholic beverages and fuel. Fees also were implemented for cultural and sports activities;

♦ Reorganization of administrative apparatus including the transformation of the National Tourism Institute into the Ministry of Tourism.

(Smith, 1996; Avella and Mills, 1996)

Fisk (2001) argued that these changes were tactical in nature and that they did not lead to 'fundamental political or economic change' (p. 101). Similarly, Cave (2003) points out that the subsequent reversal of many of these reforms in 1996 created a mixed message for budding entrepreneurs who as a result readily shifted from licensed small business operators to unlicensed black marketers. Not withstanding this slippage, the introduction of these reforms was instrumental in Cuban tourism's resilience against the US trade embargo.

The resilency of the US trade embargo

While the origin of the 1962 trade embargo was clearly based on the perception of Cuba being a security threat to the USA, the embargo's lack of success and the end of the Cold War suggest that the policy is no longer relevant. The fact that its core components have remained largely unchanged under Democratic as well as Republican Presidencies (11 in all), is also somewhat surprising.

One of the factors that has been responsible for the on-going retention of the economic embargo is the dynamic that exists between the US Presidential administration and Congress. At the time of the Cuban revolution, foreign policy was generally recognized as being in the domain of the President but since then there have been shifts in this balance in response to events such as Watergate and the Vietnam War. Vanderbush and Haney (2002) suggest that there are three types of foreign policy in the USA. The first involves policymaking in times of 'crisis' which is dominated by the President and a small group of advisors, a second is termed 'structural' policy-making inclusive of activities such as defence spending and foreign aid. Congress has considerable power over this realm. Finally, 'strategic' policy articulates the basic goals and tactics used by the US towards other countries. The President has the primary responsibility in this area, often initiating bills and exercising veto power. While it can be argued that the embargo was initiated during a time of crisis, its function has since been that of a 'strategic' policy. Congress has, however, challenged the President's authority in this area and has been especially active in terms of the embargo during periods when the Presidential Administration has been of a different political stripe than Congress. The best example of this is the Helms-Burton Law, passed by Congress in 1996, which made it clear that 'the economic embargo of Cuba is to remain in effect until a democratically elected government is in power in Cuba which, among other things, cannot include Fidel Castro or his brother Raul Castro' (Vanderbush and Haney, 2002, p. 175). One intent of the bill was to restrict the President's ability to create policy regarding Cuba.

While one might expect US Presidents of the Democrat Party to be more likely to relax the embargo than their Republican counterparts, this has not necessarily been the case. A good example of this was President Clinton's non-veto of the 1996 Helms–Burton Law. In this case, the timing of the bill just a few weeks after the downing of the 'Brothers of Rescue' Cessna flights represented a major intervening factor. Later in his presidency, Clinton did indeed relax the sanctions by easing restrictions on remittances, travel, medicine, and food aid and by reinstituting direct flights. In a 1995 policy statement, he also called for 'people-to-people' contact although he fell far short of rescinding the travel ban (McKenna, 2004). During the second President Bush's terms, most of these concessions were removed.

Since assuming office, President Obama has returned the travel and remittance regulations of the embargo back to their state under Clinton. It is noteworthy that his advisors have made it clear that changes in US policy related to Cuba 'should and can be led by the White House' (King and Spalding, 2009, p. 2). While it is doubtful that Congress agrees whole-heartedly with this view, it is apparent that there is also considerable support within Congress' Foreign Relations Committee to review the existing embargo. However, Congress' decisions will ultimately reflect or at least be influenced by views of Cuban American constituents (King and Spalding, 2009, p. 3).

A large population of Cuban Americans live in Florida. Many of these fled Cuba as a result of the revolution or are offspring of those who fled. The animosity of the original immigrants to Castro runs deep, as many of these families have suffered losses as a result of the revolution. They are a political force in the US under the Cuban American National Foundation (CANF) which has been a strident and active supporter of the economic embargo. Candidates for Congress as well as the Presidency have been subject to strong lobbying efforts by this group. Kirk (2007) argues that the CANF has exerted undue influence over US foreign policy on Cuba.

Recently, cracks have emerged in the Cuban American lobby. At the heart of these cracks is an apparent generational gap as first-generation Cuban Americans age and their children take over leadership (Fisk, 2001; Peters, 2000; Smith 1996). This second generation of Cuban Americans tends to appreciate a broader range of issues during elections and are not as single-minded about US foreign policy in Cuba (Lovato, 2004). They also tend to be less emotional about their ties to Cuba as they have grown up in America and may feel mixed loyalties. They have also suffered the brunt of the travel and remittance restrictions imposed by the second Bush administration and increasingly question the effectiveness of a foreign policy of retribution and isolation. In their assessment of this group's response to President Obama's recent initiatives to soften the economic embargo, King and Spalding (2009) state that:

> The political dynamics regarding Cuban American constituencies and the electoral power of Florida in particular are changing and arguably open greater possibilities for presidential action regarding Cuba policy. Whereas President Bush relied on the Cuban vote to carry Florida by narrow margins in 2000 and 2004, Obama won election without the Cuban American vote, winning just 38 percent of that group. (p. 3)

Conclusion

The purpose of chapter was to examine the effect on tourism as both an instrument and a target of US–Cuban foreign policy. This was done by focusing particularly on the US trade embargo which bans the travel of Americans to Cuba and restricts trade and investment.

Emotion has been as important as logic in the resiliency of the embargo. This is especially apparent given its failure to achieve the objective of destabilizing Castro's regime and because of changes in geo-politics that have reduced the security threat that Cuba once posed to the USA. A deep personal animosity to Cuba and particularly to Fidel Castro appears to have been passed down to each successive president (Perez, 2002; McKenna, 2004). There has also been effective pressure brought to bear on politicians by emotional and until recently, single-minded Cuban Americans who demanded punitive action against Castro.

While US resiliency was driven by animosity toward Castro and a desire not to lose face at home or abroad, the resiliency of the Cuban tourism industry is based on a real threat to Cuba's political and economic survival. If tourism had failed to thrive after the fall of the Soviet bloc, it is very likely that the Cuban economy would also have failed. Despite this success, there has been a price to be paid. From a tourism perspective, rapid growth in international tourism over the past 20 years has been accompanied by echoes of tourism's unsavoury state prior to the 1959 revolution, including a visible increase in prostitution. Significant tensions have also emerged in tourism's 'tangled economy of market and non-market values' (Elliott and Neiroti, 2008, p. 397). This ideological paradox will require careful strategic management.

With Obama's 2008 election in the USA and Fidel Castro's now defunct leadership role in Cuba, a repeal of the 1962 embargo or major components of it is a distinct possibility. A repeal of the travel ban would translate to more tourism revenues and hard currency. But if and when the travel ban is lifted, Cuba is going to have to deal with an American invasion of 2.5 to 3.5 million visitors a year in addition to the over 2 million non-Americans who currently visit Cuba on an annual basis. While this invasion will be much more welcome than a military one, the challenges that it will present should not be underestimated.

References

Avella, A. and Mills, A.S. (1996) 'Tourism in Cuba in the 1990s', *Tourism Management*, 17 (1), 55–60.

Cave, D. (2003) 'Havana hustle: Cuba's new socialist man learns to wheel and deal', *Reason*, 8, 38–45.

Elliott, S.M. and Delpy Neirotti, L. (2008) 'Challenges of tourism in a dynamic island destination: the case of Cuba', *Tourism Geographies*, 10 (3), 375–402.

ETN 'The Cuban tourism industry might welcome US visitors, but some Canadians don't want to share the island paradise', from: www.eturbonews.com/8716/ (19 June 2009)

Fisk, D.W. (2000) 'Cuba, the end of an era', *The Washington Quarterly*, 24 (1), 93–107.

Hinch, T.D. (1990) 'Cuban tourism and industry – its re-emergence and future', *Tourism Management*, **11** (3), 214–226.

Jayawardena, C. (2003) 'Revolution to revolution: why is tourism booming in Cuba?' *International Journal of Contemporary Hospitality Management*, **15**, 52–58.

King and Spalding (2009) *Client Alert: Government Advocacy and Policy Practice Group*, Washington, DC: King & Spalding.

Kirk, J. (2007) 'Toward an understanding of the tourism potential in Cuba', *Cornell Hotel and Restaurant Administration Quarterly*, **48**, 416–418.

Khrushchev, S. Henthorne, T. and Latour, M. (2007) 'Cuba at the crossroads: the role of the US hospitality industry in Cuban tourism initiatives', *Cornell Hotel and Restaurant Administration Quarterly*, **48** (4), 402–415.

Lovato, R. (2004). 'Rocking the Cuban vote', *The Nation*, 1 November, pp23–26.

Lowenfeld, A.F. (1996) 'Agora: The Cuban Liberty and Democratic Solidarity (Libertad) Act – Congress and Cuba: The Helms Burton Act', *The American Journal of International Law*, **90** (3), 419–434.

McKenna, P. (2004) 'Comparative foreign policies toward Cuba', *International Journal*, Spring 2004, 281–302.

Padilla, A. and McElroy, J. (2007) 'Cuba and Caribbean tourism after Castro', *Annals of Tourism Research*, **34** (3), 649–672.

Perez Jr., L.A. (2002) 'Fear and loathing of Fidel Castro: sources of US policy toward Cuba', *Journal of Latin American Studies*, **34**, 227–254.

Peters, P. (2000) 'A policy toward Cuba that serves US interests', *Policy Analysis*, D.C. Cato Institute, 384, 1–14.

Romeu, R. (2008) Vacation over: Implications for the Caribbean of Opening US –Cuba Tourism, International Monetary Fund, Working Paper.

Roque, P. (2005) 'Does the US embargo of Cuba violate international law?' *International Debates*, September 2005,172–182.

Sanchez, L. M. Fornieles (2006) 'The state of Cuban tourism with statistics', Havana Journal, http://havanajournal.com.

Schwartz, R. (1997) *Pleasure Island: Tourism and Temptation in Cuba*, Lincoln: University of Nebraska Press.

Smith, W.S. (1996) 'Cuba's long reform', *Foreign Affairs*, **75** (2), 99–112.

Sugden, J. (2007) 'Running Havana: observations on the political economy of sport tourism in Cuba', *Leisure Studies*, **26** (2), 235–251.

Turner, L. and Ash, J (1975) '*The Golden Hordes: International Tourism and the Pleasure Periphery*', London: Constable.

Vanderbush, W. and Haney, P.J. (2002) 'Clinton, Congress and Cuba policy between two codifications: the changing executive-legislative relationship in foreign policy making', *Congress and the Presidency*, **29** (Autumn),171–194.

Ward, F. (1978) *Inside Cuba Today*, New York: Crown Publishers.

Winson, A. (2006) 'Ecotourism and sustainability in Cuba: does socialism make a difference? *Journal of Sustainable Tourism* **14**, 6–23.

10 Arab Politics and Tourism: Political Change and Tourism in the Great Socialist People's Libyan Arab Jamahiriya

Eleri Jones

Introduction

Libya, formally known as the Great Socialist People's Libyan Arab Jamahiriya –– in Arabic Al Jumahiriyah al Arabiyah al Libiyah ash Shabiyah al Ishtirakiyah al Uzma (Library of Congress – Federal Research Division 2005), has enormous potential as a destination with its diverse high quality and unique tourism assets – its archaeological heritage (notably its Roman and Greek antiquities), its spectacular beaches, its mountains and its desert. However, to date these assets have not been developed for a number of reasons, not least Libya's isolation as a result of United Nations (UN) sanctions and relatively recent recognition of the importance of diversifying the Libyan economy from its reliance on oil and gas revenues. Although UN sanctions have now been lifted and Libya has re-emerged on the world stage, the challenges relating to the development of Libya into an internationally-competitive destination, both internally and externally, should not be underestimated. This chapter will explore some of the political issues relating to tourism development in Libya.

Libyan tourism

Libya is located in North Africa on the southern edge of the Mediterranean Sea and shares borders with Egypt to the East, Sudan to the south-east, Chad and Niger to the south, Algeria and finally Tunisia to the West (see Figure 10.1). Libya is 90% desert and has three distinct areas: Tripolitania, which contains the most densely-populated Western coastal strip north of the Western mountains (Jebel Gharbi); Cyrenaica, which contains the Eastern coastal strip north of the Green Mountains (Jebal Akhdar); and the Fezzan in the South. Libya's 1770 kilometres of coastline (CIA 2009) has spectacular white and golden beaches which are lapped by the crystal clear and stunningly blue waters of the Mediterranean.

Figure 10.1: Map of Libya.

The World Travel and Tourism Council (2009) provide an overview of the economic impact of Libyan tourism, showing both GDP contribution and tourism employment are expected to rise over the next ten years (Table 10.1).

Table 10.1: Ten year predictions for the contribution of tourism to the Libyan economy (World Travel and Tourism Council, 2009).

Indicator	Units	2009	2019
Tourism contribution to GDP	%	8.6	10.2
	Libyan dinars (millions)	9937.9	27,873.3
	US dollars (millions)	7703.8	21,607.2
Direct and indirect employment	Jobs	159,000	232,000
	% of total employment	8.8	10.4
	Proportion of jobs	1 in 11.4	1 in 9.6

However, despite this optimism, Libyan tourism can only be described as emerging although as Ham (2007: 5) asserts:

> *Libya has it all: ancient cities of rare splendour, the Sahara that you thought existed only in your imagination and the unmistakable cachet of being ruled by one of the 20th century's most iconic figures, Colonel Muammar Qaddafi.*

Clearly these assets provide great potential for tourism in Libya – with its beaches, archaeological (particularly Greek and Roman) heritage, mountains and deserts. These assets and the requisite infrastructure and superstructure for their effective exploitation – roads, hotels, restaurants and resorts – are underdeveloped. Some superstructural developments have taken place, e.g. the opening of the 299-room luxury Corinthian hotel in Tripoli in April 2003 (Library of Congress – Federal Research Division 2005) which was developed through Libyan–Maltese investment partnership.

Libya's tourism attractions reflect successive periods of occupation. There are thirteen major archaeological sites, of which five are inscribed on the UNESCO World Heritage list (UNESCO 2009) – Tadrart Acacus, the old town of Ghadamès, Cyrene, Leptis Magna and Sabratha – as outlined below.

- ♦ The earliest of the five World Heritage sites is the Neolithic rock art sites of Tadrart Acacus in the South-west of Libya which link to Algeria's Tassili N'Ajjer (also inscribed on the World Heritage list). Thousands of cave paintings dating from 12,000 BCE to 100 CE document changes in the Sahara's fauna and flora (UNESCO 2009).

- ♦ Ghadamès – 'the pearl of the desert' – is one of the oldest pre-Saharan cities, standing in an oasis on Libya's Western border. UNESCO (2009) describes Ghadamès as an outstanding example of a traditional settlement through which runs a network of covered passageways at ground level for men to move around the settlement.

- ♦ Cyrene, a former Greek colony, was one of the principal cities in the Hellenic world. It was later Romanized and remained an important capital until an earthquake in 365.

- ♦ Leptis Magna was originally founded by the Phoenicians around 1000 BCE, it survived the Spartans to become first a Punic and eventually (around 23 BC), a Roman city developed by Emperor Septimius Severus into one of the most beautiful cities of the Roman Empire (UNESCO 2009);

- ♦ Sabratha, a Phoenician trading-post and port serving the former Numidian kingdom of Massinissa in modern-day Algeria, was rebuilt by the Romans in the 2nd and 3rd centuries CE.

History and political structure

Ronald Bruce St John provides a select chronology of Libyan history (St John 2008). What is now Libya has, at various periods, been occupied: simultaneously by the Phoenicians in the West and the Greeks in the East, then the Romans and later the Arabs. It was part of the Ottoman Empire from 1551 to 1911 and under Italian occupation from 1911 to 1943. The three parts of Libya (Tripolitania, Cyrenaica and Fezzan) were unified in 1934 (Library of Congress – Federal Research Division 2005).

During World War II, Libya was one of the main battlegrounds of North Africa and at the end of the war fell into military administration – Tripolitania and Cyrenaica under the British, the Fezzan under the French. Post-war, the United Nations General Assembly created the United Kingdom of Libya with Idris al-Sanusi as King. In 1958 oil was discovered and by the early 1960s Libya had become an oil exporting country, transforming it from one of the poorest countries in the world to one of the richest (Library of Congress – Federal Research Division 2005)

King Idris was ousted, 1 September 1969, in a military coup led by Colonel Muammar al-Qaddafi who, aged 27 became President of the 12-person Revolutionary Command Council (RCC) which was designated as Libya's supreme executive and legislative authority (Martinez 2007). Although the RCC was dominated by Qaddafi he did not hold absolute authority and the RCC operated collegially, debating issues until consensus was achieved. The RCC established a Council of Ministers to execute general policy and legislation in accordance with RCC decisions, initially with Qaddafi as Prime Minister although he soon handed this post over to another RCC member and devoted himself to the development of his revolutionary theory.

Qaddafi's political principles form the basis of the Libyan political system and were published in 1975 in the Green Book (widely available in public places throughout Libya and in a number of languages) (Qathafi, n.d.). The Green Book comprises three parts: Part 1: The Solution of the Problem of Democracy: The Authority of the People; Part 2: The Solution of the Economic Problem: Socialism; Part 3: The Social Basis of the Third Universal Theory.

The political changes which have taken place

The Libyan political system is a local idiosyncratic ideology based on Qaddafi's Third Universal Theory, combining socialist and Islamic principles (El-Kikhia 1997). According to El-Kikhia (1997) while local idiosyncratic ideologies are not unusual, what is unusual about Libya's is its longevity. The Third Universal Theory is offered as an alternative to capitalism and communism which Qaddafi saw as failing political paradigms. It rejects political parties (illegal in Libya), and promotes people power in a 'state of the masses' or Jamahiriya – a political system designed to promote participation by the Libyan people. The Jamahiriya is organized as local congresses feeding into regional congresses and ultimately into the national GPC (Library of Congress – Federal Research Division 2005). The GPC is the primary formal instrument of government with legislative powers. It has a membership of more than 1000 and convenes twice a year. The congresses have executive bodies or Committees at local, regional and national level (Library of Congress – Federal Research Division 2005). At a national level, the General People's Committee is made up of Secretaries forming a cabinet of ministers representing different portfolios. One portfolio relates to tourism and the Secretary reports to the General People's Committee for Tourism.

Thus Libyan politics reflect a dual structure: the RCC (whose members are in power as a result of involvement in the revolution) and the Jamahiriya. In theory, Libya is governed by the people and the GPC has primary authority. However, in practice it is an authoritarian regime with Qaddafi as chief of state and several of his relatives – most notably his son Saif al-Islam – holding ultimate power either directly or indirectly through the RCC. The RCC controls the Jamahiriya ensuring that its decisions at each level conform to the Green Book. Remarkably nowadays Qaddafi holds no official title but is commonly referred to as the 'Brotherly Leader and Guide of the Revolution'. Saif al-Islam has emerged as a progressive and reforming leader and seems likely to be accepted by the Libyan people to succeed in due course. Qaddafi himself probably sits between the revolutionaries and the reformers (Martinez 2007). As the CIA World Factbook (2009, online) suggests:

Libya faces a long road ahead in liberalizing the socialist-oriented economy, but initial steps – including applying for WTO [World Trade Organization] membership, reducing some subsidies, and announcing plans for privatization – are laying the groundwork for a transition to a more market-based economy.

Qaddafi's domestic position as champion for the oppressed has been reflected in his approach to international politics and his support of liberation movements worldwide. In accordance with his Third Universal Theory, Qaddafi has sought to establish a more equitable distribution of wealth between developed and developing countries through sponsorship of terrorist and guerrilla movements world-wide, e.g. the Irish Republican Army (IRA), the Basque nationalist and separatist movement Euskadi Ta Askatasuna (ETA) and the Palestine Liberation Organization (PLO). It depends who is telling the tale as to whether Qaddafi is cast as good guy or bad guy. What is undisputable is that he has used Libya's oil wealth to assert the independence of developing nations on the international stage. Amongst many international interventions Qaddafi: supported Nelson Mandela before his release from prison; intervened in Uganda to keep Idi Amin in power; and supported Iran in the 1980–88 Iran–Iraq war (Library of Congress – Federal Research Division 2005).

The United States (US) Department of State (2008) catalogue US-Libyan relations which from 1969 and through the 1970s tell a sorry story of attack and counter-attack culminating in December 1979 with the USA designating Libya a state sponsor of terrorism following the mobbing and burning of the US Embassy in Tripoli as Libyans demonstrated solidarity with the Iranian revolution. In November 1969, Qaddafi demanded the evacuation of US air bases in Libya which was achieved by June 1970. Diplomatic relations deteriorated and in 1972 the US withdrew its ambassador. In 1973, a Libyan airliner was downed by Israeli fighters over Sinai and in response the US embassy in Tripoli was mobbed and a USA flag burned. In 1973 Libya proclaimed first a special maritime zone within 100 nautical miles of Libya and later control of the Gulf of Sidra south of $32°30'$ N, neither of which the USA recognized. US provision of military aid to Israel during the Yom Kippur war in 1973 between Israel and Egypt-Syria precipitated an embargo on Libyan oil exports to the USA.

Through the 1980s, US-Libyan wrestling over the Gulf of Sidra continued. In March 1981 Qaddafi threatened war if the USA entered the Gulf of Sidra. Later in March the USA announced exercises there within the next six months. In August 1981, two Libyan fighter planes were shot down over the Gulf of Sidra following an attack on US planes. In January 1986, following Palestinian terrorist attacks on airports in Rome and Vienna in December 1985, allegedly with Libyan support, the USA imposed economic sanctions on Libya. In March 1986, Libya fired air missiles at US aircraft flying over the Gulf of Sidra and in response the USA sank two Libyan patrol craft and attacked the missile base. In April 1986, a bomb exploded in West Berlin discotheque frequented by US soldiers, killing three people, including two US soldiers, and wounding 230 people. The USA responded by attacking five targets in Libya and killing 40 Libyans, including Qaddafi's baby daughter. The incidents of the 1980s culminated in December 1988 with the bombing of Pan Am flight 103 over Lockerbie, Scotland killing 269 passengers and crew, most of whom were Americans, as well as eleven civilians on the ground (US Department of State 2008).

The 1990s saw Libya in political and economic isolation as a result of sanctions and trade embargoes to force the transfer of two Libyan intelligence agents suspected of the Pan Am 103 bombing for trial in the USA or the UK. In June 1992, Libya agreed that these suspects could be tried abroad but it was not until April 1999 that they were transferred to The Netherlands for trial under Scottish law. The international sanctions forced rising import costs and inflation in Libya's domestic economy and standards of living deteriorated prompting several assassination attempts on Qaddafi by militant opposition groups and an army-led coup attempt in 1993. In January 2001 Scottish judges convicted one of the suspects (Abdel-Basset al-Meghrahi) but found the other not guilty. Amidst extreme controversy Al-Meghrahi, suffering from prostate cancer and allegedly with three months to live, was released in August 2009 on compassionate grounds by the Scottish Justice Minister.

During the sanctions, Qaddafi turned to the Arab world for support. When this was not forthcoming he turned to sub-Saharan Africa promoting the concept of a 'United States of Africa', again with little success (Martinez 2007). It was the US-led invasion of Iraq in March 2003 that precipitated a change of heart towards the West by Qaddafi. As Martinez (2007, 154-155) commented, what alarmed Qaddafi was:

> ... the overthrow of Saddam Hussein. Up to then, the international sanctions had not greatly concerned the regime, and Colonel Gaddafi has seemed attracted by the idea of turning Libya into a kind of Mediterranean Cuba. In 2003, a great gust of panic was felt in Tripoli, which blew away the regime's certainty that it could withstand simultaneously the pressure of Islamist violence from within at the same times as the threat of invasion from without [and] ... took care to emphasise the convergence of its interests in all spheres with those of the United States and Europe.

In August 2003, Libya officially accepted responsibility for Lockerbie, agreed to pay the relatives of each victim at least $5 million and renounced terrorism to the UN Security Council (US Department of State 2008). The US maintained sanctions but did not oppose the lifting of UN sanctions in September 2003. In December 2003, after negotiations with the USA and the UK, Libya renounced its production and use of weapons of mass destruction and agreed to unannounced inspections from international bodies. In February 2004, diplomatic relations between the USA and Libya were resumed and US passport restrictions lifted. Trade restrictions gradually eased. By June 2006 the USA formally rescinded Libya's designation as a state sponsor of terrorism and, in October 2007, the UN General Assembly elected Libya as a non-permanent member of the Security Council completing its return to the world stage. Libya is once again 'open for business' thus enhancing its tourism potential.

The implications for tourism

If Libya is to become an internationally-competitive destination then it needs to resolve a number of fundamental issues. Ritchie and Crouch (2003) discuss how a destination might turn its comparative advantage to competitive advantage using a five-layer model in which core resources and attractors are underpinned by supporting factors and resources. Destination policy, planning and development provide a strategic framework for implementation by destination management. Qualifying and amplifying determinants define the potential scale of tourism development within a particular context. Each layer will be discussed below in the context of Libya.

Core resources and attractors

Core resources and attractors are key to destination development. Ritchie and Crouch (2003) identify: physiography and climate; culture and history; a mix of activities; special events; entertainment; superstructure and market ties as important elements. Libya's physical resources in terms of its landscape are world-class and it has a good climate. It offers a fascinating mix of cultures and a rich history. There is the potential for developing hallmark events, to generate high levels of interest and enhance a Sense of Place. Libya has a diverse range of colourful community-led events which would provide entertainment and a good basis for such events. Superstructure includes accommodation facilities, food and beverage provision, transport and attractors. Although Libya has world-class attractors in its World Heritage and other archaeological sites, beaches, mountains and deserts, most other superstructure aspects need attention (World Tourism Organization 1998). The issue of market ties relates to the developing links with key source markets. Libya's colonial history offers the potential for the development of such links across Europe (UK, France, Germany and Italy) and beyond.

Supporting factors and resources

Core resources and attractors need to be underpinned by supporting factors and resources, including infrastructure, accessibility, facilitating resources and perhaps most important, political will. Infrastructure includes transportation which in Libya needs a massive overhaul. Accessibility is a challenge. Despite the advantage of geographic proximity to key tourist-generating markets with reasonable flying times, entry to Libya is problematic and potential, non-Arabic tourists to Libya must hold a passport complete with legally-certified Arabic translation, a visa and a return ticket. Facilitating resources include the availability and quality of local human, knowledge and capital resources, education and research institutions, financial institutions and an enabling public sector. Libya is a cash economy and credit cards are not widely accepted. Although the number is increasing, there are few automated teller machines in Tripoli or the rest of Libya.

CIA (2009) reports 2004 estimates of unemployment levels of 30% so the potential for tourism jobs should be welcome. However, whenever this writer has asked Libyans directly: 'Would you work in tourism or let your wife or son/daughter work in tourism?' the answer has been a resounding 'No'. There are fundamental issues in relation to the attractiveness of tourism as an employment sector. Tourism is widely seen as 'bad' and 'has been blamed for sexual permissiveness, flagrant indulgence in alcohol, gambling, drugs, pornography, voyeurism' (Din 1989: 554). Such negative images of tourism are particularly important in Muslim countries and no less so in Libya. Most Libyans are devoutly religious – 97% are Sunni Muslims (CIA 2009) – and the Islamic basis of the Green Book makes it difficult, if not impossible, to separate religion from state. It is not just a case of not drinking wine. Islam is unambiguous about alcohol, as recorded in Sunan Al-Tirmidhi Hadith 2776 narrated by Anas ibn Malik:

> *Allah's Messenger (peace be upon him) cursed ten people in connection with wine: the wine-presser, the one who has it pressed, the one who drinks it, the one who conveys it, the one to whom it is conveyed, the one who serves it, the one who sells it, the one who benefits from the price paid for it, the one who buys it, and the one for whom it is bought.*

Alcohol is prohibited in Libya as is pork. Pork is easily avoided and its absence has few implications for tourism. However, the role of alcohol in international tourism cannot be ignored and its prohibition may deter some visitors.

Another challenge, particularly relating to women's employment in tourism, is where a company requires its staff to wear uniforms that do not meet Islamic dress codes. Islamic women are required to cover their entire bodies – except for their hands and faces and not 'reveal their adornment except to their husbands, fathers, husbands' fathers, sons, husbands' sons, brothers, brothers' sons, sisters' sons, sisters in Islam, female slaves, old male servants and small children' (The Noble Qur'an 24: 31). Several conditions for Muslim women's dress have been identified:

> *Clothing must cover the entire body so that only the hands and face remain*
> *visible; the clothing should hang loose so that the shape and form of the body*
> *is not apparent; female clothing must not resemble male clothing; the design*
> *of clothing must not resemble the clothing of non-believing women; the design*
> *must not consist of bold designs which attract attention; clothing should not*
> *be worn for the sole purpose of gaining reputation or increasing one's status in*
> *society.*
>
> *(El-Sherif Ibrahim et al. 2007, p.293)*

Covering of the head with the hejab is particularly problematic in relation to women's employment in tourism across the Middle East and North Africa. As one Omani hotel manager commented in relation to waiters:

> *we cannot recruit a girl who will be wearing the hejab in a very restrictive way*
> *or totally black which might give the impression to the customer that she is*
> *a terrorist … the way that the female waitresses wear their black scarf makes*
> *the guest afraid to ask her any service … because he doesn't want to offend the*
> *culture or the religion.*
>
> *(Al-Balushi 2008, p.272)*

The attractiveness issues relating to tourism employment are exacerbated by legislation which prescribes low wages for tourism occupations (Naama 2007).

The supporting factors and resources could be unlocked if the political will were strong enough. Tourism was recognized by the Libyan government in 1986 at the Eleventh Session of the GPC for 'the significant role it can play in changing the international image of the country' (World Tourism Organization 1998, p. i). In 1987 this was followed up with a Memorandum on Tourism and People's Recreation with more detailed objectives. In the late 1990s, the General People's Committee for Tourism sought technical assistance from the World Tourism Organization acting as executing agency on behalf of the UN Development Programme to commission a nine-member team of consultants from the High-Point Rendel Economic Studies Group to develop a National Tourism Development Plan (NTDP). The NTDP aimed to provide 'a realistic and implementable base for the development of the sector through the establishment and promulgation of a policy framework, short and long term objectives, supporting strategic guidelines and a five-year action programme for the period 1999 to 2003' (World Tourism Organization 1998, p. i). The consultancy team concluded that: 'the lack of development of the tourism product, and the widely-held negative perception of the Jamahiriya among the populations of the major tourist generating markets … will necessitate tourism to be product led … [and] … strongly supported by a programme of public relations activities' (World Tourism Organization 1998, pp. 3/2). However, to date, little has happened to turn rhetoric into reality although there is much talk of partnership development of several coastal resorts, including the ambitious multi-billion pound Green Mountain Project outlined by Foster and Partners (2007) in the Cyrene Declaration signed by Saif al-Islam.

Destination policy, planning and development

An important first step in developing a tourism development plan is to define the tourism system based on an audit of the destination's resources. Whatever the final plan is it will need to be sensitively phased so infrastructure constraints can be addressed incrementally as can human resource issues. The plan must be monitored and evaluated with a set of key performance indicators integrating international best practice as far as possible, so as not to reinvent the wheel and to enable benchmarking against competitor destinations. That little has been done thus far to implement the NTDP means that it would probably be best to start again. One criticism of the NTDP (personal communication) is that it was developed by outsiders so developing Libyan consensus on an appropriate plan is crucial.

Obviously Libya's archaeological and cultural heritage will be a key element in the Libyan tourism product and spa tourism and the potential for spa resorts along Libya's coast offer opportunities for attracting high-spending market segments. Business/conference tourists are another high-spending segment although they require considerable investment, e.g. in an international calibre conference centre, a bidding unit and a trained workforce capable of delivering a high-quality product (Haven-Tang et al., 2007).

Philosophy/values are key aspects of destination policy, planning and development, especially in Libya where there are many socio-political issues. They must be interpreted sensitively and explicitly stated in a vision of what Libyan tourism would mean. The positioning of the brand in relation to Libya's competitors (probably Morocco, Tunisia, Egypt and Jordan) must then be determined. 'Brand Libya' must be consistent with the vision and its underpinning philosophy/values and there must be community consensus-building and market testing to ensure it resonates internally and externally.

Destination management

This layer of the Ritchie and Crouch model (2003) comprises: organization, marketing, quality of service experience, information/research, human resource development (HRD), finance and venture capital, visitor management, resource stewardship, crisis management. Of these marketing, information and HRD are particularly relevant to Libya.

In terms of marketing the NTDP recommended an initial first stage, perhaps of three years, focusing only to create 'awareness of, and a clear, accurate yet positive image for the Jamahiriya as a country and of Libyans as a people' (World Tourism Organization 1998: 7/1) before moving on to stimulate demand for visiting Libya.

Human Resource Development (HRD) is a key issue. There are skills shortages and gaps in the labour market, and Libyans are generally ill-equipped to take up employment opportunities in the tourism industry. This is partly a result of the outmoded curricula on offer in Libya's training institutes which make their graduates an unattractive employment option and drives employers, e.g. hoteliers, towards the employment of foreign workers (Naama 2007).

Qualifying and amplifying determinants

Qualifying and amplifying determinants are situational conditioners defining the potential scale of tourism development. This layer of the Ritchie and Crouch (2003) model includes location, safety/security, cost/value, interdependencies (with other destinations), awareness/image and carrying capacity.

Libya's location on the southern edge of the Mediterranean gives it close proximity to its key source markets and a pleasant climate. Although safety and security are key concerns, Qaddafi's police state is very safe for tourists, but Qaddafi and his former hatred of the West dominate images of Libya in the media and reinforce Libya's former involvement with the sponsorship of terrorism and high-profile isolation fuelling concerns about the security of Libya as a potential destination which are not countered by marketing and promotion activities.

There is low awareness of Libya's tourism potential in key markets. In the UK, for example, potential visitors have little awareness of Libya's potential as a destination. Akram Khalifa (personal communication), who undertook a study of images of Libya in the UK, quoted the words of one Libyan tour operator: 'In the UK there are not enough promotions and not enough effort is spent in advertising, which should be the main duty of the tourism ministry. The British have no idea about Libya'. He reported a second Libyan tour operator as saying that the Libyan image is unclear and misunderstood in the West, despite a number of media articles promoting positive images. Major marketing and promotion activities will be required to address this issue.

Conclusions

Qaddafi's local idiosyncratic ideology is based on socialist and Islamic values and uniquely defines the Libyan political context. It is therefore hard to see what lessons can be learned from Libya in relation to tourism development in other contexts. Qaddafi has now been in power for over 40 years and although there have been increasing signs of economic reform and shifts towards free trade since international sanctions were lifted, progress is slow.

Although the Libyan government has long recognised the importance of tourism in economic diversification and the NTDP was developed in 1998, there has been little progress on its implementation to turn rhetoric into reality. Qaddafi's control of all aspects of Libyan political life is so overwhelming that it is difficult to imagine that the NTDP could have been conceived without his backing. Tourism is an integral part of the reform agenda with the potential to help re-engineer images of Libya abroad. However, it is one which poses fundamental challenges to Libyan conservatism. It would seem that it is going ahead very slowly, in a controlled and contained manner through proposals for high-quality resorts in partnership with foreign developers. So, to date and despite Libya's world-class tourism resources, the infrastructure to support tourism development (roads, telecommunications, hotels and resorts), remains massively underdeveloped. Low awareness of Libya as a potential destination in key source markets, misperceptions about security, complexities around passports and visas, and currency issues are major challenges to Libya's ambition of becoming an internationally-competitive destination with tourism making a significant GDP contribution.

Libya has vast financial resources from its oil exporting activities on which it could draw to support its tourism rhetoric and turn its undoubted comparative advantage into competitive advantage. This is likely to be achieved through careful specification of high-quality distinctive tourism products implemented through a sensitively-phased development plan to address the many and varied infrastructural and other issues which are currently obstacles to progress. Such a plan should involve public and private-sector investment. It must be supported by appropriate marketing and promotion activities to tackle the low awareness of Libya even in key European source markets and change perceptions that Libya is not a safe destination. The message must be loud and clear that Libya is open for business and welcomes tourists.

References

Al-Balushi M.K. (2008) Omani employment and the development of careers in the hotel sector in the Sultanate of Oman, PhD, University of Wales.

CIA (2009) The World Factbook [Online]. CIA, from: https://www.cia.gov/library/publications/the-world-factbook/geos/ly.html (20 July 2009).

Din K.H. (1989) 'Islam and tourism: patterns, issues and opinions', *Annals of Tourism Research*, **16** (4), 542–563.

El-Kikhia M.O. (1997) *Libya's Qaddafi: The Politics of Contradiction*, Gainesville: University of Florida Press.

El-Sherif Ibrahim N.S., Pritchard A. and Jones E. (2007) '(Un)veiling women's employment in the Egyptian Travel Business', in A. Pritchard, N. Morgan, I. Ateljevic and C. Harris (eds), *Tourism and Gender: Embodiment, Sensuality and Experience*, Wallingford: CABI, pp 290–302.

Foster and Partners (2007) The Cyrene Declaration: An overview. Foster and Partners. from: http://static.dezeen.com/uploads/adverts/LibyaBrochure_30dpi.pdf (26 October 2009).

Ham A (2007) *Libya*, 2nd edn, London: Lonely Planet.

Haven-Tang C., Jones E. and Webb C. (2007) 'BESTBET: Exploiting Cardiff's capital city status in developing and shaping its business tourism offer', *Journal of Travel and Tourism Marketing*, **22** (3/4),109–120.

Library of Congress – Federal Research Division (2005) Country Profile: Libya [Online], from: http://lcweb2.loc.gov/frd/cs/profiles/Libya.pdf (20 July 2009).

Martinez L (2007) *The Libyan Paradox*, London: C Hurst and Co.

Naama A.A.A. (2007) Workforce analysis for the Libyan hotel sector: stakeholder perspectives. PhD, University of Wales.

Qathafi, M.A. (n.d.) *The Green Book*, Public Establishment for Publishing, Advertising and Distribution.

Ritchie J.R.B. and Crouch G.I. (2003) *The Competitive Destination: A Sustainable Tourism Perspective*, Wallingford: CABI.

St John R.B. (2008) *Libya: From Colony to Independence*, Oxford: Oneworld Publications.

UNESCO (2009) World Heritage. (Updated 22 August 2009), from: http://whc.unesco.org/en/list (20 July 2009).

US Department of State (2008) Significant Events in US-Libyan Relations (Released on 2 September 2008). Office of the Spokesman of the US Department of State: Washington, DC, Available: http://www.state.gov/r/pa/prs/ps/2008/sept/109054.htm (20 July 2009).

World Tourism Organization (1998) *Tourism Planning and Development (Lib/96/001) National Tourism Development Plan: Volume 1*. Great Socialist People's Libyan Arab Jamahiriya General People's Committee for Tourism/ World Tourism Organization/ United Nations Development Programme.

World Travel and Tourism Council (2009). Travel and Tourism Economic Impact 2009: Libya, World Travel and Tourism Council, from: http://www.wttc.org/bin/pdf/original_pdf_file/libya.pdf (20 July 2009).

11 From Apartheid to a 'Managed Revolution': Tourism Development and the Transition in South Africa

Peter U.C. Dieke

Introduction

South Africa's recent transition from a racist apartheid society that denied basic human rights to the majority of its citizens to a fully democratic nation is one of the most celebrated political changes of modern times. This change has implications at several levels, not least of which is its impact on the tourism sector. The phenomenal growth in this sector resulting from the end of apartheid has provided a massive boost to the country's economy (see Table 11.1).

Ahmed et al (1998: 80) have noted however that 'After years of isolation, South Africa's reemergence as a tourist destination is marked by serious challenges that may inhibit the industry's growth and development'. Given the legacies of the apartheid era, much of the concern here centres on the need, among other considerations, to change the ownership structure of the tourism sector, the involvement of local individuals and communities in the tourism development process, its operations and in benefits-sharing (Rogerson, 2003a, 2004a, 2004b).

The apartheid system was complex and intriguing and one which needs some introduction to if its wider significance is to be understood. Thus, the purpose of this chapter is threefold: first, to chronicle the background to the apartheid legacy of discrimination and inequality in South Africa and the peaceful 'event change' that ended it, described as a 'managed revolution' (Boyd, *et al.* 2001: 72). Second, the chapter reviews the effects of the change on the tourism sector, not just for South Africa but also for neighbouring countries. The chapter concludes with a discussion of the prospects of South Africa's tourism if the country is to successfully compete in the globalised tourism marketplace and turn the post-apartheid fallout into an opportunity.

Understanding the nature and scope of the apartheid system: 1948–1994

Apartheid, literally, 'apartness' or separateness, describes a policy of separating people by race, with regard to where they lived, they went to school, they worked, and where they died (Clark and Worger, 2004; Eades, 1999; McGarth, 1998). It was a conscious policy to separate physically all races within South Africa in a hierarchy of power with minority whites at the top and the majority black population at the bottom. Its structure rested on four major pillars: (1) the exclusive right to centralized political power by white politicians elected by a white electorate; (2) the division of race relations along spatial lines; (3) the regulation and allocation of coloured labourers to factories, farms and mines in South Africa; and (4) the continuance of social control in urban townships surrounding the key loci of political and economic power (Cohen, 1988: 91). This policy was introduced in South Africa in 1948 by the National Party government. Within one generation the policy wove itself into every aspect of South African life, remaining official practice until the fall from power of that party in 1994.

In the views of McGarth (1990: 92), under apartheid, the market acted 'like a malevolent invisible hand, working to the advantage of white workers and capitalists, and widening the wage differentials between black and white workers'. Not surprisingly, the ratio of per capita incomes of white to black Africans rose from 10.6: 1 in 1947 to 15:1 in 1970 (McGarth, 1998: 94).

Economic conditions, including the oil crisis of the 1970s caused major problems, and things came to a head in the 1970s and 1980s with the rise of mass resistance, first from trade union workers who organized huge strikes and, when these were crushed, a growing urban proletariat. Blacks violently protested at being shut out of the system, and the African National Congress (ANC), which had traditionally used non-violent means to protest inequality, began to advocate more extreme measures. Mob rule, as reflected in the emergence of street committees and youth groups, replaced the state in many areas and a wave of strikes and riots marked the 10th anniversary of the Soweto uprising in 1987.

By the 1990s the economy was in a real meltdown: growth was negative, capital was leaving the country at a rapid rate, and there were high levels of unemployment. Problems existed on many other fronts, including the dwindling primary product export, unsustainable import substitution as export prices plummeted, skilled labour shortage, and an insufficient domestic market. The cost of implementing apartheid was sky-rocketing, worsened by the bureaucracy structure, and further compounded by huge military and security expenditures.

In 1989, De Klerk succeeded President Botha, first as party leader, then as president. De Klerk's government began relaxing apartheid restrictions, and in 1990, Nelson Mandela was freed after 27 years of imprisonment and became head of the recently legalized ANC. In late 1991, the Convention for a Democratic South Africa (CODESA), a multi-racial forum set by de Klerk and Mandela, began efforts to negotiate a new constitution and a transition to a multi-racial democracy with majority rule. In March 1992, voters in a referendum open only to whites endorsed constitutional reform efforts by a wide margin. Despite obstacles and delays, an interim constitution was completed in 1993, ending nearly 300 years of white rule in South Africa. It marked the end of white-minority rule on the African continent. A 32-member multi-party transitional government council was formed with blacks in the majority. In April 1994, days after the Inkatha Freedom party ended an electoral boycott, the republic's first multi-racial election was held. The ANC won an overwhelming victory, and Nelson Mandela became president.

That the transition occurred relatively peacefully was the result of the exceptional statesmanship of Nelson Mandela and Frederick de Klerk, together with the existence in South Africa of an extraordinary range and depth of civil institutions. The institutions include a free press, independent judiciary, churches, trade unions, non-governmental organizations (NGOs), and a well-developed and socially engaging business community. Authors have characterised this political change as thus a 'managed revolution' rather than a supernatural phenomenon (Boyd *et al.*, 2001: 72). In sum, the dominant global political and economic forces played a significant role in shaping its subsequent political and economic strategy to which we now turn.

Macroeconomic policy adjustments since 1994

There were three main challenges which the post-apartheid government faced on accession to power in 1994. These were (a) economic growth and employment creation; (b) reduction of poverty; and (c) reduction in inequality. The government's response to the economic challenges was set out in a macroeconomic strategy document, Growth, Employment and Redistribution: A Macroeconomic Strategy (GEAR) (South Africa, 1996). Boyd *et al.* (2001: 74-84) have critically analysed the broad outline of this policy adjustment document under eight subject headings: (a) Improved access to global capital; (b) A more open economy; (c) Fiscal policy; (d) Monetary policy; (e) Competition policy; (f) Privatisation; (g) Labour-market policies; and (h) Governance.

Limited space does not allow for a detailed consideration of this and other relevant policy formulations or their outcomes. Suffice it to say that: first, this GEAR policy advocated a neo-liberal approach with a streamlining of state functions and expenditure (calling for fiscal restraint), privatization and deregulation of the financial sector. It was envisaged that this would lead to growth through the attraction of foreign direct investment and redistribution would occur through the 'trickle down' of wealth. Second, it would be expected that there would be winners and losers, the latter being declines in employment especially in the textile and manufacturing sectors. On the other hand, GEAR has led to increases in some sectors such as tourism that have been partially reversed following the strengthening of the South African rand.

The case of tourism in post-1994 South Africa

Under apartheid, tourism was essentially anti-developmental in focus and largely centred on the recreation of white South Africans. Since the 1994 democratic transition, tourism has become recognized as an increasingly important sector for South Africa's economy and achieving the government's goals for reconstruction and development (Visser and Rogerson, 2004: 201).

This statement prompts five striking reflections. First is the importance that the post-apartheid South Africa places on tourism as a nationally unifying force, and with greater emphasis being placed on the provision of 'basic needs' by increasing the nation's economic surplus which could then be used to facilitate development.

Second, development connotes an improvement of both economic opportunity and quality of social life and conditions, but includes also human and institutional changes, i.e. changes in behaviours, aspirations, and broader concerns of the quality of life, etc. In this sense, one is constantly reminded of the gap between the majority black and minority white South Africans, described by Cypher and Dietz (1997: 106): 'the enigma of extremes of wealth and poverty that attended this process and the lack of authentic development affecting a large segment of the population'. Tourism has a Herculean task in trying to bridge that gap, and it is unclear whether tourism can relieve poverty in this country.

Third, the significance of tourism as a development strategy in less developed countries is well documented (Sharpley and Telfer, 2002; Telfer and Sharpley, 2008). Tourism has been viewed as a means of earning hard currency, a source of employment and therefore income, a stimulus to inward investment, and a means of bringing wider economic benefits to regions with limited economic potential (Dieke, 2008). A fourth, and related, observation is the need to recast or rebrand the country as a shining example of an 'African Renaissance'. In their classic paper, entitled 'Repackaging the past for South African tourism', Witz et al. (2001: 277) advocated for 'the packaging of images that represent the society and its past. In the 1990s, the tourist industry consolidated an image of South Africa as a "world in one country" '. This move has led to a flurry of such catchphrases as: 'discover our new world', 'a rainbow nation'. In the main, it is expected that through tourism the wrongs of the past might be put right.

Finally, there is a need to compare and contrast tourism in South Africa in the pre- and post-1994 era and explain variations. This comparative insight will clarify the contention that tourism under apartheid was anti-developmental implying that the much hated system did undermine the cause of tourism.

Tourism in South Africa

The focus in this section will be on three main points: trend patterns; constraints on development; and policy response and the regulatory framework.

Trend patterns

As a basis for analysis, trend patterns examine the way tourism has developed and the nature of tourism activities. This is because such trends are a necessary and influencing parameter to analyse future prospects.

The historical context

Before 1994, South Africa was relatively unknown as a tourist destination. The low priority given to the sector was not surprising, in part because of the apartheid system and in part also because conventional mass tourism in this country is barely 40 years old (Ahmed *et al.*, 1998; Visser and Rogerson, 2004). It was small-scale and very domestic in scope (Table 11.1).

This situation was exacerbated by the economic sanctions by Western countries against the country because of the apartheid regime. The effect was to depress demand for South Africa's tourism. Visser and Rogerson (2004: 202), citing Cassim (1993), summed up the crucial moment thus: 'the period of the early 1990 represents a crucial watershed for it is at this important juncture of South Africa's development history that tourism first enters the realm of policy debate'.

Table 11.1: Overseas visitor arrivals to South Africa, 1987–97. Source: Central Statistical Services (CSS), cited in Ahmed *et al.* (1998: 82)

Year	Annual Arrivals	Change from previous year (%)
1987	339,307	14.2
1988	388,102	14.4
1989	472,076	21.6
1990	498,712	5.6
1991	521,257	4.5
1992	559,913	7.4
1993	618,508	10.5
1994	704,630	13.3
1995	1,071,839	52.0
1996	1,172,394	9.5
1997	1,400,000	19.4

The current situation

South Africa's current tourism situation can be described by reference the product, market mix and expenditure profile.

The tourism product is defined as facilities, amenities and services which attract visitors, and includes: game viewing, beaches, conferences and seminars, activity/adventure pursuits, shopping, cultural events, hotel-based gambling and sports events. Game viewing based on wildlife and its natural habitat is the most significant asset of the natural endowments, and is available within the 212 national parks and reserves, of which 17 are major ones, such as the 2 million hectare Kruger National Park.

The product spectrum merits some brief comments about the distinction between primary and secondary attractions vis-à-vis market fit and the competitive environment. In the first place, the products reflect specialist interests, for example, adventure pursuits appeal to the youth market; wildlife appeals particularly to American tourists, many of whom are travelling on multi-destination tours. Second, these features are not unique; the product elements (with the exception of gambling, sports events) are available in neighbouring countries (Kenya, Zambia, Botswana, Tanzania). Many of these destinations will be competing with South Africa. Third, as tourism marketers (Jefferson and Lickorish, 1991; Seaton and Bennett, 1996) suggest, no one activity is adequately attractive to motivate visitors, but together, they provide a basket of options available to tourists.

Data from United Nations World Tourism Organisation (UNWTO) (2008: 8) indicate the extent and impact of the South Africa's tourism (between 2005 and 2007), in terms of market mix and earnings profile. It is estimated that 9.090 million tourists visited South Africa in 2007, a growth rate of 8.3% compared to 2006 and 13.9% over 2005. It is further estimated that $8.418 million were generated in international receipts in 2007 (or $543,000 more than 2006).

Rogerson (2007) indicates the main tourist flows to South Africa, in order of importance, include: Europeans; residents of African countries; visitors from the Americas, from the Middle East, and from Asia. Long-haul visitors comprised about 80% of the total arrivals in 2007 most from the United Kingdom (22%), the USA (18%), Germany (18%), France (8%), the Netherlands (7%), and the Republic of Ireland (3%). Residents of other African countries constituted about 30% of arrivals.

A synthesis

Based on the demand figures, we can draw the following brief conclusions. First is the extent to which South Africa has now become a significant tourist destination for foreign travellers following the end of apartheid, and the competitive nature of the tourist activity in which it is fiercely competing to increase its share of the market. Second, there is the recognition that international tourism has become a high-volume industry and a major feature in the South African economy and society. Third, Western European countries and the USA maintain their dominance of both visitor arrivals and receipt figures. Fourth, there is recognition of the importance of regional tourism for the tourism economy of post-apartheid South Africa as demonstrated by government policy. Regional tourism is defined here as: 'tourism flows, by land or air, from other countries in sub-Saharan Africa' (Rogerson, 2004c).

In conclusion, there are two basic questions which need addressing: (1) what are the constraints hampering the development of tourism in South Africa? (2) how are the new relevant authorities responding to these constraints through the policies formulated for the tourism sector?

Constraints on tourism development

There were a number of structural challenges facing the South African economy and society after the country's democratic transition in 1994. While the factors were common or generic and can be found in most young democracies, they were also supplemented by the special situation in South Africa, and collectively, they were themselves barriers to development of the tourism sector. These problems can be summarised as:

1   The need to re-integrate South Africa into the global economy and to establish new regional economic linkages within Africa (Ajam and Aron, 2007; Rogerson, 2004c).

2   The need to transform and provide access to ownership, jobs and other income generating opportunities for black South Africans (Kaplan, 2004; Kingdon and Knight, 2007).

3   The need to generate economic growth, alleviate poverty and address the apartheid legacy of discrimination and inequality (Agüero, et al, 2007; Binns and Nel, 2002).

Within tourism, they have been summed up as follows:

- Central constraints relate, among others, to the fact that tourism had been inadequately resourced and funded by government;
- The short-sightedness of the private sector towards the nature of the South Africa tourism product;
- The limited integration of local communities and Black South Africans into tourism; inadequate or non-existent tourism training, education and awareness;
- Inadequate protection of the environment through environmental management;
- Poor level of service standards within the industry;
- The lack of infrastructure in rural areas; the lack of appropriate institutional structures;
- And, the immediate problems of violence, crime and security.

(Rogerson, 2002a: 33-42).

There are five important features: marketing, image, institutional structures, budgets, and expertise, which need tackling in order to progress tourism development. It has been suggested in a different context (Dieke, 2000), that many of these issues are similar to those facing most countries in sub-Saharan Africa, as studies of Namibia (Jenkins, 2000a), Zambia (Zambia, 1995) and other Southern African countries (Jenkins, 2000b) show.

In a nutshell, the problems are interrelated and they will not go away by merely postponing the finding of solutions to them. Without addressing the root cause of violence, crime and security, i.e. unemployment, confidence in South Africa's tourism will be undermined. International tourism is highly competitive, and destinations offer similar products, and a lack of consumer confidence means that tourists will substitute South Africa with another destination.

Policy response and the regulatory framework

In this section we present the policies which were formulated to combat these problems to lay a foundation for the South African tourism system that is developmental in focus. Attention is given to major four initiatives:

1 White Paper on the Declaration and Promotion of Tourism in South Africa (South Africa, 1996);

2 Tourism in GEAR (Growth, Employment and Redistribution): Tourism Development Strategy 1998–000 (South Africa, 1998);

3 Responsible Tourism Handbook: A Guide to Good Practice for Tourism Operators (DEAT, 2003); and

4 Black Economic Empowerment (BEE) (DTI, 2003a, 2003b).

These together form the 'building blocks' to actualize national policy objectives, and articulate the role of tourism in this process and represent relevant inputs to tourism development strategies, the key elements being policy, planning and implementation (Jenkins, 2007); to re-shape the future direction of tourism in South Africa, by creating an 'enabling environment' to facilitate sector development.

1   White Paper on the Declaration and Promotion of Tourism in South Africa (South Africa, 1996)

This pioneering document sets out the broad guidelines or parameters for development action, the centrepiece of which is to make a new tourism economy through the promotion of 'responsible tourism'. The main features are that: tourism will be private sector driven; government will provide the enabling framework for the industry to flourish; effective community involvement will form the basis of tourism growth; tourism development will be underpinned by sustainable environmental practices; tourism development is dependent on the establishment of co-operation and close partnerships among stakeholders; and lastly, tourism will be used as a development tool for the empowerment of apartheid's neglected communities and should particularly focus on the empowerment of women in such communities.

2   Tourism in GEAR (Growth, Employment and Redistribution): Tourism Development Strategy 1998–2000

This is a successor document to 'top up' the ideas articulated earlier in the 1996 White Paper, with one major caveat; to consolidate the objectives within the framework of a neo-liberal economic policy agenda. Key points are: the comparative advantages of South Africa's natural and cultural resources; the country's tourism attractions complement global trends towards alternative tourism; the ability of tourism to attract substantial private sector investment, as well as to accommodate small and medium enterprises (SMEs) development; the employment-intensive nature of tourism; its potential catalytic role for major infrastructure investment; its ability to stimulate linkages with other production sectors; and its value as an export earner.

3   Responsible Tourism Handbook: A Guide to Good Practice for Tourism Operators (DEAT, 2003)

This sets out a number of benchmarks to measure outcomes. It provides practical guidance to what South Africa's 'new' or 'responsible' tourism system should constitute and highlights parameters for giving opportunities for local communities by emphasising a need to develop partnerships and joint ventures in which communities have a significant stake and, with appropriate capacity building, a substantial role in management. Second, there is the need for private sector enterprises to buy locally made goods and use locally provided services from locally owned businesses without compromising quality or consistency. Finally, enterprises should recruit and employ workers in an equitable and transparent manner and maximize the proportion of workers from the local community.

This publication emphasizes five imperatives: to sustain growth in tourism arrivals, especially of high income tourists; to stimulate and support emerging tourism entrepreneurs and maximize opportunities for the SME sector; to integrate tourism development within the strategic framework for infrastructure investment; to ensure a quality tourism experience, quality products and services; and lastly, to address fundamental questions of leadership, ownership and job creation.

4   Black Economic Empowerment (BEE) (DTI, 2003a, 2003b).

BEE (or Black Economic Empowerment) is the latest policy change in the reintegration process and is a mechanism to rescue black South Africans from the 350-year long legacy of colonialism, economic exploitation, poverty and social degradation. In response to these challenges, in 2003, the government formulated the Black Economic Empowerment Act to facilitate change and address some of the ills of black economics (In terms of the act that set up BEE, 'black people' meant African, coloured or Indian South Africa citizens, and those entitled to become citizens.)

Drawn up by the Department of Trade and Industry, BEE covered several economic sectors including tourism. The tourism industry is one of the key sectoral drivers for economic development and transformation of the country over the next two decades (Rogerson, 2002a, 2002b). The Department of Environmental Affairs and Tourism contends that an urgent challenge that confronts the South African tourism industry is that of 'changing the nature of the South African tourism industry from one that is pre-dominantly white-owned to one that is increasingly owned by the majority of South Africans' (DEAT, 2000: 1).

Future possibilities

In looking into the future there are many factors which need to be considered if tourism is to act as one of the basic pillars in South Africa's global re-integration process, to return the country to a 'proper' economic development path and thus become a viable member of such a system, and to act as a locomotive for its economy and, provide a just and prosperous society, devoid of fear, tension and suspicion. One critical question in all this is: what else does South Africa need to do in order to enhance the role of tourism in development, broadly defined?

1 The 3a's: attractions, accommodations, and access

 One prerequisite for reaching these development scenarios is to develop the tourism product (attractions, accommodation and access) simultaneously with the arrival of tourists. The main tourism product of South Africa includes top quality natural and built attractions, high standards of accommodation and infrastructure and excellent transport network.

The main requirement in the future, however, is to clearly identify and market new facilities for the local and regional markets, such as self-catering facilities. For overseas customers it is necessary to improve existing facilities and to separate the two major market segments.

2 Growing regional competition

Here, 'region' refers specifically to the 14 southern African countries, comprising the Southern African Development Community (SADC); Angola, Botswana, Democratic Republic of Congo, Lesotho, Malawi, Mauritius, Mozambique, Namibia, Seychelles, South Africa, Swaziland, Tanzania, Zambia and Zimbabwe. Another regional forum, with a specific tourism charge or remit is the Regional Tourism Organisation of Southern Africa (RETOSA), a combination of 14 SADC countries including participants from government and private sectors from each country.

Competition will ensure that standards and value-for-money will eventually determine which countries and destinations will be successful and tourism development in South Africa will not be divorced from regional African trends.

Another important consideration here will be how to improve service standards in a world where tourists are becoming more discerning and frequent travellers and accumulating tourism experience which allows them to determine value-for-money destinations and to compare service standards. In the long term it will be the availability of trained human resources which may be the determining factor between success and failure of tourism investment (Dieke, 2001). At present much of the labor force in tourism is expatriate. Any programme to facilitate indigenous employment will require careful planning, a change in cultural perceptions and encouragement from the political hierarchy.

3 Investment capital

It is evident that in South Africa there is no shortage of investment capital but perhaps a reluctance to invest in the tourism sector. To a large extent such caution is linked to current experience where growth in tourism has been slowed, and in some cases, stopped by the 'threats' described earlier. However, trend data has demonstrated that in the medium and long term tourism is a robust industry and one which has greater sustainability than others. Creating a destination in a highly competitive market is not a short-term objective; it is essentially an incremental activity like development in general. The strategic vision has to be long term, and the huge investment in infrastructure is a long-term commitment without which tourism will not develop adequately or appropriately.

4 The private sector

It has been acknowledged that the country's infrastructure has been provided by government. In the southern African region there are signs that governments are moving to a more supportive and facilitating role in the tourism sector and leaving the development to private companies, or through public–private partnerships. But as a representative or custodian of the people, government is the ultimate arbitrator of what type of tourism should be developed, where and on what scale, all important considerations in the sustainability of the industry.

5 The environment

There is a close relationship between tourism and the environment within which it takes place. Environmental quality is a factor which is not only fundamental to the development of tourism but also to the lives of residents. Those destinations offering environmental quality can often charge higher prices for services. In terms of South Africa, much tourism development has been based on the existence of high-quality environmental attractions, including wildlife. Most policy statements include explicit objectives to protect and carefully utilize environmental and other natural assets. Many of the prime areas for tourism are ecologically and sometimes socially fragile, and care has to be taken in selecting the appropriate scale and type of development. Tension exists between environmentalists and tourism developers and to resolve this, one of the main tasks for the country will be to seek a balance between tourism development and conservation needs to ensure that the national objectives of economic progress with sustainability are met.

6 Market demand

As a leisure activity, tourism is heavily influenced by economic conditions in the main generating regions, primarily, the United States and Europe. But tourism is also affected by non-economic factors, with the main ones being personal threats, which are of two categories; security and health-related. As a general proposition it can be said that perceived threats to tourists will decrease international tourism flows and cause a substitution effect. Tourists will not travel to countries or areas within large countries where they feel threatened. This has high applicability in South Africa.

Conclusion

South Africa is the most complex country in sub-Saharan Africa, with. a complex history of human relations over the last 400 years. Its state of development and real economic power has, for historical reasons, been deliberately designed and implemented to favour white-dominated areas. The black African reservations are poor, over-populated, and dominated by poverty-related crimes. The elections of 1994 that ushered in universal adult suffrage and democratic government opened the door for revolutionary changes since then. This chapter has dealt with the roots of these changes and their ramifications for tourism, and has also identified the main issues of concern. Major consideration has been given to government policy responses, identifying items which might constitute action agenda for the 21st century.

References

Agüero, J., M.R. Carter and J. May (2007) 'Poverty and inequality in the first decade of South Africa's democracy: what can be learnt from panel data from KwaZulu-Natal?' *Journal of African Economies*, **16** (5): 782–812.

Ahmed, Zafar U., Victor L. Heller, Kevin A. Hughes (1998), Tourism in South Africa: Uneven Prospects, *Cornell Hotel and Restaurant Administration Quarterly*, 39(6): 80-90.

Ahmed, Z.U., V.L. Heller and K.A. Hughes (1998) 'Tourism in South Africa: uneven prospects', *Cornell Hotel and Restaurant Administration Quarterly*, **39** (6), 80–90.

Ajam, T. and J.Aron (2007) 'Fiscal renaissance in a democratic South Africa', *Journal of African Economies*, **16** (5), 745–781.

Binns, T. and E.N. (2002) 'Tourism as a local development strategy in South Africa', *Geographical Journal*, **168** (3), 235–247.

Boyd, L., M. Spicer and G. Keeton (2001) 'Economic scenarios for South Africa: a business perspective', *Daedalus*, **130** (1), 71–98.

Cassim, R. (1993) 'Tourism and development in South Africa', *Economic Trends, Working Paper No 18*. Cape Town: University of Cape Town.

Clark, N.L. and W.H. Worger (2004) *South Africa: The R and F of Apartheid*, London: Pearson Longman.

Cohen, R. (1988) *The Endgame in South Africa: The Changing Structure and Ideology of Apartheid*, Trenton, NJ: Africa World Press, Inc.

Cypher, J.M. and J.L. Dietz (1997) *The Process of Economic Development*, London: Routledge.

(2000), *Unblocking Delivery on Tourism Strategy by Government Departments*. Pretoria: DEAT.

DEAT: Department of Environmental Affairs and Tourism (2003), *Responsible Tourism Handbook: A Guide to Good Practice for Tourism Operators*. Pretoria: DEAT.DTI: Department of Trade and Industry (2003) South Africa's Economic Transformation: A Strategy for Broad-Based Economic Empowerment. Pretoria: DTI, from: www.thedti.gov.za/bee. (18 August 2009).

DTI: Department of Trade and Industry (2003b) Broad Based Black Economic Empowerment Bill, from: www.thedti.gov.za/bee. (18 August 2009).

Dieke, P.U.C. (ed.) (2000) *The Political Economy of Tourism Development in Africa*. Elmsford, New York: Cognizant Communication.

Dieke, P.U.C. (2001) 'Human resources in tourism development: African perspectives', in D. Harrison (ed.), *Tourism and the Less Developed World: Issues and Case Studies*, Wallingford: CABI, pp. 61–75.

Dieke, P.U.C. (2008) 'Tourism development in Africa: challenges and opportunities', *Tourism Review International*, **12** (3/4), 167–315.

Eades, Lindsay M. (1999), The End of Apartheid in South Africa. Westport, CT: Greenwood Press.

Jefferson, A. and L.J. Lickorish (1991) *Marketing Tourism: A Practical Guide*, Harlow, UK: Longman.

Jenkins, C.L. (2000a) 'The development of tourism in Namibia', in P. Dieke (ed.), *The Political Economy of Tourism Development in Africa*, Elmsford, New York: Cognizant Communication, pp. 113–128.

Jenkins, C.L. (2000b) 'Tourism policy formulation in the Southern African region', in P. Dieke (ed.), *The Political Economy of Tourism Development in Africa*, Elmsford, New York: Cognizant Communication, pp. 62–74.

Jenkins, C.L. (2007) 'Tourism development: policy, planning and implementation issues in developing countries', in J. Cukier (ed.), *Tourism Research: Policy, Planning and Prospects, Occasional Paper #20*, Canada: University of Waterloo, pp. 21–30.

Kaplan, L. (2004) 'Skills development in tourism: South Africa's tourism-led development strategy', *GeoJournal*, **60** (3), 217–227.

Kingdon, G. and J. Knight (2007) 'Unemployment in South, 1995-2003: causes, problems and policies', *Journal of African Economies*, **16** (5): 813–848).

McGarth, M. (1990) 'Economic growth, income distribution and social change', in N. Natrass and E. Ardington (eds), *The Political Economy of South Africa*, Cape Town: Oxford University Press.

McGarth, M. (1990), 'Economic Growth, Income Distribution and Social Change', In *The Political Economy of South Africa*, N. Natrass and E. Ardington (eds). Cape Town: Oxford University Press.

Rogerson, C.M. (2002a) 'Driving developmental tourism in South Africa', *Africa Insight*, **32** (3), 33–42).

Rogerson, C.M. (2002b) 'Tourism – a new economic driver for South Africa', in Lemon A. and Rogerson C. M. (eds.), *Geography and Economy in South Africa and its Neighbours*, Aldershot: Ashgate, pp. 95–110.

Rogerson, C.M. (2003) 'Tourism and transformation: small enterprise development in South Africa', *Africa Insight*, **33** (1/2), 108–115.

Rogerson, C.M. (2004a) 'Tourism and small firm development and empowerment in post-apartheid South Africa', in R. Thomas (ed.), *Small Firms in Tourism: International Perspectives*. Amsterdam: Elsevier, pp. 1–33.

Rogerson, C.M. (2004b) 'Transforming the South African tourism industry: the emerging black-owned bed and breakfast economy', *GeoJournal*, **60** (3), 273–281.

Rogerson, C.M. (2004c) 'Regional tourism in South Africa: a case of "mass tourism of the South"', *GeoJournal*, **60** (3), 229–237.

Rogerson, C.M. (2007) 'Reviewing Africa in the global tourism economy', *Development Southern Africa*, **24** (3), 361–379.

Seaton, A.V. and M.M. Bennett (1996) *Marketing Tourism Products*, London: Chapman and Hall.

Sharpley, R. and D. Telfer (eds.) (2002) *Tourism and Development: Concepts and Issues*. Clevedon: Channel View.

South Africa, Republic of (1996) *White Paper on the Declaration and Promotion of Tourism in South Africa*, Pretoria: Department of Environmental Affairs and Tourism.

South Africa, Republic of (1998) *Tourism in GEAR: Tourism Development Strategy 1998-2000*, Pretoria: Department of Environmental Affairs and Tourism.

Telfer, D. and R. Sharpley (2008) *Tourism and Development in the Developing World*, London: Routledge.

UNWTO: United Nations World Tourism Organization (2008) *Tourism Highlights 2008 Edition*, Madrid: UNWTO.

Visser, G. and C.M. Rogerson (2004) 'Researching the South African tourism and development nexus', *GeoJournal*, **60**, 201–215.

Witz, L., C. Rassool and G. Minkley (2001) 'Repackaging the past for South African tourism', *Daedalus*, **130** (1), 277–296.

Zambia, Republic of (1995) *Medium-Term National Tourism Strategy and Action Plan for Zambia*. Lusaka: Government of Zambia.

12 Tourism and Political Transition in Reform-Era Vietnam

Wantanee Suntikul

Introduction

In 1986, the Congress of Vietnam introduced an economic programme called *doi moi* (Renovation), which can be compared to Gorbachev's contemporaneous *glasnost* campaign in the Soviet Union. The Vietnamese Communist Party's new policy called for measures including the decentralisation of the planning system, a reduced number of government ministries and bureaucracies, reliance on the private sector as an engine of economic growth, allowing state and privately owned industries to trade directly in foreign and international markets, and long-term land leases for farmers.

With these political and economic shifts, Vietnam has become a much more accessible and attractive destination in the international tourism market and has been 'rediscovered' by tourists from around the world. Consequently, Vietnam's tourism industry has experienced a period of meteoric growth in recent years. According to the website of the Vietnamese National Administration of Tourism (VNAT) (www.vietnamtourism. com/index/e_index.asp), over 4.2 million international tourists arrived in Vietnam in 2007, compared to 1.3 million in 1995: an increase of over 200% in 12 years. A 2007 prognosis for 2010 foresaw tourist arrivals reaching 6 million and tourism receipts US$ 4 billion, with a tourism industry workforce of 1.4 million, as compared with 250,000 in 2007 (Hodgson, 2007). Aside from this quantifiable growth, tourism in Vietnam has also changed in character since 1986. Vietnam's tourism industry is experiencing the emergence of new tourism niches, new kinds of attractions and businesses, new breeds of tourists and unfamiliar types of tourism such as eco-tourism and war tourism.

This explosion of tourism is unprecedented in Vietnam, and the Vietnamese government faces the necessity of balancing its socialist ideology and methods on the one hand, with the globalising and commercializing influence of the international tourism market on the other. Not merely a side effect of economic and political changes in Vietnam, growth and change in the tourism sector also generates significant effects on politics, economics and Vietnamese society in general.

The primary purpose of this chapter is to identify relationships between political changes in Vietnam since the beginning of the *doi moi* programme and changes in Vietnam's tourism sector during the same period.

Tourism development before Doi Moi

During the era of French control of Vietnam (1884–1954), the colonial regime attempted to remodel Vietnamese cities to resemble cities in France to give French residents the feeling of being at home while living in an exotic land. The success of the French programme of urbanism in Vietnam is shown by the nicknames 'Pearl of the Far East' and 'Paris of the Orient' by which the cities of Saigon and Hanoi, respectively, came to be known (Lam, 2000: 52). Many buildings from this time are now famous tourist attractions in Vietnam's cities. In 1935, the Government General of Indochina established an official Information Tourist Bureau in Saigon under the name of Office Central du Tourisme Indochinoise, to publicise Indochina tourism by advertising in newspapers in Hong Kong, Singapore, Ipoh and Kuala Lumpua (ibid.: 19) where large numbers of Western foreigners resided, in an attempt to attract Western colonial expatriates living in the region to come to Vietnam as tourists. Indochina lay on a crossover route for businessmen travelling from Siam or Penang to Japan or China (Office Central du Tourisme Indochinoise, 1938:26). Air Vietnam, the national airline of Indochina, was formed on 1 October 1951, by a French-Vietnamese consortium.

Even though Vietnam had attracted European tourists since the 19th century, the break-up of the French colony and the political instability during the period of partition following the Geneva Conference of 1954 proved to be major constraints on tourism development. Tourism relations with foreign nations were affected by the political polarisation of the two quasi-states of divided Vietnam. Just as France had tried to mould its colony into a home-away-from-home, the USA and the Soviet Union left their own imprint on the character of developments in the two Vietnams during partition. The influence of the USSR in Hanoi can be seen in buildings from the 1950s and 1960s such as the Ho Chi Minh Mausoleum, the Ho Chi Minh Museum and the Soviet-Vietnamese Friendship Culture Palace. The tourist flow to North Vietnam during this period was mainly from the Eastern bloc (EIU, 1993: 62). During the US/Vietnam War, tourism in North Vietnam came to a virtual standstill. The Civil Aviation Administration of Vietnam (CAAV) was founded on 1 January 1956 at Hanoi's Gialam Airport. The first scheduled flights (between Hanoi and Beijing) began on 20 April of the same year, using planes donated by the Soviet Union, with training and aircrew from East Germany. Services expanded very slowly and were re-dedicated to military uses after 1961. In 1967, service between Hanoi and Moscow was initiated (Smith, 2002: 811).

In 1960, the Vietnam Tourism Company was established under the control of the South Vietnamese Ministry of Trade (EIU, 1993: 70). The presence of many thousands of American and Allied servicemen, foreign correspondents and foreign businesses (Saigon Tourist and Saignon Tourism Association, 1990: 11) made Saigon a dynamic and developing city, even during the War years. However, US military flights made up most of the air traffic during this time, and figures from the latter years of the war show a constant decrease in activity by Air Vietnam itself, from 24,000 airline departures and over a million travellers in 1971 to 16,000 departures and 553,000 passengers in 1974 (Airline Traffic, 1976). New business such as restaurants, bars and cinemas opened for the entertainment of military personnel.

Many of the elements of Vietnam's pre-partition tourism landscape were degraded or destroyed in the course of the War. After reunification under communist rule in 1975, the major tourism flow to Vietnam came from Eastern Europe. These tourists had lower buying power and less demand for luxurious accommodation than tourists in the colonial era. For this reason, between 1975 and 1988, the significance of French accommodation and cuisine declined considerably (EIU, 1993: 62). It was only in the post-reunification era that tourism became a conscious focus of governmental policy. In 1978, the General Department of Vietnam Tourism was established to oversee 14 tourist companies and 30 provincial and rural enterprises. Ironically, despite the explicit worsening of the political conditions for tourism development, the 1980 Constitution is the first version in which tourism is addressed and, at least at the level of rhetoric, promoted as an important factor in economic development. Article 49 states that '(t)ourism is encouraged and adequately organised'. In the 1980s, efforts began to remedy Vietnam's isolation from the global tourism market and, in 1985 Vietnam was represented at the Internationale Tourismus Börse (ITB) in Berlin for the first time (ITB Berlin, 2001). The realisation of the internal contradictions between the goals and means expressed in the 1980 Constitution may have played a role in preparing the way for the *doi moi* reforms of the later 1980s.

Doi Moi and changing political and economic alignment

Beginning with *doi moi* and intensifying with the decline of communism in the late 1980s the source of monetary and material assistance, as well as tourists, to Vietnam shifted from the Soviet bloc to the developed capitalist industrial nations of East Asia and the West. Incrementally throughout the 1990s, especially as a result of the lifting of the US trade embargo in 1994, Vietnam established or re-established normal political relations with other countries at the regional and global scale. The 1991 adoption of the new slogan 'Vietnam befriends all' signalled a new attitude of openness towards foreign policy. Japan and China normalised relations with Vietnam in 1991 and 1993, respectively. This was significant as China had historically been a threat to Vietnam, with periods of occupation 111 BC – AD 939, 1407–1427, and 1884 (contesting French claims to Vietnam) and Japan occupied Vietnam during the Second World War. US/Vietnamese political relations were normalised in 1995, the same year that Vietnam became an ASEAN member. By 1996, Vietnam had diplomatic relations with 163 countries, compared to only 23 non-communist states in 1989 (Thayer, 1997: 365).

The end of the trade embargo also allowed Vietnam to invest in Western-manufactured equipment to bring its tourism infrastructure up to the standard of international tourism. In the tourism-related transportation sector, for instance, the replacement of Russian economic assistance and Soviet-built planes with Western aircraft and the assistance of Air France, as well as the acquisition of Siemens locomotives by Vietnam Railways, are signs of this changeover of economic affiliations.

Regional connections and affiliations have begun to play a larger part in the support of Vietnam tourism in many different ways. As a member of ASEAN, Vietnam is provided with guidelines for the development of human resources as well as the development and marketing of its tourism industry. There are also promotional agreements among ASEAN countries that encourage tourists to other ASEAN countries to continue their travels to Vietnam and vice versa without a visa for up to 14 days. In such ways, Vietnam is being integrated into a regional culture of common practice in tourism, and the links between Vietnam and its regional neighbours are being solidified, replacing the pre-*doi moi* network of COMECON countries (Council for Mutual Economic Aid: corresponding roughly to the former Soviet bloc) as Vietnam's 'family' of related destinations.

Vietnam has become a new destination on the international tourism circuit as barriers to tourism (both those imposed by Vietnam itself and those imposed by other nations upon Vietnam) have been lifted since the beginning of *doi moi*. Before 1986, most foreign tourists to Vietnam came from COMECON countries (EIU, 1993). With the introduction of the open door policy, the Vietnamese government turned its attention to making Vietnam more open to tourists from all nations. In order to encourage tourists to the country, the government relaxed the conditions for entry visas for foreigners of all nationalities (Elliott, 1997: 228). As a result, the number of tourist arrivals to Vietnam from non-COMECON countries increased sharply in only a few years, from 4581 in 1986 to 40,966 in 1989, surpassing the number of tourists from COMECON countries (Theuns, 1997: 306-307).

This section has discussed changes in the Vietnam economy and government's relations with the world. Subsequent sections will discuss contemporaneous changes in the internal workings of the government and economy related to tourism development.

Changing governmental roles in tourism sector

The *doi moi* policy called for the decentralisation of the planning system, a decrease in the number of government ministries and bureaucracies, increased reliance on the private sector as an engine of economic growth, and allowing state and private industries to trade directly in foreign and international markets. According to Kokko (1998: 2), *doi moi* has succeeded remarkably in moving the country from a stagnant, centrally planned Soviet-style economy with macroeconomic instability to a mixed market-oriented economy.

The Vietnam National Administration of Tourism (VNAT) was formed in 1992. The VNAT is not a ministry, but occupies an analogous level in the government hierarchy (VNAT, 2001), responsible directly to the Prime Minister. The VNAT also plays a role as an investor and commercial operator in the tourism industry (Vietnam, 2001), and is responsible for setting tourism regulations and classification criteria, conducting research, owning and operating hotels, and joint venturing with foreign investors. Some policies have been changed to allow more decentralisation of state influence. Uniformity is no longer perceived to serve the best interest of the tourism industry or its stakeholders and the central government has been handing over control to the provinces in some areas of tourism which were previously controlled by central government agencies. For instance, the VNAT is no longer involved in the licensing of tourism transport operators, previously the joint responsibility of the VNAT and the local Ministry of Transport (VNAT, 2001).

Tourism activities in each of Vietnam's 64 provinces are administered either by the province's Department of Tourism, Department of Trade, or Department of Tourism and Trade, depending on the significance of the tourism industry in a province. Tourism is usually combined with trade in in provinces lacking many great attractions or tourism activities (personal communication, 2004). A large number of provinces now set their own regulations regarding tourism, inevitably resulting in variations in scope and emphasis, and some inconsistencies in quality and standards. As of 2001, 44 of the provinces had their own Departments of Tourism (VNAT, 2001). Despite Vietnam's nominal status as a 'centrally-planned' economy, in reality, regional authorities have always been accustomed to a high degree of autonomy from central control, and the imposition of national plans has always been met by resistance at the local level. Thus, legislation and national policies by no means guaranty enforcement by lower levels of government (Elliott, 1997: 232). A VNAT document points out a lack of synchronisation of planning and investment in different sectors and regions, overlapping rights of ownership, and authorisation procedures that complicate and hinder development. This document found that, parallel to decentralisation of some facets of tourism administration, there are reasons for the strengthening of central planning in other facets. It made a case for more macro-level planning to optimise resource use and competitiveness (VNAT, n.d.).

The change in the nature of the central government's involvement in state enterprises within *doi moi* is epitomised by the shift from state-run to state-owned as the preferred model. Parallel to the withdrawal of government from direct involvement in the running of tourism operations, a series of ordinances laid out, in increasing scope and detail, a set of mechanisms for government regulation of tourism activities run by state, domestic private and foreign enterprises. The years since *doi moi* have seen the role of government change from being a provider to a regulator. This is an unfamiliar role for the government, not only because of the added complication of regulating others as opposed to the built-in self-regulation inherent in former state-run enterprises, but also because the criteria, standards and goals of Vietnam's post-*doi moi* tourism industry are vastly different from those under which the government operated its monopoly.

Foreign direct investment (FDI) in tourism

Because it is a developing nation, Vietnam is reliant on foreign investment for much of its tourism development. The nearly bankrupt Vietnamese government is not able to provide much of the required investment capital itself (Mok and Lam, 1996). In 1987, one year after the beginning of *doi moi*, the state issued the Law on Foreign Investment, which encouraged foreign direct investment in Vietnam, especially in the tourism industry. The State Committee for Cooperation and Investment (SCCI), founded in 1989, became responsible for encouraging foreign investment in five priority sectors, of which tourism is one. Parallel to the rush of foreign investment that followed, private enterprises have increased in number, ending the government monopoly in the provision of tourism services, although the government still owns a large number of hotels.

FDI in tourism in Vietnam grew from US$7.4 million in 1988 to US$1.9 billion (30.7% of total FDI) in 1995 (Erramilli, *et al.*, 1997: 227-228). The number of projects remained more or less constant, but the average size of projects grew, from US$1.4 million in 1988 to US$66.7 million in 1995. An increase in the average duration of tourism FDI projects from 9 years to 27 years over the same period reflects the growth in the size of projects undertaken and indicates an increase in investor confidence in the Vietnam tourism market during the early years of *doi moi* (ibid.). By 2004, 239 FDI tourism projects had been registered in Vietnam, with total capital of US$6.1 billion, including 13 projects with US$64.7 million in foreign investment in 2003 alone (VN Welcomes over 2.2 Mil Foreign Tourists this Year, 2003).

Hoping to encourage tourism to the country, the Vietnamese government declared 1990 as 'Visit Vietnam Year', but its ambitious programme was considered by the Economist Intelligence Unit (EIU) to have failed due to a shortage of hotel rooms, suitable tourist facilities, services and airline seats (EIU 1993). Consequently, the Vietnamese government became more aware of the importance of tourism infrastructure. In order to spur development while encouraging opportunities for transfer of capital and expertise, the Vietnamese government had been prioritising joint venture investment over other kinds of FDI in tourism (EIU, 1993: 63; Ngo Ba Thanh, 1993: 95). By 2000, 182 of the 194 foreign-invested hotel and tourism projects were joint ventures, with six fully foreign-funded projects and six business cooperation contracts. A 1999 ruling allowed foreign investors to own a stake of up to 30% in so-called 'equitised' state-owned enterprises in several sectors, including hotels (*Saigon Times Daily*, 30 June 1999).

Changes in the accommodation sector

Until *doi moi*, the Vietnamese government was the only owner of tourist accommodation in Vietnam. The tourist influx at the beginning of *doi moi* caused problems due to a lack of infrastructure and skilled staff, and inadequate quantity and quality of accommodation to meet the expectations of international tourists (Tourism Development Master Plan, 1991). At the beginning of the 1990s, accommodation of international standard in Vietnam was very limited (VNAT, 2001). The EIU reported that in 1989 there were 18,877 tourist rooms in Vietnam (1993: 69), but a UNDP and WTO document identified only 1565 rooms that met international standards in 1990 (Tourism Development Master Plan, 1991: 20).

The joint venture Saigon Floating Hotel became the only five-star hotel in Ho Chi Minh City when it opened in 1989, bringing a standard of service and amenities previously unknown in Vietnam. Other high-standard joint-venture hotels followed in the early 1990s. By 2001, most of the large international hotel chains had opened hotels in Vietnam, with many of the hotels in the biggest cities being operated by Vietnamese/foreign joint ventures (VNAT, 2001).

Having previously received guests primarily from Eastern bloc countries, state-owned hotels had to adjust to the higher standards of service and facilities expected by Western travellers who have made up an increasing number of their customers since 1986. Many older urban hotels dropped their Vietnamese names and reverted to their pre-1975 Western-sounding names after *doi moi* (Travel Business Analyst, 1992: 26), presumably to appeal to the foreign market. The proliferation of international standard foreign joint-venture hotels poses another challenge for existing state-owned hotels, which must now compete against hotels in a quantity and of a quality that did not exist in their market before *doi moi*.

In response to growing competition, some state hotels have established sales or marketing departments where previously a reservation department was deemed sufficient (interviews with the Directors of two state-owned hotels 2004). The first sales department in a state-owned hotel was set up by the Majestic Hotel in Ho Chi Minh City in 1995, in direct response to the stiff competition brought by the highly profitable joint-venture Floating Hotel and Omni Saigon Hotel. These hotels served as both the impetus and the model for progressive management thinking in the state-owned hotels that were their direct competitors. The Director of Sales and Marketing at a state-owned hotel freely admits to learning about pricing and promotion from the hotel's joint-venture rivals (Interview with the Director of a state-owned hotel, 2004).

The deputy general manager of another state-owned hotel in Hanoi noted that the concept of guest-oriented thinking was unknown to the hotel management before 1993. Until that time, occupancy had been guaranteed by an undersupply of hotel rooms, and the government could be counted on to provide subsidies. With increasing competition and the slow withdrawal of government support, this hotel began to accept credit cards in 1995 and a policy of seasonal pricing was adopted for the first time in 1998 (Interview, with the deputy general manager of a state-owned hotel, 2004).

Changes in the use of nature areas

Like the business paradigm that has driven a renaissance in accommodation provision in Vietnam, forcing a change in government policy and practice, the conservation paradigm could also be called a Western import, the introduction of which was eased by attractive conservation funds. Vietnam's forested land is divided into the categories of Protection Forest, Special-use Forest and Production Forest. In the past, the governmental State-Forest Enterprises managed most production forests. Most economic activity in national parks was in the form of logging, and national parks received financial support from the government (Suntikul, *et al.*, forthcoming). However, in 1997 the Vietnamese government eliminated logging activities in 300 of the 400 State-forest enterprises because degradation of forest resources and the inaccessibility of commercially valuable forest stands were compromising their economic viability. With this re-designation, most State-Forest Enterprise lands moved from production to protection forestry and infrastructural development tends to take priority over conservation measures in terms of funding allocation (ICEM, 2003).

Because of this lack of government funding, many of the funds for conservation management in Vietnam are provided by international donors. Since *doi moi*, the most significant among these donors have been international conservation organisations such as the World Wildlife Fund (WWF), International Union for Conservation of Nature (IUCN) and Birdlife International (Nguyen Nhu Phuong and Vu Van Dung, 2001). McElwee (2001) has cynically identified international development funding from international donors as a new and lucrative source of income for the government. For example, the money obtained from international donors in a few years before 2001 for the Vu Quang Nature Reserve on Vietnam's north central coast alone was ten times the government budget for all protected areas in Vietnam in 1991 (McElwee, 2001: 10).

Between 1996 and 2002, 17 major conservation projects in which foreign governmental and non-governmental organisations were the primary sponsors were begun in Vietnam (Rambaldi *et al.*, 2001: 46). The European Commission alone invested 30 million Euros in conservation projects in Vietnam from 1997 to 2005 (ibid.: 47). A number of the 'nature reserves' on State-Forest land have been largely denuded of their forest cover by years of logging and one could suspect that the decision to convert them to protection uses had to do primarily with the allure of eligibility for conservation funding as a way of making the land economically productive after the timber had been extracted.

The number of national parks in Vietnam has increased greatly during the period of political transition since the beginning of *doi moi*. As has been noted, much impetus for the establishment of protected areas and national parks in Vietnam has been provided by the potential international funds for which such nature preserves are eligible and the interest of international conservation organisations and their money. The re-designation of so many logging areas as protected forests after *doi moi*'s inception can be more convincingly explained in this way than by any sudden government concern for nature conservation. Tourism seems to play at best a secondary role as a driving inspiration for the founding of parks.

Levelling of pricing policies

In the earlier years of *doi moi*, uneven pricing policies for domestic and foreign tourists existed in many government-controlled operations, especially transport. For instance, in 1995, a domestic tourist would pay US$60 for a one-way domestic flight from Hanoi to Ho Chi Minh City with Vietnam Airlines, while a foreigner would be charged US$170 for the same ticket. The Deputy Director of Vietnam Airlines explained the reasons for this discrepancy in pragmatic terms: 'We are the national carrier, and our mission is not only to make profit, but to serve as a public utility. We are allowed to compete with other airlines on international routes, but for our domestic network, there are certain government fare controls according to local income levels' (Lewis, 1995). As of 1 January 2004, however, the split fare scale was abolished and a flat fare of VND3 million (US$190) was charged all passengers, domestic or foreign (Vietnam Airlines Plans Sole Fare, 2003).

Vietnam Railways also used to have a dual pricing policy that charged foreigners and overseas Vietnamese a surcharge of 375% and 480% respectively on tickets compared to prices for domestic travellers (EIU, 1993: 68). This policy was introduced by the government, not by Vietnam Railways, which succeeded in convincing the government to do away with this practice in 2003 in order to conform to international standards of pricing (personal communication, 2004).

Dual pricing policies for foreigners and Vietnamese also used to apply to foreign tour operators, but also have been abolished. For instance, a policy that institutionalised the practice of charging foreign tour operators substantially higher prices for services and market access was abolished in 1999, causing the fee for a representative office to fall from US$5000 to US$70 (Watkin, 1999).

Double-tiered pricing policies and other rules and situations that discouraged foreign tourists and businesses seem as a rule to have been imposed by the government rather than the individual attractions or operators. This implies that the government took a much shorter-term view of profitability in the sector than individual attractions and operators, who may be more concerned with the sustainability of their business over the long term. Such practices also point to a naïve idea of the workings of a capitalist market by the government, which appears to be slower to learn than operators who are immersed in the market and most have now been abolished.

Conclusion

Vietnam's modern history has been one of constant political change, from colonisation to war and division to reunification and subsequent reform, with all of these changes affecting tourism. While the government of Vietnam has not fundamentally altered its ideological stance since the birth of the modern united Vietnam in 1975, the world has changed drastically during this period. The Cold War polarisation of the latter half of the 20th century influenced all aspects of Vietnam's foreign policy, including tourism. Now that this situation no longer holds sway, the government of Vietnam is striving to develop a tourism policy to best position Vietnam for development within the new world order, while remaining true to the nation's core ideological foundations.

Vietnam's tourism industry has been going through dramatic changes since the beginning of the *doi moi* programme. In pursuit of the economic benefits of tourism, the Vietnamese government has relinquished some modes of control, thus loosening restrictions, abandoned discriminatory practices such as dual pricing and passed new laws to encourage tourism development and attract visitors to the country. Whereas socialist ideological agendas have always been at the centre of the government's vision for tourism in Vietnam, the government has been incrementally experimenting and learning how best to design and implement a policy that would achieve its free-market-driven economic agenda as well. Some earlier measures aimed at achieving short-term gains from tourism, such as dual pricing policies, have been abandoned in favour of a longer view towards developing Vietnam as a sustainably attractive destination.

In moving from the role of a provider to a regulator of tourism services, the government is realising that Vietnam's changing tourism industry will not subjugate itself to governmentally-imposed strictures nor fit neatly within predefined programmes, but that government policy will have to adjust itself to deal with the new issues being introduced by the evolving modes of tourism in Vietnam, as well as with the demands and practices of foreign investors and private enterprises with whom the government is sharing the liberalised tourism market. The results can be observed in the reform of pricing and visa policies, the raising of accommodation standards, the removal of ideological and bureaucratic restrictions, and in terms of compelling reforms of state tourism (accommodation) providers in order to become competitive.

Vietnam is still in a state of transition, and none of the characteristics of Vietnam's current tourism sector can be expected to have reached a state of stasis or resolution. This chapter has demonstrated that the relationship between political change and change in tourism in Vietnam is complex. Just as political change is inspiring change in tourism development, changes in tourism development are also catalysts affecting political change. Ongoing interactions between the government, operators in the tourism industry, and tourists to Vietnam can be expected to continue to drive further evolution. However, more recent developments and changes in tourism in Vietnam and in government tourism policy are much less drastic than developments in the early years of *doi moi* and take the form of refinements to established and tested structures, rather than revolutionary shake-ups or reversals. *Doi moi*'s overall effect on Vietnam's tourism sector has been positive for the government, for business interests in the country, and for tourists visiting this emerging destination.

References

Airline Traffic (Reported Traffic, by Airline) (1976) Volume 1, 1971–1975, Montreal: International Civil Aviation Organisation.

Travel Business Analyst (1992) 'Country Inbound Profile Special Report on Vietnam'. Hong Kong.

Economist Intelligence Unit (EIU) (1993) *Indochina-Vietnam, Cambodia and Laos*, International Tourism Reports, No 2, pp. 59–82.

Elliott, J. (1997) *Tourism: Politics and Public Sector Management*, London: Routledge.

Erramilli, M., Luu, T., Gilbert, L. and Hooi, D. (1997) 'Foreign direct investment patterns in the Vietnamese tourism sector', Conference Proceedings for International Conference on Sustainable Tourism Development Hue, pp. 276–310.

Saigon Times Daily (1999) Foreigners Can Buy Stakes in Equitized Stated Companies, June 30.

Hodgson, A. (2007) 'Vietnam to be among the world's top ten tourist destinations by 2016', Euromonitor International, from: http://www.euromonitor.com/Vietnam_ to_be_among_the_worlds_top_ten_tourist_destinations_by_2016. (20 August 2009).

ICEM (2003) 'Vietnam: national report on protected areas and development', in *Review of Protected Areas and Development in the Lower Mekong River Region*, Queensland: Indooroopilly.

ITB Berlin (2001) *Chronik der Internationalen Tourismus-Börse ITB Berlin*. Berlin: ITB.

Kokko, A. (1998) Vietnam – ready for Doi Moi II?, Stockholm School of Economics: SSE/EFI Working Paper Series in Economics and Finance No. 286, from: http://swopec. hhs.se/hastef/abs/hastef0286.htm. (20 February 2003).

Lam, B.T. (2000) *Colonialism Experienced: Vietnamese Writings on Colonialism, 1900–1931*, Ann Arbor: University of Michigan Press.

Lewis, P. (1995) 'Vietnam Airlines is finally coming into its own as a regional, and international, carrier', *Flight International*, 15 November.

McElwee, P. (2001) 'Park or people: exploring alternative explanations for protected areas development in Viet Nam', Workshop on Conservation and Sustainable Development Comparative Perspectives: Yale University.

Mok, C. and Lam, T. (1996) 'Hotel and tourism development in Vietnam. An overview of its potential and constraints', Conference Proceedings for Tourism in Indo-China: Opportunities for Investment, Development and Marketing, HCMC: University of Housten and University of Angers, pp. 23–40.

Ngo Ba Thanh (1993) 'The 1992 Constitution and the rule of law', in C. Thayer, and D. Marr, (eds), *Vietnam and the Rule of Law*, Canberra: Australian National University, pp. 81–115.

Nguyen Nhu Phuong and Vu Van Dung (2001) 'Assessment of legal documents and policies relating to management of special-use forest in Vietnam, Technical Report No.1. WWF. Hanoi.

Office Central du Tourisme Indochinoise (1938) *Glimpses of a Great Tourist Country: French Indo-China at the Beginning of 1938*, Saigon: Government Information and Publicity Bureau.

Rambaldi, G., Bugna, S., and Geiger, M. (2001) 'Review of the protected area system of Vietnam. Special Report', *Asean Biodiversity*, pp 43–51.

Saigon Tourist and Saigon Tourist Association (1990) *Guide Book for Foreign Tourists and Business People*, Saigon: Saigon Tourist and Saigon Tourist Association.

Smith, M. (2002) *The Airline Encyclopedia 1909-2000, Vol. 1*. Oxford: Scarecrow Press.

Suntikul, W., Butler, R. and Airey, D., (forthcoming) 'Implications of political change on national park operations: Doi Moi and tourism to Vietnam's national parks'. *Journal of EcoTourism*.

Thayer, C. (1997) 'Vietnam and ASEAN: a first anniversary assessment', *Southeast Asian Affairs*, pp. 364–374.

Theuns H. (1997) 'Vietnam: tourism in an economy in transition', in F.M.Go and C.L.Jenkins (eds), *Tourism and Economic Development in Asia and Australia*, London: Cassell, pp. 304–318.

United Nations Development/WTO (1991) Tourism Development Master Plan, Socialist Republic of Vietnam Summary Report, United Nations Development/WTO.

Vietnam (2001) *Country Report No. 2. Travel and Tourism Intelligence*, pp. 85-99.

'Vietnam airlines plans sole fare' (2003) December 3, from: http://edition.cnn.com/2003/BUSINESS/12/03/vietnam.airlines.reut/ (17 February 2004).

'VN welcomes over 2.2 mil foreign tourists this year' (2003) December 24, from: http://english.vietnamnet.vn/biz/2003/12/146033/ (30 August 2009).

Vietnamese National Administration of Tourism (VNAT), from: www.vietnamtourism.com/index/e_index.asp (17 August 2009)

VNAT (n.d.) 'Overview of Vietnam tourism', unpublished document from VNAT.

VNAT (2001) *Revised National Tourism Development Plan for Vietnam 2001–2010, Draft Report*, Hanoi: VNAT/UNDP/WTO.

Watkin, Huw (1999) 'Foreigners wary of Vietnam dual price reforms', *South China Morning Post*, 30 June.

Part IV
Political Unrest

13 Tourism and Political Change in Nepal

Sanjay Nepal

This chapter examines tourism development in the context of political changes in Nepal distinguished by four different political eras: Era I – dawn of democracy (1951–61); Era II – authoritarian democracy (1962–88); 3) Era III – People's Movement (1989–95); and Era IV – People's War (1996–2009). The nature and level of tourism development in the country is discussed in the context of key political events during the four eras, with the focus on the last era during which political upheaval has had unprecedented impacts on tourism development.

Introduction

The development of tourism in Nepal has been rapid, considering that Nepal opened its borders to the outside world only in 1949. Visitor statistics show a steady growth through the 1970s followed by a levelling-off period until 1985, followed by periods of growth and decline, with a fifth phase of dramatic decline in visitor numbers after 1999; and the current phase of slow recovery since 2006 (Figure 13.1).

Tourism has been an important source of revenues for the government, in 2008 total earnings from tourism were US$351 million, which is 7.2% of total foreign exchange of the country. Thousands of businesses providing services to the tourism industry create

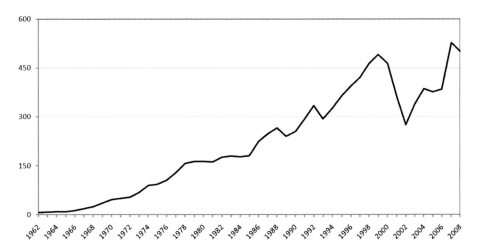

Figure 13.1: Tourist arrivals to Nepal between 1962 and 2008 (thousands). Source: NTB 2008

jobs and income for people who directly or indirectly work in this sector. For many local residents in Nepal's major tourism destinations such as the Annapurna and Everest regions, tourism is the only source of income and employment opportunities. Therefore the economic viability of tourism is of paramount importance not just to the government but also to the people who depend on it. Any uncertainty in tourism growth and development has critical impacts on the livelihoods of many. Since the beginning of the Maoist-led 'People's War' in 1996, tourist arrivals have declined significantly causing a major upheaval within the industry itself.

Era I: dawn of democracy and decade of instability (1951–61)

Prithivi Narayan Shah founded the kingdom of Nepal 240 years ago by unifying dozens of principalities and kingdoms. Led by Jang Bahadur Rana in 1846, the Ranas usurped absolute power and reduced the monarch to a mere figurehead. The Ranas ruled Nepal as their personal fiefdom for 104 years (1846–1950), isolating the country from outside and forbidding anyone to visit it (Thapa and Sizapati 2007). Aside from occasional scholars and royalty invited by the ruling Ranas, Nepal was the 'forbidden kingdom' and it is estimated that between 1881 and 1925, only 153 Europeans entered the country (Aditya and Shrestha, 1998). However, the isolationist policy was one-sided, as Nepalese migrated to India in search of better livelihood opportunities.

With the revolutionary changes in the government in 1951, involving the establishment of diplomatic relations with several countries, and participation in international forums, Nepal opened its borders to foreign officials, businessmen and tourists. The post-Rana regime introduced democratic governance in the country. The Interim Constitution promulgated in April 1951 provided various democratic safeguards including establishing an independent judiciary and limiting the King's role to a constitutional one. The Nepali Congress Party was invited to form a government as it was the largest political party at that time; however, instead of appointing its leader B.P. Koirala as the Prime Minister, King Tribhuvan nominated Koirala's elder brother Matrika Prasad. Analysts suggest that the nomination of Matrika was made in order that the king could exercise his authority better than he could have with a more influential figure in the Prime Minister position (Thapa and Sijapati 2007). The Congress–Rana coalition was beset with difficulties from the very start, as there were continuing political disturbances in various parts of country and tensions between the two coalition partners were frequent (Whelpton 2005). King Tribhuvan died in March 1955, and his successor Mahendra turned out to be a shrewd politician who consolidated the political position of the monarchy and the governments appointed by Mahendra served in office at the King's pleasure. The struggle for power between various political leaders, and between the leaders and the King, continued until 1959 when the King agreed to parliamentary elections. However, the elections were not to be for a constituent assembly as promised by the late King, but for a parliament under a Constitution that was to be granted by the King as the repository of the country's sovereignty (Thapa and Sijapati 2007). The Constitution of the Kingdom of Nepal 1959 was promulgated on February 12. It was nominally prepared by a Drafting Commission, but in reality was drafted in accordance with the

King's wishes by a British constitutional lawyer (Whelpton 2005). The Constitution stated explicitly that executive authority rested with the King, and 'shall be exercised by him either directly or through ministers or other officers subordinate to him' (quoted in Whelpton 2005: 93). Nepal's first democratically elected government took office in May 1959 with B.P. Koirala as Prime Minister, but his government lasted less than two years, as Mahendra dissolved parliament and arrested Koirala and some of his cabinet colleagues under the emergency power vested in him by the Constitution. The King was now in total control of the country and according to one Indian analyst, for Mahendra, 'Nepal was an idea and none but he could realize what it was destined to be' (Chatterji 1977: 110 cited in Whelpton 2005).

During this era, tourism development focused on climbing expeditions. In 1950 Maurice Herzog and Louis Lachenal reached the summit of Annapurna, and in 1953 Edmund Hillary and Tenzing Norgay climbed Mt Everest. In 1955 Thomas Cook offered the first organized tour of Nepal for western visitors (Karan *et al.*, 1994), and a Russian entrepreneur opened the Royal Hotel in what was formerly a Rana palace (Sunquist and Sunquist 2002). In the same year the Tribhuvan Highway was completed, which linked the capital city to the Terai lowlands. The Royal Nepal Airlines Corporation was established in July 1958 with one Douglas DC-3 aircraft offering its services from Kathmandu to a few other Nepali cities and to the Indian city of Patna. By 1961, the number of annual visitors to Nepal had reached 4000. Conversations with some former Everest climbers (three Swiss and two British nationals) with whom this author is acquainted suggest that there was very little development of tourism infrastructure at that time.

Table 13.1: Tourism development and political events in Nepal – Era I. (Compiled from various sources)

	Tourism development	Political events
1881– 1923	A total of 153 Europeans allowed into the country	Nepal is under autocratic Rana regime
1951		Formal end of Rana regime and establishment of coalition government
1953	Edmund Hillary and Tenzing Norgay climb Mt Everest	The Nepali Congress party forms government after the coalition fails
1955	Thomas Cook offers organized tour packages to Nepal; first tourist hotel (The Royal Hotel) is opened by Boris Lissanevitch	Death of King Tribhuvan in Switzerland; Mahendra's accession
1958	Royal Nepal Airlines Corporation is established	
1959–60	Directorate of Tourism established; Nepal joins the World Tourism Organization; First travel agency opened	First time voting in general election; B.P. Koirala is elected Prime Minister; King Mahendra removes Congress from government and imposes direct rule

Era II: the Panchayet years of authoritarian democracy (1962–89)

The takeover by Mahendra laid the foundation for three decades of direct rule by the monarchy. A single party system that the King himself had envisioned was implemented and all other political parties were banned and their leaders either jailed or exiled to India. Those who escaped to India regrouped and launched an armed struggle against the King's regime, limited mostly to border towns. The pressure was enough to force the King to compromise, but his situation became much more critical when India imposed an economic blockade in September 1962. To the King's good fortune, war between India and China broke out on October 16 and upon the request of India's Prime Minister Nehru, the Nepalese agitation was called off. This gave Mahendra the opportunity to consolidate his power. The Panchayat system was modelled as a 'guided democracy' such as those then existing in Pakistan, Indonesia, Yugoslavia and Egypt (Whelpton 2005). The system provided for directly elected village or town councils (*panchayat*), whose members formed an electoral college to choose district level representatives. These latter in turn selected from among themselves the majority of members of the national legislature (Rastriya Panchayat), the remainder being either representatives of government sponsored 'class organizations' or royal nominees. The national legislature's powers were limited and the whole arrangement was designed to allow an element of popular representation while the King ruled unhindered by the pressures of parliamentary democracy (Whelpton 2005). Because of the immense power the King wielded, the separation of powers between the legislature, the judiciary, and the executive became thoroughly blurred (Thapa and Sijapati 2007). Apart from minor acts of resistance mostly outside the capital, civic life was peaceful, development proceeded slowly and the system continued unchallenged (Table 13.2). In 1979, in response to the hanging of two Congress party fighters for an attempted assassination of the King, students, already unhappy about changes made to the education system, were mobilized for nationwide protests. As protests continued, universities were closed for a year. Bowing to the pressures, Birendra called for a national referendum asking citizens if they preferred the current system or a multi-party system; results favoured the current system.

As to tourism development, the government started including tourism-specific objectives in its five year plans beginning with the Third Plan (1965–70). The Tourism Act of 1964 was enacted, and an advisory committee formed, which was replaced by the Nepal Tourism Development Committee in 1969 (Touche Ross 1990). A major boost was given to building new hotels to accommodate the growing number of overseas visitors; although most hotels were restricted to Kathmandu and Pokhara. Expansion of air services was also a priority during this period. Completed in 1972, the First Tourism Master Plan recognized the importance of developing Nepal as a distinct tourist centre, and suggested improvements in existing tourist sites, services and facilities, expansion of tourist areas outside Kathmandu, and publicity in the international tourism market (HMG 1971). Subsequent plans stressed the need for increased foreign exchange earnings from tourism, employment creation, broader geographical distribution of tourist activities, and establishing regional tourist centres. Tourism received separate ministry status in 1977. Within a short span of time, tourism became one of the most important sources of foreign exchange in the country. The Sixth Plan (1980–85) emphasized identification of tourist centres, promotion of off-season tourism, development of mountain tourism and remote area tourism, development of resorts and tourist information centers, and tourism research and surveys as central priorities, and invested US$23 million in various tourism related projects (Pradhan 1997). The Seventh Plan (1985–90) stressed the need to attract high value tourists, simplified tax and tariff structures, government and private investments in tourism, and intensify marketing and promotion in Asian countries. It also emphasized heritage conservation and diversification of basic infrastructure required for tourism. The Nepal Tourism Development Programme (NTDP), formulated in 1990, provided a comprehensive review of all aspects of tourism and proposed a long-term strategy for tourism development (Touche Ross 1990).

With the growth in tourist numbers, Nepal quickly established its reputation as an adventure tourism destination. The country's first national park – Royal Chitwan National Park – was established in 1973, followed in 1976 by Mt Everest National Park; both were later designated as UNESCO World Heritage sites. Around the same time, Nepal became an attractive destination to budget tourists, and soon Kathmandu became famous for its hippies. The Hotel Eden in Jhonche became notorious for its shady dealings (in drugs). The 'hippie' tourists were resented by local residents, which may be a reason for their deportation just before Birendra's coronation ceremony.

Table13. 2: Tourism development and political events in Nepal – Era II. Compiled from various sources

	Tourism development	Political events
1962-64	Annual number of visitors increases to 4,000 Tourism Act of 1964 enacted	Promulgation of Nepal's new Constitution
1965-68	Mountaineering banned	Political dissidents continue their agitation from India
1972	"Hippie" tourists are deported	Death of King Mahendra and accession of King Birendra; Nepali Congress launches armed raid from India
1973-74	Nepal's first national park (Royal Chitwan National Park) established	Naxalite-style campaign of violence; Bomb attempt on Birendra's life
1979-80	1977 - Ministry of Tourism established 1980 – Chitwan and Everest national parks are declared World Heritage sites	Two Congress fighters are hanged for attempted murder of the King; nationwide protests cripple government apparatus; universities remain inoperative for almost a year during 1979; Birendra announces referendum on current system (Panchayat) of multi-party government – referendum favours single party system
1985-86	Annapurna Conservation Area Project implemented; launch of Nepal's first community-based tourism programme	Congress launches civil disobedience campaign; bomb explosions in Kathmandu's Hotel de l'Annapurna

Era III – people's movement or the second coming of democracy (1989–95)

With the death of B.P. Koirala in 1982, leadership of the Congress Party was assumed by Ganesh Man Singh, Krishna Prasad Bhattarai, and Girija Prasad Koirala. However, the party lacked direction, as several of its former members had already joined the ruling government after the referendum in 1980, and were now in conflict with the party leaders. Members from other left wing parties including the Marxist-Leninist communist party also joined the government. In 1985 the three Congress leaders launched Satyagraha (a civil disobedience campaign) while the communist groups organized a parallel agitation. The campaign was called off after four bombs went off in Kathmandu's Hotel de l'Annapurna killing three staff. Average citizens were growing disenchanted with the heavy-handedness of the Palace. There was discontent among members of the royal family; for example, the King's youngest brother Dhirendra renounced his royal title in a dispute with the Queen, while a key figure loyal to the palace was convicted of smuggling. Towards the end of 1989 political parties began hectic parleys to prepare for a new stage of struggle against the King's autocracy (Thapa and Sijapati 2007). The opposition was emboldened with what was going on inside the Palace, and were greatly helped when India imposed an economic blockade on Nepal in March 1990 as a result of a dispute arising from the 1950 Trade and Transit Treaty (Whelpton 2005). The Movement for the Restoration of Democracy was launched in February 1990 (Whelpton 2005). Congress was joined by the United Left Front, an alliance of seven communist groups, and despite the lack of a common strategy the opposition parties were united in their common goal to restore democracy in Nepal. On 6 April, some 200,000 demonstrators took to the streets in Kathmandu demanding an immediate end to the ban on political parties, violent clashes occurred in many parts of the Valley, especially in Patan and around the Palace. On April 8 the ban on political parties was lifted. On 19 May Krishna Prasad Bhattarai was declared Prime Minister, and several cabinet ministers from other parties including two royalists were appointed to his government, restoring multi-party democracy after almost three decades of authoritarian or 'guided' democracy.

Drafting of a new Constitution and holding parliamentary elections under the new Constitution were the two main goals of the newly formed government. The election results favoured Congress and Girija Prasad Koirala became the Prime Minister. However, in-fighting within the Congress Party and growing opposition from the Communist Party led to various events culminating with mid-term elections in November 1994 and a hung parliament. The Communist Party of Nepal (United Marxist-Leninist) emerged with the largest number of seats while the United People's Front (UPF; one of its factions was later known as the Maoists) failed to win a single seat. For the first time, a Communist leader (Man Mohan Adhikari) became the Prime Minister; however, the government did not last long. In September 1995 the Nepali Congress formed a coalition government under Sher Bahadur Deuba. After splitting from the United People's Front, Pushpa Kamal Dahal (aka 'Prachanda' – or the fierce one) together with Baburam Bhattarai renamed his party as the Communist Party of Nepal (Maoist) and adopted the 'Plan for the Historic Initiation of the People's War' in September 1995 (Thapa and Sijapati 2007). In November, Nepali Police launched Operation Romeo against Maoist supporters in the western part of the country (Whelpton 2005).

The Eighth Plan (1991-96) aimed to develop Nepal as a final destination for tourists and to implement the tourism industry as a major source of employment generation (HMG 1992). It also stressed the need for greater private sector participation. One significant achievement in 1992 was the establishment of several domestic airlines with private sector involvement. However, despite the strong emphasis on tourism development, improvements in infrastructure and government tourism investment beyond Kathmandu and Pokhara did not materialize. The government issued a new tourism policy in 1995 seeking to develop tourism as an important sector of the national economy, diversify tourism products, and opening new areas for tourism. The policy called for greater local participation in identifying and marketing rural tourism resources, and recommended setting up a Tourism Council with public and private sector participation.

Table 13.3: Tourism development and political events in Nepal – Era III. Compiled from various sources

	Tourism development	Political events
1989-90	A comprehensive Tourism Development Program is formulated	Start of 'People's Movement'; dissolution of the Panchayat system; Nepali Congress leader Krishna Prasad Bhattarai appointed Prime Minister
1991-	Free market system adopted in the domestic airline sector – several private air lines	Communist Party of Nepal formed after a merger of two far-left parties; establishment of United People's Front as electoral vehicle for the Unity Centre
1994-96	A new Nepal Tourism Policy formulated	Baburam Bhattarai's faction splits from United People's Front; Prachanda's faction of Unity Centre renames itself CPN (Maoist) and adopts 'Plan for the Historic Initiation of the People's War'

Era IV: People's War or Maoist Insurgency (1996-2009)

The Maoist insurgency started on 13 February 1996 with an attack on a police post in western Nepal (Table 13.4). The genesis of the insurgency in western Nepal has been attributed to several factors such as poverty and landlessness, long-standing grievances against the government, and the crackdown on the Maoist activists (Do and Iyer 2007). By 2004, the Maoist insurgency had engulfed the entire country with the exception of Mustang and Manang districts. The Maoists' main objectives were to establish a people's republic and set up a constituent assembly to draft a new constitution. The 75-point manifesto released by the Maoists in November 2001 listed several other aims including the distribution of land to poor and landless people, equal treatment of all ethnic groups and languages, and equal rights for women. The political situation in the country changed dramatically in 2001 when Crown Prince Dipendra allegedly killed his father King Birendra and most members of his immediate family including himself. With a remarkable twist of events, Gyanendra, whom the Rana regime had declared King when he was three years old, became the new King of Nepal. The then Prime Minister Sher Bahadur Deuba declared a truce with the Maoists and held a first round of talks.

Table 13.4: Tourism development and political events in Nepal – Era IV. Compiled from various sources.

	Tourism development	Political events
1996		Commencement of 'People's War'
1998–2000	'Visit Nepal Year' declared Nepal Tourism Board, a public-private entity, established. 1999 record number of visitors to date	May 98 - beginning of police operation against the Maoist insurgents; Sep. 99 – violence erupts in western Nepal; Sep 00 – Maoists kill 14 policemen, Hijacking of Indian Airlines plane from Kathmandu airport by Pakistani nationals
2001	Foreign arrivals decrease by 20%	Birendra approves ordinances setting up an armed police force and system of regional governors; Maoists adopt the 'Prachanda Path' as party doctrine; Maoists kill 70 policemen in Rukum and Dailekh attacks; government announces plans for Integrated Security and Development Program involving key role for army; Crown Prince Dipendra shoots himself, king, queen and seven other members of the royal family; accession of King Gyanendra; Declaration of state of emergency throughout Nepal and full mobilization of army against rebels
2002–04	23% decline in tourist numbers in 2003 from the year before; for the first time Thai Airways surpasses Nepal Airways in passengers flying to Nepal	Gyanendra dismisses the elected government, postpones elections and assumes executive powers; Maoist gunmen assassinate head of Armed Police Force; ceasefire announced between rebels and government; Maoist bomb ACAP headquarters in Ghandruk
2006–07	Government-run Nepal Airlines close to collapse; 2007, tourist arrivals surpass previous record of 1999 reaching 527,000	Nov 06 – Peace accord signed between government and rebels; end of Maoist insurgency
2008–09	Nepal Airlines carriers the lowest number of passengers of four major airlines flying international passengers to Nepal; a 5% decline in tourist numbers	Maoists win the constituency elections; 239-year old monarchy is dissolved, Nepal is declared a republic, Prachanda becomes Prime Minister; Maoists lose coalition support after eight months in power; a new coalition government under Madhav Kumar Nepal (Communist Party of Nepal – Unified Marxist-Leninist) formed; Maoists threaten to derail the peace agreement, announce a parallel government; country turns restless again

However, the Maoists unilaterally broke the truce in 2001, when they simultaneously attacked army barracks in the mid-western and eastern regions. Deuba imposed a state of emergency, declared the Maoists a terrorist group, and mobilized the Royal Nepal Army to counter the insurgency. The intensity of the conflict escalated and continued through February 2005, when Gyanendra dismissed the Prime Minister, placed major political figures under arrest and seized power; events remarkably similar to those of

1960. The Maoists began talks with the major political parties in November 2005 in an attempt to present a united front against the monarchy. In April 2006 Gyanendra gave up absolute power, and Nepal was declared a republic. The Maoists joined the seven party coalition and won the highest number of constituent assembly seats in the election of April 2008. However, since they did not have a significant majority, Prachanda was declared the Prime Minister, heading a coalition government formed in August 2008. The Nepali Congress was represented by the President, and a party from the lowlands was represented by the Vice President. But after only nine months in power Prachanda's government failed in May 2009 and Madhav Kumar Nepal of CPN (UML) took over. All told, the Maoist insurgency cost the Shah Dynasty its monarchy, took 13,000 lives and caused a decade of political violence and unrest. Now that the Maoists are out of the government, they have threatened to launch yet another stage of political unrest creating a state of uncertainty. While tourism development in Nepal in the years preceding the Maoist insurgency was not affected by political changes, dramatic impacts were felt in the industry during the insurgency. With the exception of 'forced solicitation' of donations by the Maoists, tourists were generally safe, but numbers declined in 2000 by 5.7% compared to 1999 (see Figure 13.1). Arrivals plunged further in 2001 (-23%) and 2002 (-23.7%). Numbers stayed low until 2006, and surpassed 1999 arrivals in 2007 only after the insurgency ended. The decline in numbers from Asian countries in particular has been attributed to the hijacking of an Indian Airlines plane from Kathmandu's airport in 1999 by Pakistani nationals, which resulted in suspension of all Indian Airlines flights to Nepal for six months (Adhikari 2005).

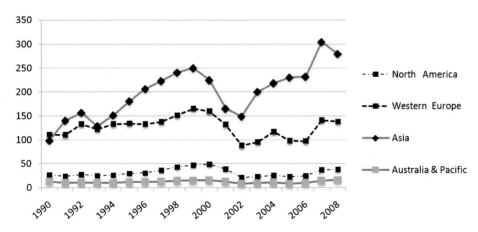

Figure 13.2: Tourist arrivals by major region – 1990-2008 (thousands). Source: NTB 2008

Figure 13.3 shows tourist arrivals by three main purposes of visit over an 18-year period; revealing significant drops in all three categories after 2000, being most pronounced for holiday and pleasure seeking tourists. Similarly, tourist visits to protected areas since 2000 have also decreased sharply; for example, the Everest region saw its trekking numbers decline from a peak of 26,790 in 2000 to only 14,000 in 2002 (Figure 13.4). It should be noted that two hill districts (Mustang and Manang) which are within the boundaries of ACA were not affected by the Maoist insurgency, but other areas were affected greatly after the 2004 bombing of the ACA headquarters in Ghandruk.

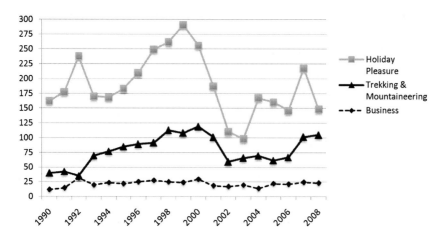

Figure 13.3: Tourist arrivals by purpose of visit – 1990-2008 (thousands). Source: NTB 2008

A major effect of the political turmoil and frequent changes in government was that Nepal's national airline suffered greatly (Figure 13.5). The Nepal Airlines Corporation (NAC) is currently in a sorry state and has been mismanaged by various politicians for their own benefits. It is depressing to note that NAC which was founded in 1958, might close its international operations. During its peak years it carried almost 150,000 tourists; in 2008 it carried only 21,000 tourists.

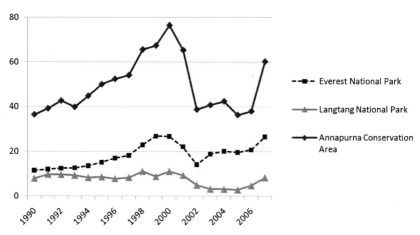

Figure 13.4: Protected area visitors between 1990 and 2007 (thousands). Source: NTB 2008

Surprisingly, the effect of insurgency on the national economy has not been extreme. Nepal's national economy has shown positive growth, mostly due to the remittances sent home by overseas workers. Prior to 1995 less than 100,000 Nepalese were going abroad; after the insurgency in 1996 the number increased to close on 415,000 in 2006 – an increase of almost 250%. It further rose to more than 560,000 in 2008. During 2003–04 remittances sent by overseas workers contributed to 12% of Nepal's gross domestic product (World Bank 2009). Similarly, total foreign exchange earnings did not suffer a decline even during the years of turmoil; total earnings declined only in 2001 and 2002 even though growth remained negative in seven of the 13 years since 1996 (Figure 13.6).

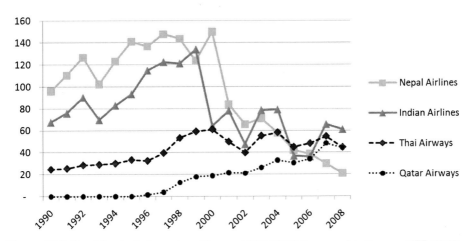

Figure 13.5: Tourist arrivals by major airlines – 1990-2008 (thousands). Source: NTB 2008

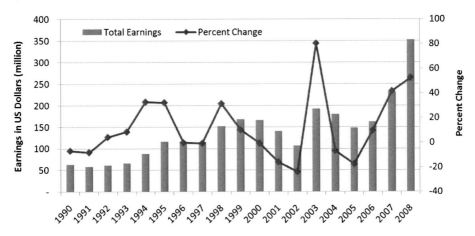

Figure 13.6: Foreign exchange earnings from tourism –1990–2008. Source: NTB 2008

Conclusions

The post 1950s political situation in Nepal has been unstable, uncertain and fluid at the same time. It is interesting that apart from the opening of its borders to the outside world, which was a radical departure from the past, political changes in Nepal generally did not affect tourism development significantly. The only other event that had a decisive impact on tourism was the Maoist-led insurgency, unprecedented in Nepal's history as it was the first time violence was brought upon civilians. It is ironic that tourism development prospered during the era of authoritarian democracy, perhaps because it at least provided some sense of normalcy and stability. With democracy and an associated free market economy, tourism has seen a glut in hotels (more than 900 registered hotels), accommodation capacity (36,000 beds), travel agencies (656), and trekking agencies (487) (Adhikari 2005). When, how, and under what political circumstances these will thrive is subject to speculation.

Political analysts have interpreted the Maoist insurgency as a crisis caused by vast inequalities in wealth and access to resources, widespread rural poverty, regionally imbalanced economic development, and deeply entrenched corruption and abuse of government authority. However, it is also a reflection of a disenchanted public tired of the major political parties of Nepal, which are more interested in consolidating their power than working for the people and country. Poverty, corruption and underdevelopment have undermined the legitimacy of any government, royal or democratically elected, creating a chaotic situation, on which the Maoists capitalized for their interests. Tourism provided livelihood opportunities for people who were entrepreneurial and hard working. Indeed, the industry had provided direct employment to 300,000 people (Adhikari 2005). Ethnic minorities like the Sherpa from Everest region, the Loba (Manangi) from Mustang, and the Gurung from ACA prospered primarily due to tourism. One might wonder if the Maoist insurgency would have even taken roots if rural areas of western Nepal had been as prosperous as those identified above, as Mustang and Manang were the only two Districts in Nepal that were spared the bloodbath?

It is interesting to consider why despite several policies, adequate tourism development failed to materialize. The policies that were formulated over the last 25 years have repeatedly raised the same concerns without resultant concrete actions. Aditya and Shrestha (1998) identified key issues of tourism development in Nepal, including its peripheral position in the international tourism market, its failure to attract a substantial proportion of visitors traveling primarily to India or Thailand, two main gateways to Nepal; its reliance on India for imports related to the industry; external leakage of revenues; and environmental and social costs. The Maoist problem completely overshadowed those concerns. The post-insurgency conditions are volatile and will likely prevent sustained growth and development of tourism in Nepal.

References

Adhikari, R. (2005) 'Building confidence in tourism through crisis management', Economic Policy Network – Policy Paper 9, Kathmandu: Ministry of Finance.

Aditya, A. and Shrestha, S. (1998) 'Indian tourists in Nepal: the potential and pitfalls of accelerated neighborhood tourism from the south', Draft Report, Geneva: United Nations Research Institute for Social Development

Chatterji, B. (1977) *Nepal's Experiment with Democracy*, New Delhi: Ankur.

Do, Q. and Iyer, L. (2007) 'Poverty, Social divisions and Conflict in Nepal'. Working Paper, Washington, D.C.: World Bank.

HMG (His Majesty's Government of Nepal) (1971) *The Fourth Plan (1970–75)*, National Planning Commission (NPC), Nepal.

HMG (His Majesty's Government of Nepal) (1992) *The Eighth Plan (1992-97)*, NPC, Nepal.

Karan, P.P., Ishii, H., Kobayashi, M., Shrestha, M., Vajracharya, C., Zurick, D. and Pauer, G. (1994) *Nepal - Development and Change in a Landlocked Himalayan Kingdom*, Tokyo: Tokyo University of Foreign Studies.

Nepal Tourism Board (NTB) *Tourism Statistics 2008* (2008), Kathmandu: NTB.

Pradhan, K.M. (1997) *Planning Tourism in Nepal*, New Delhi: Vikash Publishing House.

Sunquist F. and Sunquist, M. (2002) *Tiger Moon - Tracking the Great Cats in Nepal*, Chicago: University of Chicago Press.

Thapa, D. and Sijapati, B. (2007) *A Kingdom under Siege: Nepal's Maoist Insurgency, 1996 to 2004*. Kathmandu: The Printhouse.

Touche Ross Management Consultants (1990) Nepal Tourism Development Programme: A Report for the Asian Development Bank and Ministry of Tourism, Kathmandu.

Whelpton, J. (2005) *A History of Nepal*, Cambridge: Cambridge University Press.

World Bank (2009) Macroeconomics and Economic Growth in South Asia, from: http://web.worldbank.org/ (9 September 2009).

14 Political Change and Tourism: Coups in Fiji

David Harrison and Stephen Pratt

Introduction

This chapter focuses on the relationship between tourism development in the Fiji Islands and political change. Political unrest has had a negative impact on tourist arrivals, employment, earnings and investment over the last two decades, but the tourism industry has been resilient and the effects, though serious, have been relatively short-term. However, political uncertainties have also affected the wider socio-economic context of tourism, leading to emigration of Indo-Fijians and an increasingly obvious mismatch of the Fiji promoted by the tourism industry and the social and economic reality.

Fiji: the background

When Fiji became a British colony in 1874, the colonial government attempted to shield indigenous Fijians from incorporation into a market economy by insisting that more than 80% of the land was retained under the communal ownership of *mataqali* (exogamous patrilineages) (Legge, 1958: 170–201; Prasad, 1997: 17). From 1879 until 1918, some 60,000 indentured labourers from India were imported to work in the sugar industry, of whom 40,000 remained after their indentures (Lawson, 1996: 51). These two policies, along with the colonial establishment of a Council of Chiefs (Bose Levu Vakaturaga), which much favoured chiefs in the east of Viti Levu (Lawson, 1996: 44–57), laid the foundations for the present socio-cultural and economic nature of modern Fiji, and the social tensions that continue to beset it.

By 1956, the Indo-Fijian population had outstripped that of indigenous Fijians and in 1966, the last census before independence (1970), revealed that of a population of 480,000, 43.4% were indigenous Fijian, 50.5% Indo-Fijian, and 3.4% European and part-European, with other minorities making up the remainder (Bureau of Statistics, 2009: 3). This ethnic mix was characterised by Fisk (who arguably failed to recognise that 'the poor' came from all non-European groups, and that some (chiefly) indigenous Fijians were highly privileged), as 'three Fijis', where Europeans/Chinese managed and operated large corporations, mainly for foreign owners, Indo-Fijians owned medium and small-scale enterprises, including commercial farms, and indigenous Fijians communally owned most land and were primarily subsistence farmers (Fisk, 1970: 42).

Ethnic divisions were reinforced in the 1966 Constitution, which established communal rolls for elections (favouring indigenous Fijian constituencies), which survived constitutional changes in 1970, 1990 and 1997. Consequently, Indo-Fijian disadvantage was institutionalised (Fisk, 1970: 34–36; Lawson, 1996: 57–74). Thus, at independence, Fiji was (and might still be considered) a prime example of a 'plural society' (Norton, 1990: 1-5; Lawson, 1996: 42–44), containing ethnic groups with different cultures and forms of association, and differential access to civil and political rights, meeting primarily in the market place, where 'they mix, but do not combine' (Harrison, 1997: 170).

The point was not lost on astute observers at the time, and Fisk prophetically noted that 'the two main engines of economic growth' in Fiji, tourism and foreign investment, were 'virtually dependent on the absence of serious racial disturbance' (1970: 48).

Political change in post-indepence Fiji

By 1946, Indo-Fijians were in the majority, a situation that remained until 1986, when they constituted 49% of the population, with indigenous Fijians at 46% (Bureau of Statistics, 2009: 3). The perceived significance of such demographic changes explains why, since 1970, Fiji has (so far) seen nine general elections, four coups and three Constitutions, and events since independence have graphically demonstrated the validity of Fisk's apprehension.

Indigenous Fijians dominated government until 1987, when a coalition of the (mainly Indo-Fijian) National Federation Party and the (mixed-race) Fiji Labour Party was formed, with a Fijian Prime Minister and a racially mixed Cabinet. Soon afterwards, claiming the 'pro-Indo-Fijian' government was leading Fiji into disaster, Sitiveni Rabuka, an army officer, carried out two (relatively bloodless) coups (or arguably, one in two parts), formed a military government, oversaw a changed (1990) Constitution, which reinforced the supremacy of indigenous Fijians, and remained in power until 1992. Then, when the newly formed Fijian Political Party was elected, he was reinstated, this time as legitimate Prime Minister, and again oversaw amendments to the Constitution (1997). However, in 1999 he was electorally defeated by the Fiji Labour Party, led by Mahendra Chaudhury, who became the country's first Indo-Fijian Prime Minister, only to be overthrown in 2000 in a violent and prolonged pro-Fijian coup. These coup leaders themselves were then arrested by the military, led by Commodore Bainimarama, who subsequently invited Laisenia Qarase to form an interim government. In March 2001 Qarase and his new party, the Soqosoqo Duavata ni Lewenivanua Party (SDL), were elected and remained in power until 2006, when Qarase and Bainimarama disagreed over what Bainimarama considered were excessively pro-Fijian policies, and the former's support for leaders of the 2000 coup. Bainimarama again instigated military government and later, in April 2009, abrogated the 1997 Constitution, vowing to hold elections in 2014 after the introduction of a non-racist constitution, guided by a People's Charter, collated by aNational Council for Building a Better Fiji (NCBBF, 2008). As a consequence, Fiji was suspended from the regional Pacific Forum and, on 1 September 2009, from the (British) Commonwealth of Nations – which it had rejoined only in 1997 after its membership had been withdrawn on becoming a Republic in 1987.

While there were clear differences in the nature, circumstances and aims of the various coups (Lal, 2000, 2008; Naidu, 2008), the language and ideology of race and ethnicity have consistently been to the fore, though they have undoubtedly detracted attention from class and regional factors (Durutalo, 2000; Lal, 2008: 17). Less in doubt is the fact that Fisk's 1970 concerns over the possible impacts of domestic unrest on the economy, especially tourism and investment, have been amply justified.

Tourism and the coups in Fiji: the figures

Mahadevan's description of the performance of Fiji's post-independence economy as 'sluggish and unstable' (2009: 2) is supported by other commentators (Prasad and Tisdell, 2006: 61, 69; Robertson, 2008: 26), and it is commonly agreed that 'political instability...has not allowed Fiji to achieve its full potential for economic growth' (Prasad and Tisdell, 2006: 75). Noting that 1987, 2000 and 2006 were the 'years of the coups,' the macroeconomic data seem to support this view (Table 14.1).

Table 14.1: Macroeconomic indicators for Fiji, 1971-2008 (%). Source: Mahadevan, 2009: 2

Indicator	1971–86	1987–90	1991–99	2000	2001–05	2006–08
Real GDP growth	4.12	-0.94	2.76	-1.66	2.45	-1.0
Inflation rate	3.53	6.56	3.7	3.0	2.82	5.0
Unemployment rate	8.9	7.5	6.4	7.6	8.2	8.6

Tourism's potential was recognised as early as the mid-1960s (Harris, Kerr, Forster and Co., 1965: 5) and stressed in virtually all later development and tourism development plans (e.g. Central Planning Office, 1970: 179–188; Belt, Collins and Associates, 1973; Sustainable Tourism Development Consortium, 2007). By the early 1990s, it had replaced sugar as the major earner of foreign exchange, though sugar remains vital to the economy and has fewer leakages than tourism (Ram and Singh, 2003).

Table 14.2: Average annual arrival and earnings: Growth rates by decade. Source: Bureau of Statistics (various issues)

Decade	Annual growth rates	
	Arrivals (%)	Tourism earnings (%)
1952-1959	12.6	n/a
1960-1969	21.5	n/a
1970-1979	9.1	n/a
1980-1989	3.8	12.2
1990-1999	5.2	7.7
2000-2008	5.0	6.5

The relative success of Fiji tourism over the last four decades in attracting increased numbers of visitors and substantial foreign exchange is evident in the figures (Table 14.2). In 1952 (the earliest available arrival statistics), international visitor arrivals totalled 5605. Throughout the 1950s, arrivals grew at a yearly rate of about 13% to reach 12,632 by 1959. The 1960s averaged 22% growth a year. By 1969, there were

85,163 arrivals, a 6.7-fold increase over the past decade. Arrivals continued to increase during the 1970s at a rate of 9% per annum, slowing to 4% in the 1980s but rising to 5% in the 1990s, a rate maintained at the beginning of the new millennium.

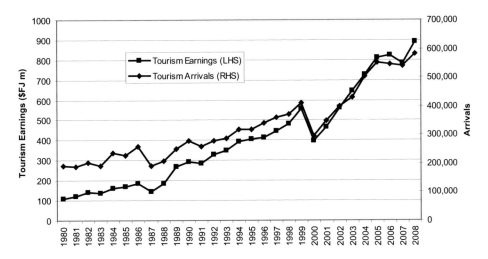

Figure 14.1: Tourism arrivals and tourism earnings: 1980-2008

In terms of tourism earnings, Fiji earned F$108.0 million from tourists in 1980, almost tripling to F$294.6 million in 1990. Growth then slowed to an average of 8% per annum in the 1990s and continued at an average of 7% per year from 2000, reaching F$892.0 million in 2008, by which time tourism was directly or indirectly supporting some 50,000 jobs and was explicitly considered 'the key driver for economic recovery' (Reddy, 2009).

Tourism's general sensitivity to political unrest is well demonstrated (Richter and Waugh, 1986; Clements and Georgiou, 1998; Sonmez, 1998; Sonmez *et al.*, 1999) and also true for Fiji. The coups in 1987, 2000 and 2006 resulted in decreased visitor numbers in the following years and retarded growth in tourism in general (Table 14.3).

After the 1987 coup, the first in Fiji, visitor arrivals fell 26% and tourism earnings dropped by 21%. Similarly, after the 2000 coup, which was notably violent and prolonged, arrivals fell by 28% and earnings by 29%. By contrast, arrivals after the 2006 coup decreased by only 1%, though earnings fell by 5% – an indication that significant discounting occurred in the accommodation sector resulting in a contribution of tourism to the economy that was disproportionate to the marginally reduced number of arrivals.

Not only macro tourism indicators were adversely affected by the coups in Fiji. After the 2000 coup, for example, hotel turnover decreased 21% from the previous year, room nights sold decreased 23%, and domestic tourism (overnight stays by Fiji residents) fell by 5% (Bureau of Statistics, 2009: 114,115). With the sharp drop in tourism demand, lay-offs and shortened working hours were common, and several accommodation enterprises went out of business. The total number of rooms available dropped 9%, and room-night capacity and bed-night capacity fell 3% and 2% respectively from the previous year (Bureau of Statistics, 2009: 114).

Table 14.3: Arrivals and earnings in the years of the coups and surrounding years. Source: Bureau of Statistics (various issues)

	Visitor arrivals	% change from previous year	Tourism earnings ($FJ million)	% change from previous year
1986	257,824	13	184.9	10
1987	189,866	-26	145.7	-21
1988	208,155	10	186.5	28
1999	409,955	10	558.6	16
2000	294,070	-28	397.0	-29
2001	348,014	18	463.9	17
2005	549,911	9	812.7	12
2006	545,168	-1	822.5	1
2007	539,255	-1	784.2	-5
2008	583,319	8	892.3	14

Changes in arrivals and earnings from tourism following the coups reveal only partially the impact of political unrest on Fiji tourism. Calculations of losses can be made with the focus on those forgone during the recovery period after the coup (scenario 1) and, more conjecturally, of what would have occurred without the coups, had the average growth in arrivals and earnings over the five years continued (scenario 2).

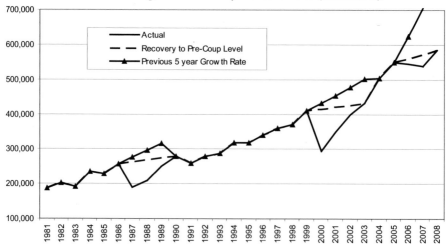

Figure 14.2: Imputed impacts on tourism arrivals

Such approaches are indicated in Figure 14.2 and Table 14.4. In 1987, the year of the first coup(s), arrivals dropped by nearly 68,000 to 189,866. It was not until 1990 (the end of the recovery period) that pre-coup arrival figures were surpassed. In the five years before the 1987 coup, for example, the average annual growth rate in arrivals was 7.0%. Had arrivals continued to increase at the same rate, as indicated by the diamond marker line in Figure 14.2, by 1989 they would have been approximately 316,208, i.e. the difference between actual arrivals (solid line) and the forecast line of arrivals across the recovery period.

A similar analysis can be undertaken for the coups of 2000 and 2006. In Figure 14.2, the solid line represents actual visitor arrivals, the dashed line represents a line of best fit from the pre-coup level of arrivals to the year arrivals surpass their pre-coup level, and the 'diamond' line indicates the likely level of arrivals based on the previous 5-year average growth rate. These data are provided numerically in Table 14.4, where column 2 is the level of actual arrivals, column 3 shows the trend from the pre-coup level of arrivals to the end of the recovery period, and column 4 indicates the difference between this line of best fit and actual arrivals (scenario 1). By contrast, column 5 represents arrivals foregone based on the previous five-year pre-coup average, and column 6 shows the difference between actual and forecast arrivals (scenario 2).

Table 14.4: International arrivals to Fiji, actual and forecast: 1986–2008. Source: Bureau of Statistics (various issues); authors' calculations

Year (1)	Actual visitor arrivals (2)	Scenario 1			Scenario 2	
		Recovery to pre-coup level (3)	Difference (4 = 3 − 2)		Previous 5 year growth rate (5)	Difference (6 = 5 − 2)
1986	257,824	257,824			257,824	
1987	189,866	263,117	73,251		275,977	86,111
1988	208,155	268,410	60,255		295,408	87,253
1989	250,565	273,703	23,138		316,208	65,643
1990	278,996	278,996			278,996	
1991	259,354	259,354			259,354	
1992	278,534	278,534			278,534	
1993	287,462	287,462			287,462	
1994	318,874	318,874			318,874	
1995	318,495	318,495			318,495	
1996	339,560	339,560			339,560	
1997	359,441	359,441			359,441	
1998	371,342	371,342			371,342	
1999	409,955	409,955			409,955	
2000	294,070	415,166	121,096		431,321	137,251
2001	348,014	420,378	72,364		453,801	105,787
2002	397,859	425,589	27,730		477,452	79,593
2003	430,800	430,800			502,336	71,536
2004	504,000	504,000			504,000	
2005	549,911	549,911			549,911	
2006	545,168	561,047	15,879		623,651	78,483
2007	539,255	572,183	32,928		707,279	168,024
2008	583,319	583,319			802,121	218,802
Total	–		426,641		–	1,098,484

A similar analysis can be completed for tourism earnings, as indicated in Table 14.5. Had previous growth rates in arrivals continued, and the coups not occurred, between 427,000 and 1.1 million extra visitors would have come to Fiji during the 'recovery' years. The earnings forgone are estimated to be between F$373 million (scenario 1) and F$986 million (scenario 2).

Table 14.5: Summary of estimated losses in arrivals and earnings. Source: Authors' calculations

| | | Arrivals | | | Earnings F$ Million) | |
| | | Scenario 1 | Scenario 2 | | Scenario 1 | Scenario 2 |
Coup	Years to reach pre-coup level	Estimated 'loss' during recovery period	Estimated 'loss' assuming pre-coup growth rates	Years to reach pre-coup level	Estimated 'loss' during recovery period	Estimated 'loss' assuming pre-coup growth rates
1987	3	156,644	239,007	1	40.0	89.2
2000	3	221,190	394,168	2	260.2	611.2
2006	2	48,807	465,309	1	73.2	285.1
Total	–	426,641	1,098,484	–	373.4	985.5

It took three years after the 1987 and 2000 coups for arrivals to recover, while the 2006 coup resulted in a two-year setback. The decline in arrivals and earnings after the 2000 coup was steep because it was especially protracted. By contrast, the aftermath of the 2006 coup was milder: encouraged by shrewd, albeit contested, marketing (King and Berno, 2001: 8–9), visitors perceived the coup to be relatively non-violent and unthreatening to them, and losses were minimised.

While the previous estimates, based on pre-coup arrivals and earnings patterns, are based on conjecture, they are not unrealistic, and suggest that over all, the coups could have cost Fiji more than one million tourists and F$986 million (Table 14.5).

Finally, a caveat, which might indicate the above estimates are on the high side. It is possible tourists planning to visit Fiji when the coups occurred might have deferred their visit until the situations were resolved. Evidence for this would be a relatively strong increase in arrivals and earnings after the coups, compared with that in the pre-coup period, which is indeed noticeable. For example, over the period 1988–90, the average growth rate of arrivals was 13.8%, but this slowed to an average of 4.5% per year for the period 1991–99. Such a 'catch-up' occurred after every coup.

The wider socio-economic environment

Figures of changing tourist demand give some indication of the relationship of tourism in Fiji to political unrest but they must be situated in the wider socio-economic and historical context. From the outset, tourism to Fiij was developed by overseas interests for overseas visitors, and it is still owned and/or operated primarily by non-Fijians, though such bodies as the Fiji National Provident Fund and the Fiji Teachers' Association have invested in major transnational-operated hotels. In addition, numerous budget resorts are owned and operated by Indo-Fijians and indigenous Fijians (the latter primarily in the islands north-west of Viti Levu). All function in a context that has clearly been affected by domestic politics, but tourism stakeholders have also played an active part in the political process.

Indigenous Fijian people and culture have long been, and remain, the focus and image of Fiji tourism – a highly conscious, political strategy (Harrison, 1998). Nevertheless, the interests of the industry have often clashed with those of indigenous Fijians. Many hotels, for instance, lease land from native owners and historically there have been many acrimonious disputes over access to and rights over such land (Sofield, 2003: 285-289). Access to marine resources (*qoliqoli*) is similarly the subject of much acrimony, frequently expressed over which *matiqalis* are entitled to authorise and benefit from transporting tourists to well-known surfing spots. These issues became especially prominent when the Qarase's SDL government of 2001–06 proposed a Qoliqoli Bill, which would transfer

> '*all proprietary rights to and interests in qoliqoli areas within Fijian fisheries waters and vest them in the qoliqoli owners.*' *By this process, the marine area from the foreshore to the high water mark would be declared 'native reserves', for the unfettered use and enjoyment of [native] resource owners.*
>
> (Lal, 2009a: 24).

Not surprisingly, this prospect was vigorously opposed by tourism interests, which feared immediate financial uncertainty and catastrophic loss of investment. Qarase later alleged that the American owner of Turtle Island, a boutique resort in the Yasawas temporarily occupied during the 2000 coup, led the opposition, lobbying Commodore Bainimarama and funding the Bill's opponents (2009: 368). That suggestion was not new, but opposition to the Qoliqoli Bill extended far beyond the Yasawas and was not restricted to the tourism sector. The Bill was subsequently branded by Bainimarama as racist and Qarase's refusal to withdraw it given as one of the reasons for the 2006 coup (Lal, 2009a: 33–34). When the new military government halted the bill's progress, there was much relief throughout the business sector.

Bainimarama's 2006 coup generated considerable publicity and international opposition, especially from Australia and New Zealand, whose travel advisories (like that of the USA) continue to depict (perhaps exaggerate) a seriously volatile Fiji and urge travellers to be cautious. However, the tourism industry in Fiji has become adept at countering unfavourable publicity (King and Berno, 2001). Ever since the initial shock of the 1987 coups, Crisis Action Plans and Tourism Action Groups have been activated, and while tourist arrivals and earnings have decreased after every coup, and have been accompanied by job losses, reduced working hours, decreased occupancy rates and heavy discounting, the industry has (correctly) emphasised that Fiji remains a safe tourist destination (Trnka, 2008: 153) and – as indicated earlier – after recovery periods continued an upward trajectory.

In fact, the tourist lobby, most notably the Fiji Islands Hotel and Tourist Association (previously the Fiji Hotel Association) has become a highly effective pressure group, in that the population generally has become aware of the impact of political unrest on the image of their country (Trnka, 2008: 147–149). Ironically, given its success in countering 'negative publicity,' the Government's marketing arm, now known as Tourism Fiji, has only recently achieved a substantial increase in its marketing budget (as indicated in Figure 14.3), and in the government-sponsored NCBBF's 2008 'State of the Nation' report, tourism receives only a passing mention!

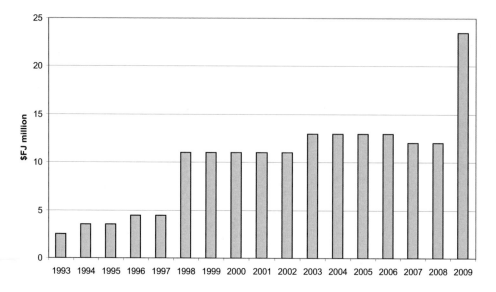

Figure 14.3: Tourism Fiji's marketing budget: 1993–2009

The coups also had internal consequences, which crucially fed back into and changed the environment within which tourism operated. The first major result was that they exacerbated Indo-Fijian emigration, mainly to Australia, North America and New Zealand (Mohanty, 2006; Naidu, 2008: 156–158). Although already a feature of pre-independence Fiji, after 1987 Indo-Fijian emigration doubled and again increased after the 2000 coup (Table 14.6), though in recent years more indigenous Fijians have also emigrated.

Whereas in 1986, Indo-Fijians were 49% of the population, compared to indigenous Fijians at 46%, by 1996 the ratios were 44% to 51%, and by 2007, Indo-Fijians constituted only 38% of the population, with indigenous Fijians at 57% (Bureau of Statistics, 2009: 3).

As a consequence of the high rates of emigration, remittances became increasingly important to the Fijian economy, and are now second only to tourism as a source of foreign exchange (Mohanty, 2006: 115–116). In addition, there was (and continues to be) a loss of skilled and professional human resources. Between 1987 and 2004 an estimated 14,000 (13%) out of over 110,000 emigrants were in either professional or technical occupations, mainly young Indo-Fijians, with 3800 alone leaving between the 2000 coup and the end of 2004 (Mohanty, 2006: 112). The loss to the Fiji economy through emigration has been estimated to be on average, F$44.5 million annually ... mainly through loss of skill, re-training new appointees, and delayed appointments. The figure is much higher – F$274.7 million – if account is taken of the output lost if the emigrant's work is not carried out by a replacement (Lal, 2009b).

Among the sectors to suffer from their departure is tourism, a multi-occupational industry which, in Fiji, as elsewhere in the region, lacks educated personnel (Sustainable Tourism Development Consortium, 2007: 125–128; Asian Development Bank and Pacific Islands Forum Secretariat, 2008: 12–13; Pacific Islands Forum Secretariat, 2008: 15–16).

Table 14.6: Emigration from Fiji: 1978-2008: Selected tears. Source: Mohanty, 2001: 57; Bureau of Statistics, 2009: 101 and personal communication, 7 September)

	Fijian	Indo-Fijian	Total	% Indo-Fijian	Annual average
1978-1986	1,242 (E)	17,358	20,703	83.8	2,300
1986	178	2,362	2,799	84.4	
1987	351	4,294	5,118	83.9	
1988	263	4,808	5,496	87.5	
1989	249	4,981	5,510	90.4	
1990	307	5,020	5,650	88.8	
1991	280	4,911	5,432	90.4	
1992	248	4,184	4,621	95.6	
1993	268	3,707	4,107	90.3	
1994	252	3,748	4,155	90.2	
1995	285	4,473	4,931	90.7	
1996	319	4,527	5,030	90.0	
1997	324	3,999	4,493	89.0	
1998	362	4,273	4,829	88.5	
1999	418	4,244	4,837	87.7	
1978-1999	3,926 (6.1%)	57,159	64,209	89%	4,939
2000	468	4,568	5,275	86.6	
2001	511	5,550	6,316	87.9	
2002	421	4,831	5,480	88.2	
2003	585	4,964	5,771	86.0	
2004	557 (E)	4,730 (E)	5,500 (E)	86.0 (E)	
2005	545 (E)	4,644 (E)	5,400 (E)	86.0 (E)	
2006	535 (E)	4,558 (E)	5,300 (E)	86.0 (E)	
2007	525 (E)	4,472 (E)	5,200 (E)	86.0 (E)	
2008	522 (E)	4,448 (E)	5,172	86.0 (E)	
1997-2008 (E)	4,343 (9%)	41,977	48,250	87% (E)	5,361

Second, the coups are said to have reinforced the already pervasive racism in Fiji, and increased levels of poverty and social inequality. Naidu (2008), for instance, suggests the pro-indigenous Fijian coups of 1987 and 2000 (which involved considerable hostility to Indo-Fijians) contrast with the ostensibly social inclusive aims of that in 2006, which was supported by a high proportion of Fiji's minorities and opposed by most indigenous Fijians. Echoing Fisk's 'three Fijis' analysis of 1970, Naidu notes the current dominance of foreign-owned corporations in the private sector, a strong Indo-Fijian presence in large and medium-sized companies, and a highly favoured (but relatively small) indigenous Fijian middle class with jobs in the public sector and state-owned companies (2008: 163).

Third, it has been argued that the coups led to increased poverty, crime and prostitution (Naidu, 2008: 168–169; Rolls, 2002: 87–94). Newspaper reports and anecdotal evidence suggest prostitution has increased (e.g. Fiji Sun, 18th October 2008, Fiji Times 14th November 2008, 4th January and 29th June 2009) but there is little evidence of increases in crime (Bureau of Statistics, 2009: 125) or poverty (Narsey, 2008: 115–120). However, Fiji's position relative to some other tourist-reliant economies has deteriorated over the years (Table 14.7). From 1991 to 2007/8, for example, its ranking in UNDP's Human Development Index dropped from 71 to 92, and over that period it was overtaken by Samoa (and the Dominican Republic, Tunisia, Philippines, Ecuador, Jordan, Lebanon, Peru, Libya and China), remaining behind Barbados, Mauritius, Seychelles and Tonga.

Table 14.7: UNDP human development position of selected countries: 1991–2007/08. Source: UNDP, 1991: 119-120 and 2007/08: 229-231

Level of human development			HDI position	
1991	2007/8		1991	2007/08
high	high	Barbados	22	31
high	high	Mauritius	47	65
medium	medium	Jamaica	59	101
medium	high	Seychelles	63	50
medium	medium	Fiji	71	92
medium	medium	Samoa	81	77
medium	medium	Solomon Islands	96	129
n/a	high	Tonga	–	55

Plus ça change, plus c'est la même chose?

Is it the case that the more political change occurs in Fiji, the more things stay the same? After all, the coups have clearly had significant short-term effects, but after two or three years the upward trajectory of Fiji tourism has continued and, compared with other regions, its performance is quite similar. Over the period 1990 to 2007, for example, international arrivals grew by 93%, compared with 106% in Oceania and in 107% in global tourism (Table 14.8).

Fiji's tourism industry is demonstrably resilient and its future, though still shrouded in political uncertainty, may not be bleak. However, as Table 14.8 also shows, tourism growth over the last two decades in Papua New Guinea, Samoa, Tonga and Vanuatu has been more impressive, and Samoa and Vanuatu, especially, have often benefited from Fiji's problems, clearly demonstrating (and aiming for) the substitution effect. Recent figures confirm the trend. From January to April 2009, global tourism suffered an 8% decline because of the financial crisis and fears of the H1N1 pandemic. At the same time, Western Fiji was recovering from severe floods, and arrivals to Fiji (despite massive discounting) decreased by some 20% (and by even more in French Polynesia and the Marshall Islands). However, increased arrivals were recorded in Samoa (10.3%), Solomon Islands (32.4%), Cook Islands (2.5%), Tonga (9.7%) and Vanuatu (19.1%) (southpacific.travel: personal communication 8 September 2009).

Finally, despite all the 'negative publicity' of coups, rumours of coups, and the many holidays cut short by anxious tourists, one aspect of Fiji has remained the same. As virtually every stakeholder in the country's tourism continuously emphasises, Fiji remains a 'safe destination' (Trnka, 2008: 153). The reason is quite simple: tourism in the Fiji Islands is highly concentrated in Viti Levu – on the Coral Coast, in the West and in the N.W. islands of the Mamanucas and Yasawas – all areas far from centres of population. Except for one or two resorts during the 2000 coup, tourists have never been directly affected by domestic unrest. Even Suva, the capital and scene of most political activity, has rarely been off-limits to visitors or, indeed, to local residents, though the latter may experience a continued and palpable sense of unease.

Table 14.8: Tourism in the South Pacific, 1985-2008: selected years. Sources: World Tourism Organisation (1990, 1991, 1995, 2006 and 2008)

Country	1985	1990	1995	2000	2005	2007	% change 1990-2007
Cook Islands	29,000	34,000	49,000	72,994	88,405	97,019	185.4
Fiji	228,000	279,000	336,000	294,070*	549,911	539,255**	93.3
French Polynesia	122,000	140,000	186,000	233,326	208,067	218,241	55.9
Kiribati	3,000	3,000	3,900	4,377	4,137	4,709	57.0
New Caledonia	51,000	87,000	100,000	109,587	100,412	103,363	18.8
Niue	–	3,000	2,500 (est)	2,010	2,793	3,463	15.4
Papua New Guinea	30,000	41,000	42,000	58,429	69,251	104,122	154.0
Samoa	39,000	48,000	68,000	87,688	101,807	122,250	154.7
Solomon Islands	12,000	12,000 (est)	12,000	10,134	12,533	13,748	14.6
Tonga	14,000	21,000	29,000	34,694	41,862	46,040	119.2
Tuvalu	–	1,000	900	1,504	–	–	
Vanuatu	25,000	35,000	44,000	57,591	62,082	81,345	132.4
Oceania (million)		5.2	8.1	9.2	10.5	10.7	105.8
Global tourism (million)	332.7	436.0	536.0	683.0	803.0	903.0	107.1

* Decrease was result of 2000 coups.

** Decrease as result of 2006 coup

Paradoxically, while many citizens are concerned at the impact of domestic unrest on the international image of their country, and the tourist industry uses 'negative publicity' to claim more funds for marketing, in its dealings with successive governments it seems remarkably coy. In public industry-wide discussions, at least, it echoes government claims that it is this same 'negative publicity' that caused reduced tourist arrivals, and all that this entails. Perhaps this is inevitable: were it to do otherwise, it would go against its own marketing programme and jeopardise its marketing budget. However, this diplomatic position is also highly political: to deny tourism has any relationship to politics is, itself, a political stance!

And yet... successful advertising campaigns, along with a general willingness to promote and internalise the tourist image of Fiji, and the physical separation of most tourist areas from population centres, have ensured that, over the long term, such tensions have had little or no impact on the tourist experience of Fiji. Commentators may dispute how many Fijis there are, but we can perhaps add another: the isolated tourist world, that 'slice of heaven on earth' made for 'relaxed adventure,' where smiling Fijians continue to wait on overseas guests anxious to experience the sun, sea and sand attractions of this island Paradise – a Paradise which, for them, at any rate, is not lost but found.

References

Asian Development Bank and Pacific Islands Forum Secretariat (2008) *Skilling the Pacific: Technical and Vocational Education and Training in the Pacific: Executive Summary*, Manila: Asian Development Bank.

Belt, Collins and Associates Ltd (1973) *Tourism Development Programme for Fiji*, Washington: United Nations Development Programme/International Bank for Reconstruction and Development.

Bureau of Statistics (various years) Fiji Tourism and Migration Statistics, Suva: Fiji Islands Bureau of Statistics, from: http://www.statsfiji.gov.fj/Publication/Reports.htm, (11 September 2009).

Bureau of Statistics (2009) *Key Statistics, June 2009*, Suva: Fiji Islands Bureau of Statistics.

Central Planning Office (1970) *Fiji's Sixth Development Plan: 1971–75*, Suva: Ministry of Finance.

Clements, M. A., and Georgiou, A. (1998) 'The impact of political instability on a fragile tourism product', *Tourism Management*, 19 (3), 283–288.

Durutalo, A. (2000) 'Elections and the dilemma of indigenous Fijian political unity', in B.V. Lal (ed.), *Fiji Before the Storm: Elections and the Politics of Development*, Canberra: Asia Pacific Press at the Australian National University, pp. 73–92.

Fisk, E.K. (1970) *The Political Economy of Independent Fiji*, Canberra: Australian National University Press.

Harris, Kerr, Foster and Co. (1965) *Report on a Study of the Travel and Tourist Industry of Fiji*, (Legislative Council of Fiji, Council Paper No. 32) Suva: Government Printer.

Harrison, D. (1997) 'Globalization and tourism: some themes from Fiji', in M. Oppermann (ed.), *Pacific Rim Tourism*, Wallingford: CAB International, pp. 167–183.

Harrison, D. (1998) 'The world comes to Fiji: who communicates what, to whom?' *Tourism, Culture and Communication*, 1, 129–138.

King, B. and Berno, T. (2001) 'Trouble in paradise: managing tourism after the coups in Fiji', Paper presented at the CAUTHE National Research Conference Capitalising on Research, Canberra, February.

Lal, B.V. (ed.) (2000) *Fiji Before the Storm: Elections and the Politics of Development*, Canberra: Asia Pacific Press at the Australian National University.

Lal, B.V. (2008) 'The loss of innocence,' in B.V. Lal, G. Chand and V. Naidu (eds), *1987: Fiji, Twenty Years On*, Lautoka: Fiji Institute of Applied Studies, pp. 1–24.

Lal, B.V. (2009a) 'Anxiety, uncertainty and fear in our land: Fiji's road to military coup, 2006', in J. Fraenkel, S. Firth and B.V. Lal (eds), *The 2006 Military Takeover in Fiji: a Coup to End All Coups?* Canberra: Australian National University Press, pp. 21–41.

Lal, B.V. (2009b) Fiji Islands: From Immigration to Emigration. Migration Information, from: www.migrationinformation.org/Profiles/display.cfm?ID=110 (5 September 2009).

Lawson, S. (1996) *Tradition Versus Democracy in the South Pacific: Fiji, Tonga and Western Samoa*, Cambridge: Cambridge University Press.

Legge, J.D. (1958) *Britain in Fiji: 185-1880*, London: Macmillan.

Mahadevan, R. (2009) 'The rough global tide and political storm in Fiji call for swimming hard and fast but with a different stroke', *Pacific Economic Bulletin*, 24 (2), 1–23.

Mohanty, M. (2001) 'Contemporary emigration from Fiji: some trends and issues in the post-Independence era', in V. Naidu, E. Vasta and C. Hawksley (eds.), *Current trends in South Pacific Migration*, Working Paper No. 7, Asia Pacific Migration Research Network, University of Wollongong: 54–73.

Mohanty, M. (2006) 'Globalisation, new labour migration and development in Fiji', in S. Firth (ed.), *Globalisation and Governance in the Pacific Islands*, Canberra: Australian National University, pp. 107–121.

Naidu, V. (2008) 'Social consequences of coups in Fiji', in B.V. Lal, G. Chand and V. Naidu (eds.), *1987: Fiji, Twenty Years On*, Lautoka: Fiji Institute of Applied Studies, pp.155–172.

Narsey, W. (2008) *The Quantitative Analysis of Poverty in Fiji*, Suva: Fiji Islands Bureau of Statistics and the University of the South Pacific.

NCBBF (National Council for Building a Better Fiji) (2008) *Fiji: The State of the Nation and the Economy Report*. Suva: NCBBF

Norton, R. (1990) *Race and Politics in Fiji*, 2nd edn, St Lucia: University of Queensland Press.

Pacific Islands Forum Secretariat (2008) Forum Communique, Thirty-ninth Pacific Islands Forum, Alofi, Niue, 19–20 August.

Prasad, B.C. (1997) 'Property rights, governance and economic development, in G. Chand and V. Naidu (eds.), *Fiji: Coups, Crises and Reconciliation, 1987–1997*. Suva, Fiji Institute of Applied Studies, pp. 7–31.

Prasad, B.C. and Tisdell, C. (2006) *Institutions, Economic Performance and Sustainable Development: A Case Study of the Fijian Islands*. New York: Nova Science Publishers.

Qarase, L. (2009) 'From fear and turmoil to the possibilities of hope and renewal once again', in J. Fraenkel, S. Firth and B.V. Lal (eds.), *The 2006 Military Takeover in Fiji: a Coup to End all Coups?* Canberra, Australian National University Press, pp. 353–373.

Ram, S and Singh, J. (2003) 'Multiplier effects of the sugar and tourism industries in Fiji', Economics Department Working Paper 2003–2005, Suva: Reserve Bank of Fiji.

Reddy, S. (2009) 'National economic update and path to sustainable tourism growth', Presentation to Fiji Tourism Forum, Inter-Continental Hotel, 14 August.

Richter, L.K., and Waugh, W.L. (1986) 'Terrorism and tourism as logical companions', *Tourism Management*, 7 (4), 230–238.

Robertson, R.T. (2008) 'Coups and development', in B.V. Lal, G. Chand and V. Naidu, (eds), *1987: Fiji Twenty Years On*, Lautoka: Fiji Institute of Applied Studies, pp. 25–38.

Rolls, L.M. (2002) 'Civil conflict and development: a case study approach to evaluating the economic and social costs of the 2000 civil conflict to Fiji's garment industry and society', Unpublished MA thesis, Suva: University of the South Pacific.

Sofield, T. (2003) *Empowerment for Sustainable Tourism Development*, Oxford : Elsevier Science Ltd.

Sonmez, S. (1998) 'Tourism, terrorism and political instability', *Annals of Tourism Research*, **25** (2), 416–456.

Sonmez, S., Apostolopoulos, Y. and Tarlow, P. (1999) 'Tourism in crisis: managing the effects of terrorism', *Journal of Travel Research*, **38** (1), 13–18.

Sustainable Tourism Development Consortium (2007) *Fiji Tourism Development Plan: 2007-2016*, Suva: Department of Tourism.

Tourism Fiji (2009) Tourism Fiji's Marketing Budget 1993-2008, personal communication, 8 September 2009.

Trnka, S. (2008) 'Tourism or terrorism?' in B.V. Lal, G. Chand and V. Naidu, (eds.), *1987: Fiji, Twenty Years On*, Lautoka: Fiji Institute of Applied Studies, pp. 143–172.

UNDP (United Nations Development Programme) (1991) *Human Development Report 1991*, New York: Oxford.

UNDP (United Nations Development Programme) (2007) *Human Development Report, 2007/8*. Houndmills, Basingstoke: Palgrave Macmillan.

World Tourism Organisation (WTO) (1990) *Compendium of Tourism Statistics: 1985–1989*, Madrid: WTO

World Tourism Organisation (WTO) (1991) *Current Trends and Tourism Indicators*, Madrid: WTO

World Tourism Organisation (WTO) (1995) *Compendium of Tourism Statistics: 1989–1993*, Madrid: WTO.

World Tourism Organisation (WTO) (2006) *World Overview and Tourism Topics, 2005*, Madrid: WTO.

World Tourism Organisation (WTO) (2008) *Tourism Highlights: 2008 Edition*. Madrid: WTO.

15 Iran or Persia: What's in a Name? The Decline and Fall of a Tourism Industry

Tom G. Baum and Kevin D. O'Gorman

Introduction

Iran is a combination of Persia and Islam, it is a complicated, often confused, if not diametrically opposed mix of two ideologies, but also, from a tourism perspective, unrivalled in the cultural attributes that it can offer to the more intrepid traveller. Historically, modern Iran has its roots in ancient Persia and therefore it is unsurprising that the contemporary nation attempts to trace its cultural heritage back for at least 5,000 years. Hegel considered the ancient Persians to be the first historic people:

> In Persia first arises that light which shines itself and illuminates what is around...The principle of development begins with the history of Persia; this constitutes therefore the beginning of history .
>
> (Hegel, 1857: 147)

However, Hegel's historicism is questionable on two grounds. First, that Persia was identifiable. As Garthwaite has commented,

> 'Persia' is not easily located with any geographic specificity, nor can its people, the Persians, be easily categorized. In the end Persia and the Persians are as much metaphysical notions as a place or a people .
>
> (Garthwaite, 2007: 1)

Indeed, despite the long antecedence of civilisation in the area, until the late sixth century BC, there are no known historical materials that are written by Persians identifying themselves as Persian. Second, Hegel's historicism is questionable because modern Iran is not one people in terms of customs, but a multinational and multicultural Asian state, comprising groups that on the one hand are Iranian in an ethno-linguistic sense (Persian – Tajik, Kurdish, Balochi), and on the other, of other people who are not, notably Turkish (Azerbaijani, Turkmen, Qashqai) or Arabic. As Curatola and Scarcia (2004: 11) have commented, 'Numerous ethnic groups now inhabit Iran, within the framework of a morphologically unequal territory, in an original, somewhat culturally cohesive mosaic'. The contribution of Persian culture has been fundamental for the development of Iranian civilisation, but it has also had an impact far wider than the area inhabited by ethnic Iranians or the present political boundaries of Iran. The mosaic of contemporary Iran has also felt the impact of conflicts in neighbouring states with the consequence that, over the past 20 years, the country has hosted the largest refugee population in the world, primarily rooted in the influx of over 2.6 million Afghans following the Soviet invasion of Afghanistan in 1979, and 1.2 million Iraqis who left Iraq during the 1980–88 Iran-Iraq War and the 1990–91 Gulf War. The impact of these incomers, both temporary and long-term, has been felt in economic and also cultural terms.

Iran became the officially universal title for the country in 1935 when the Shah decreed that it was to be used in all international correspondence and official documents. In the English-speaking West, Iran had been traditionally known as Persia. Indeed, the name Persia commonly conjures up quite different images to the name Iran. Under the last Shah, Mohammad Reza Pahlavi, Iran was seen as the playground of the European rich, famed for a liberal ideology, an excellent climate and wonderful natural resources (Pahlavi, 1980). Travel and tourism to Iran is not just a 20th century concept, there are early 17th Century accounts of intrepid travellers. Sir Anthony Sherley, for example, was received by the Shah, Abbas the Great, who made him a Mirza, or prince, and granted certain trading and other rights to all Christian merchants (Sherley, 1613). John Cartwright recorded details about the buildings of Esfahan and Persepolis and wrote extensively about the nature of the Persian peoples (Cartwright, 1611). By the 19th century, Iran was still seen as an exotic destination for the adventurer and explorer, as the *Journal of the Royal Geographical Society* attests. There are a number of papers presenting travellers accounts including: Biddulph (1891); Gibbons (1841); Goldsmid (1890).

Iran is incredibly rich in cultural and heritage resources and has in total eight listed World Heritage sites, and an additional 49 on the UNESCO tentative list (UNESCO, 2009). Of the eight listed sites, four are ancient historical sites: Bisotun, Pasargadae, Persepolis and Tchogha Zanbil (Table 15.1). The other listed sites are either historical towns or religious sites. The profile of the tentative list is very different. Of the 49 sites, 15 are historic towns, nine are historical landscapes and eight are natural landscapes. In addition, built heritage is further emphasised with six religious sites, one historical village, one garden, two bazaars and two military sites. Only four of the 49 are ancient historical sites and one is a prehistoric site. The emphasis of the tentative list is clearly towards more recent historical sites than the existing World Heritage list for Iran. There is a clear emphasis on the Islamic Period in the tentative list, with great attention to the cultural evolution of Iran as an artisan production and trading nation. Such sites include Yazd, the Ghaznavi-Seljukian Axis, Uramanat, Masouleh and Siraf.

This inventory reflects both ancient and more modern facets of Iran's cultural heritage but provides the basis for cultural tourism visitation experiences that, potentially, can be set alongside 'leading brand' destinations such as Egypt, Greece, India, Italy and Turkey in terms of both their historical importance and their visual splendour. That modern Iran does not enjoy such status in tourism terms is the consequence of a number of factors but none stands out as strongly as the political consequences of the country's recent history, a theme which forms the backbone of our discussions in this chapter.

The remainder of this chapter is in three sections based on key historical and political phases in the evolution of modern Iran: the Shahanshah and the Ayatollah, President Khatami and the Dialogue of Civilisations, and President Ahmadinejad and the rise of the neo-conservatives. Our purpose is demonstrate the relationship between the dramatically changing political tableaux of the country over the past 40 years, the challenges faced by a country at conflict within itself and with its neighbours and the development of a tourism destination on the basis of, primarily, natural and cultural resources.

Table 15.1: Iranian monuments inscribed on the World Heritage List.

Name	Inscription date	Date (approx)	Description
Bam and its cultural landscape	2004	7th – 11th century	Medieval Mud Town – Built at crossroads of important trade routes and known for the production of silk and cotton
Bisotun	2006	521 BC	Archaeological site with bas-relief and cuneiform inscription – Located along the ancient trade route linking the Iranian high plateau with Mesopotamia
Meidan Emam, Esfahan	1979	17th century	Isfahan's famous square built during Shah Abbas Safavid (I) – bordered on all sides by monumental buildings
Pasargadae	2004	6th century BC	The first dynastic capital of the Achaemenid Empire founded by Cyrus (II) the Great. Also known as the capital of the first great multicultural empire in Western Asia – located in Pars – homeland of Persians
Persepolis	1979	518 BC	Founded by Darius (I). It was the capital of the Achaemenid Empire inspired by Mesopotamian models
Soltaniyeh	2005	1302-12	The mausoleum of Oljaytu which was constructed in 1302–12 in the city of Soltaniyeh situated in the province of Zanjan
Takht-e Soleyman	2003	6th and 7th and 13th century	The site includes the principal Zoroastrian sanctuary partly rebuilt in the Ilkhanid (Mongol) period as well as a temple of the Sasanid period dedicated to Anahita. Located in northwest of Iran in a valley set in a volcanic mountain region
Tchogha Zanbil	1979	1250 BC	Ruins of the holy city of the Kingdom of Elam

The Shahanshah and the Ayatollah

In order to understand the shape of tourism in contemporary Iran, it is necessary to review the recent political history of the country and reflect upon how this history has shaped attitudes to modern tourism as well as the development of the sector alongside other economic priorities in the country. In 1925, General Reza Khan led a revolt and became the Shahanshah (king of kings), founding the country's final dynasty. The title Shahanshah evoked the ancient mystique of monarchy, the paramount ruler who had subdued other kings. The Pahlavi family created the bases of the modern-day Iranian nation-state, through nationalism, centralisation and modernisation (Savory, 1992; Garthwaite 2007). In turn, the Islamic Revolution led by Ayatollah Khomeini forced the last Shah into exile in January 1979 (Homan, 1980) and the foundation of the contemporary Islamic Republic was speedily laid. Initially, the popular Revolution was more about economic rights and workers' democracy than it was about an Islamic revolution in terms of its values (Malm and Esmailian, 2007), but within two years of the revolution, theocratic values and behaviour were enforced on Iranians and visiting foreigners alike. Common interests found in opposing the Pahlavis collapsed once the last Shah was forced to leave Iran, and competing interest groups once again asserted their power against each other. As Savory (1992, 256) notes in relation to the outcome:

> One of the most striking features of the [Khomeini] regime has been its policy of attempting to destroy the distinctive Iranian culture ...and to replace its symbols by Islamic ones. The monarchy has been replaced by the mosque as the cultural symbol of Iran.

The 1979 Revolution was a revolution of values. The replacement is reflected in how non-Islamic heritage has been regarded since the Revolution, in turn impacting on present day tourism development.

Tourism, heritage and politics became entwined in the Revolutionary process. In 1971 the last Shah invited emissaries from about 70 countries to celebrate 2500 years of the monarchy and symbolically staged this extravaganza beside the ancient ruins of Persepolis. According to contemporary reports, the guests watched 6000 costumed marchers representing ten dynasties of Persian history pass in review, in a spectacular tent city that hosted kings, sheikhs and sultans and was billed as the greatest cultural gathering in history. The party provoked a backlash from the Shah's political opponents that eventually swelled into the movement that shaped the revolution. Less than a decade later the Islamic revolution lead by Ayatollah Khomeini forced the Shah into exile on 16 January 1979 (Homan, 1980). During the revolution, leading clerics called for the destruction of the tomb of Cyrus the Great and remains of Persepolis (Sciolino, 2000) and according to Molavi (2005, 14) a local Ayatollah came to Persepolis with 'a band of thugs' and gave an angry speech demanding that 'the faithful torch the silk-lined tent city and the grandstand that the Shah had built' but was driven off by stone-throwing local residents. However, the 65-hectare (160-acre) site, which featured 51 luxurious air-conditioned tents organised in the shape of a star, fell into ruin after the revolution.

The pre-revolutionary regime invested in more than this one event in the development of tourism in Iran. Politically, the regime created an environment within which visitors, particularly from the West, were welcomed to facilities with a level of comfort that was on par with the best in their home countries. Although Iran was recognised as a country with a predominantly Islamic ethos, from the international visitors' perspective, this was benign Islam, tolerant and welcoming to outsiders, providing they were willing to observe appropriate respect for local culture and beliefs. Investment in tourism infrastructure was in line with the high-end tourism destination image that the Shah's regime sought to cultivate. Thus, hotel investment was supported by management contracts with major international brands such as Hilton, Hyatt, Intercontinental and Sheraton and the aspirations of the national airline, Iran Air, were significantly greater than those of airlines from comparable developing economies in the region and elsewhere. In 1965, Iran Air took delivery of its first jet aircraft, the Boeing 727-100, followed by the Boeing 737-200 in 1971, the stretched Boeing 727-200 in 1974 and three variants of Boeing 747s (747-100, -200 and SP), starting in 1975. By the mid-1970s, Iran Air was serving a wide range of cities in Europe and there were over 30 flights per week to London alone. The pinnacle of this aspiration was announced in 1972.

A 'preliminary purchase agreement' was signed in Teheran last week between Iran Air and BAC for two Concordes, with 'an intention to purchase a third', which is being retained on option at present. The first Iran Air Concorde is scheduled to be delivered by the end of 1976 and the second by early 1977. The third, now on option, is earmarked for delivery in 1978. General Khademi says his airline is anticipating operation on Far East routes as well as some to the western hemisphere.

(Flight International, 1972, 482)

By the late 1970s, Iran Air was the fastest growing airline in the world and one of the most profitable. By 1976, it was ranked second only to Qantas, as the world's safest airline, having been accident-free for at least ten consecutive years.

The impact of the Islamic revolution was immediate and dramatic for Iran Air as it was throughout the fledgling tourism sector. In the wake of the revolution in 1979, Iran Air began to reorganise its international operations, discontinuing service to a range of foreign destinations. Tehran was designated as the only official gateway to Iran, with Shiraz as an alternate, only in case of operational requirements. All other cities in Iran lost their international status. Concorde orders were cancelled in April 1980, ironically making Iran Air the last airline to cancel such orders.

With the revolution, there was the nationalisation of all foreign assets, seizure of all the wealth of the Shah's court including cinemas, factories and real estate in New York. These assets subsequently formed part of the Bonyad-e Mostazafan va Janbazan, originally called Bonyad-e Mostazafan (foundation for the oppressed), referring to those oppressed by the Shah. In 1989 Janbazan (those who sacrifice themselves) was added to the title referring to the martyrs of the Iran/Iraq war. In popular parlance is it still known as Bonyad-e Mostazafan or more commonly just Bonyad (the foundation). It is a religious foundation, under the direct control of the Supreme Leader, set up in the aftermath of the revolution. By 1989 it was the biggest holding company in the Middle East (Ehteshami, 1995). It consists of six different organisations each holding several related groups of companies as subsidiaries: Civil Development and Housing; Recreation and Tourism; Industries and Mines, Agriculture, and Transportation; and Commerce. The affiliated organisations managed about 400 companies and factories (Parsa, 1989). Within Iran, it was active in the major industrial and business sectors: food and beverage, chemicals, cellulose items, metals, petrochemicals, construction materials, dams, towers, civil development, farming, horticulture, tourism, transportation, five-star hotels, commercial services, financing, joint ventures, etc (Abrahamian, 1991). The workforce of Bonyad is estimated at 700,000 employees and their annual turnover seems to range from 2% to 10% of GDP (Maloney, 2000).

As part of the newly formed Bonyad's Recreation and Tourism organisation all the international hotel companies were taken over. In Tehran the Grand Hyatt became the Azadi (freedom), The Royal Tehran Hilton the Esteghlal (independence) and the Intercontinental the Laleh (tulip), in reference to the mythical red flower that grows in the blood of the Shia martyrs. One property, the Sheraton, was allocated to a hotel chain operated by Iran Air and re-branded as the Homa. Kentucky Fried Chicken was rebranded 'Our Fried Chicken,' Pepsi was 'Zam-Zam'. The Bonyad controlled the soft-drinks market, very lucrative in a dry country, without rivals. Maloney (2000, p. 159) notes that in 1993 when Coca-Cola, through franchisers, attempted to break into the market, the head of the Bonyad stated 'God willing we will soon drive all foreign Coca-Cola plants out of Iran'; and, indeed, the Foundation for the Oppressed exiled Coca-Cola from their land!

Immediately after the revolution the number of international tourists fell from 680,000 in 1978 to a low of 9300 in 1990 (ITTO, 2001). The Iran-Iraq War lasted from September 1980 until August 1988 and included religious schisms, border disputes, and political differences; conflicts included centuries-old religious and ethnic disputes, and personal animosity between Saddam Hussein and Ayatollah Khomeini. Primarily Iraq launched the war in an effort to consolidate its rising power in the Arab world and to replace Iran as the dominant Gulf state. At the end of the War the Bonyad was responsible for the decommissioned military personal, a considerable number of whom were found work in its hotels and resorts.

President Khatami and the dialogue of civilisations

In May 1997 Hojjatoleslam Muhammad Khatami won an overwhelming victory against all odds and expectations and began a reformist movement. President Khatami una-shamedly championed reform of the governing system in Iran, proposed comprehensive changes to the country's civil–state relations, and sought to make the Islamic system more in tune with the aspirations of the people (Ehteshami and Zweiri, 2007). Shortly after his election, in 1998, Khatami addressed the United Nations General Assembly in New York to delineate his idea for a 'Dialogue of Civilisations' (Khatami, 2001), probably as a challenge to Samuel Huntington's 'Clash of Civilisations' (Huntington, 1998). His dialogue of civilisations had several goals: laying the ground for peaceful, constructive debate among nations; providing a context in which civilisations can learn from each other; replacing fear, blame, and prejudice with reason, fairness, and toler-ance; and facilitating a dynamic exchange of experiences among culture, religions, and civilisations aimed at reform and amelioration.

As part of this dialogue there was a clear plan to increase and enhance hospitality and tourism through a groundbreaking agreement between Iran's main hotel and tourism training centre, INSTROCT (part of the Bonyad), and the University of Strathclyde. This was the first international educational collaboration between Iran and a western country since the Islamic revolution in 1979. The Strathclyde programme (as it was known) evolved out of a series of short courses, which commenced in 1996, into the delivery of the University's undergraduate degree in Hotel and Hospitality Management on site in Tehran. This initiative owned much to the vision and foresight of the tourism leadership within Bonyad who recognised the management skills deficiencies within their hotels and the wider tourism sector.

In 1999, it was estimated that Iran's international and domestic transportation system and related tourist facilities and services handled the requirements of 1.3 million inter-national visitors and 32.5 million domestic tourists. International tourism generated estimated receipts of US$773 million (ITTO, 2001). By 2004, the numbers of inbound international visitors had grown to over 1.6 million (UNWTO, 2006). The trend points to significant growth in international visitors from a low point in the aftermath of the war between Iran and Iraq (ITTO, 2001). Many of these tourists were expatriate Iranians returning home to Iran for holidays or business tourists. Separate figures for cultural heritage tourists are unavailable. Subject to the wider geo-political context, growth in cultural heritage tourism can be expected to continue. The current ICHHTO Tourism Development Master Plan targets for training places in tourism demonstrate a commitment to growth in tourism provision to match this expected growth in demand. For 2010 these targets are projected at 236,780 places; for 2026, at 1,569,769 places. In 2010 just under six out of ten (58.1%) are targeted for handicrafts, but by 2026 this proportion is to fall slightly to 50.3%. Demonstrating a commitment to enhancing strategic skills, university places are to increase more rapidly than vocational training in all three sub-sectors, handicrafts, tourism and cultural heritage.

Khatami's government also made encouraging moves to welcome foreign tourists, including creating a major programme to encourage international visitors to watch the solar eclipse in Iran in 1999. However isolated incidents led to western headlines: 'Tourists kidnapped in Iran'. 'Three Spaniards and one Italian were abducted by an armed gang' and 'Official inquiry into Iran eclipse harassment'. Foreign tourists visiting to view the eclipse, particularly women, were subjected to hostile slogans and harassment by Islamic hardliners (BBC, 1999). The George Bush 'axis-of-evil' speech in 2002 led to a BBC feature on 'my holidays in the axis-of-evil' (BBC, 2003) where a journalist ventured into the six countries mentioned, with the intent of showing the non-threatening character of day-to-day life in these areas. While this seemed to be the case in five of the countries (Iraq, North Korea, Cuba, Syria and Libya), in Iran the journalist was 'detained and intimidated' as the cameras, tapes and tourist visa were viewed as the instruments of spies. This type of behaviour towards visitors by Iranian authorities quickly undermined the work done by official tourism organisations.

President Mahmoud Ahmadinejad and the rise of the neo-conservatives

In August 2005 Mahmoud Ahmadinejad was elected president, President Muhammad Khatami having served the maximum two consecutive terms in office. While Khatami and the reformists were trying to bring back concepts such as Islamic democracy, political rights of the nation and building a civil society based on Islamic roles, Ahmadinejad and the neo-conservatives are more focused on and interested in the battle of populist ideals. In addition, the audiences are also different. Khatami's followers were intellectuals, academics: moderates. Ahmadinejad's followers are more religious, traditional and idealistic in terms of the Islamic Revolution.

As O'Gorman *et al.* (2007) observe, the growing recognition of, first, the links between tourism and the protection of Iran's national cultural heritage and, second, of the potential importance of tourism, was reinforced with the election of Ahmadinejad in 2005. The Iran Touring and Tourism Organisation (ITTO) was merged with the Iran Cultural Heritage Organisation (ICHO) to form the Iran Cultural Heritage and Tourism Organisation (ICHTO). This combined institution is under the strong influence of the central government, with direct authority for the new organisation resting with the Vice

President of the Islamic Republic. Formerly, these institutions were separate departments of the Ministry of Culture, and lacked prominence and influence. Subsequently, handicrafts were added to the new organisation, having been removed from the Industry Ministry, which further emphasises the links between tourism and cultural heritage. The expanded organization is called the Iran Cultural Heritage, Handicrafts and Tourism Organisation (ICHHTO).

The latest examples of ideology coming before the development of tourism from non-Islamic markets are focused on President Mahmoud Ahmadinejad, and the representation in the West of the anti-Zionism of Iran, its nuclear programme and its public executions. In 2006, the President made his infamous remarks on the Holocaust and subsequently hosted an international conference questioning the historicity of the Holocaust (BBC, 2006). Iran is commonly in the forefront of calling for the elimination of Israel and is presented in the West as seeking to destabilise the Middle East. The United Nations' Security Council has imposed successive trade sanctions on Iran over its refusal to halt uranium enrichment, fearing that Iran is seeking to become a nuclear military power. Iran, in contrast, insists that it has the right to enrichment to make nuclear fuel to meet the country's energy needs and that it is not intent on developing nuclear weapons. At the date of writing, the International Atomic Energy Agency has found no evidence to support a charge of nuclear military ambitions on the part of Iran, but the controversy continues. Associating the UN with the USA, it is not uncommon to hear Iranians privately express their fear that the USA will attack their country with nuclear weapons to eliminate what it perceives as an Iranian nuclear threat.

Capital punishment, particularly public hangings and stonings, provides a further dimension of controversy negatively affecting tourism markets. Murder, rape, drug trafficking, armed robbery, extreme corruption, adultery and homosexuality are punishable in Iran by the death penalty. Public executions have generally been for crimes that have provoked public outrage, and are sometimes televised network wide through Iran. In 2008 the chief of the Iranian judiciary, Ayatollah Mahmoud Hashemi Shahroudi, attempted to substantially reduce the number of public executions, which had risen to around 300 in 2007 (Tait, 2007). He has sought to require all public executions to be approved by himself, and that those sentenced to death are usually to be killed in private. Images of homosexuals being publicly hanged from cranes have added to Iran's negative image in the West, and limited its development of tourism from these markets.

Today, Iran is a country where many Western governments seek to guide the travel intentions of their nationals. For example, the British Foreign and Commonwealth Office issues clear travel warnings for visitors to Iran. They strongly advise against all travel to within 100km of the entire Iran/Afghanistan border or to within 10km of the entire Iran/Iraq border, and advise that the Pakistan border area is also insecure (FCO, 2009). They further advise against any travel east of the line running from Kerman to Bandar Abbas, which includes all travel to the World Heritage site of Bam (Table 15.1). Dangers listed for visitors to these areas include banditry, drug-traffickers, violent attacks and kidnapping. Even in the cities that are 'safe' there is the stern warning that Iran has one of the highest rates of road accidents in the world, due to dilapidated vehicles and/ or reckless driving, and tourists are warned to exercise great care when crossing streets (FCO, 2009).

Reflections

In terms of a staged model of tourism growth Iran is in the first stage of international cultural and heritage tourism development, despite the long antecedence of business tourism within the country and domestic tourism for relaxation. Moreover, Iran provides an interesting challenge to the application of Butler's (1980) tourism area life cycle in terms of how radical political change may interrupt expected progression within the lifecycle. Prior to the Islamic revolution, it is fair to assess that Iran's tourism development equated to the late involvement or early development stage within Butler's model, having moved beyond the exploration and early involvement stages as a result of significant public sector engagement and political will. Such progression ended dramatically in 1979 as a result of the revolution and subsequent political ambivalence to tourism combined with the effects of the Iran – Iraq war has meant that there has been an enforced stagnation of development at an exploration level. Notwithstanding the political will in some quarters, there is little evidence of real progress into the development phase.

The future of tourism in Iran depends on the tenor of the government, whether it be Islamic traditionalist or Islamic liberalist. In Iran religion and politics are inescapably intertwined and inseparable, with the priority of religion over politics. This is highlighted in the changing emphasis of the UNESCO list where cultural heritage is being reshaped according to current religious and political ideology. President Jimmy Carter, during a State dinner in Tehran in late December 1977, described Iran 'an island of stability in one of the more troubled areas of the world'; this serves as a salient warning to those tempted to make predictions about the future of Iran. Anti-Israeli rhetoric, Holocaust denial, uncertain nuclear aims and ambitions, pollution, traffic, false imprisonment, hangings and stoning all serve to undermine the attractiveness of Iran as a destination and have their origins in the political and religious changes that have taken place in Iran in recent times.

References

Abrahamian, E. (1991) Khomeini: fundamentalist or populist? *New Left Review*, **186**(1), 102–119.

BBC (1999) World: Middle East - Tourists Kidnapped in Iran, from: http://news.bbc.co.uk/1/hi/world/middle_east/420953.stm (25 May 2009).

BBC (2003) My Holidays in the Axis of Evil, from: http://news.bbc.co.uk/1/hi/uk/2705627.stm (25 May 2009).

BBC (2006) Iran defends Holocaust conference, from: http://news.bbc.co.uk/1/hi/world/middle_east/6167695.stm (25 May 2009).

Biddulph, C.E. (1891) 'Journey across the Western portion of the Great Persian Desert, viâ the Siah Kuh Mountains and the Darya-i-Namak', *Proceedings of the Royal Geographical Society and Monthly Record of Geography*, **13** (11), 645–657.

Cartwright, J. (1611) *The preachers trauels: Wherein is set downe a true iournall to the confines of the East Indies, through the great countreyes of Syria, Mesopotamia, Armenia, Media, Hircania and Parthia. With the authors returne by the way of Persia, Susiana, Assiria, Chaldæa, and Arabia. Containing a full suruew of the kingdom of Persia: and in what termes the Persian stands with the Great Turke at this day*, London: Printed by William Stansby for Thomas Thorppe.

Curatola, G., and Scarcia, G. (2004) *The Art and Architecture of Persia*, New York: Abbeville.

Ehteshami, A. (1995) *After Khomeini: The Iranian Second Republic*. London: Routledge.

Ehteshami, A., and Zweiri, M. (2007) *Iran and The Rise of its Neoconservatives: The politics of Tehran's silent revolution*. London: IB Tauris.

FCO (2009) The Foreign and Commonwealth Office's Travel Advice Notices: Iran, http://www.fco.gov.uk/en/travelling-and-living-overseas/travel-advice-by-country/middle-east-north-africa/iran (25 May 2009).

Flight International (1972) 'Iran Air Buys Concord' (12th October 1972) p 482–483 Available from http://www.flightglobal.com/pdfarchive/view/1972/1972%20-%202699.html (accessed 15 March 2010).

Garthwaite, G.R. (2007) *The Persians*. Malden, MA: Blackwell.

Gibbons, R. (1841) 'Routes in Kirman, Jebal, and Khorasan, in the years 1831 and 1832', *Journal of the Royal Geographical Society of London*, **11**, 136–156.

Goldsmid, F. (1890) 'Lieutenant H. B. Vaughan's recent journey in Eastern Persia', *Proceedings of the Royal Geographical Society and Monthly Record of Geography*, **12** (10), 577–595.

Hegel, G. W. F. (1857) *Lectures on the Philosophy of History* (Translated from 3rd German Edition by J. Sibree), London: Henry G. Bohn.

Homan, R. (1980) 'The origins of the Iranian revolution', *International Affairs*, **56** (4), 673–677.

Huntington, S. (1998) *The Clash of Civilisations and the Remaking of World Order*, London: Touchstone.

ITTO (Iran Touring and Tourism Organisation) (2001) *Master Plan for Tourism in Iran*, Tehran: Ministry of Culture and Islamic Guidance.

Khatami, M. (2001) *Goftogu-ye Tamaddon-ha [Dialogue of Civilisations]*, Tehran: Tarh-e No Publications.

Malm, A., and Esmailian, S. (2007) *Iran On the Brink*, London: Pluto.

Maloney, S. (2000) 'Agents or obstacles? Parastatal foundations and challenges for Iranian development', in P. Alizadeh and M. Karshenas (eds), *The Economy of Iran: Dilemmas of an Islamic state*, 145-203, London: IB Tauris and Co Ltd.

Molavi, A. (2005) *Soul of Iran: A Nation's Struggle for Freedom*. New York: Norton.

O'Gorman, K., Baum, T.G., and McLellan, L.R. (2007) Tourism in Iran: central control and indigeneity, in T. Hinch and R. Butler (eds), *Tourism and Indigenous Peoples: Issues and Implications*, London: Butterworth-Heinemann.

Pahlavi, M.R. (1980) *Answer to History*, New York: Stein and Day.

Parsa, M. (1989) *Social Origins of the Iranian Revolution*, London: Rutgers University Press.

Savory, R. M. (1992). 'Land of the lion and the Sun'. In B. Lewis (Ed.), *The World of Islam*. (pp. 245-272). London: Thames & Hudson.

Sciolino, E. (2000) *Persian Mirrors*. New York: Touchstone.

Sherley, A. (1613) *Sir Antony Sherley his Relation of his Travels into Persia: The dangers, and distresses, which befell him in his passage, both by sea and land, and his strange and unexpected deliuerances*, London: Printed by Nicholas Okes for Nathaniell Butter, and Ioseph Bagfet.

Tait, R. (2007) Tehran's standoff with west sees tourists snub Persian treasures. *The Guardian*, 12 March, from: http://www.guardian.co.uk/travel/2007/apr/12/travelnews.iran.iran (24 February 2009).

UNESCO (2009) Properties inscribed on the World Heritage List: Iran, from: http://whc.unesco.org/en/statesparties/ir (25 May 2009).

UNWTO (United Nations World Tourism Organisation) (2006) *Compendium of Tourism Statistics*, Madrid: World Tourism Organisation.

Part V
Changes
in Political
Relations

16 Does Tourism have a Role in Promoting Peace on the Korean Peninsula?

Bruce Prideaux, Jillian Prideaux and Seongseop Kim

Introduction

In recent decades the potential for global war has eased as Cold War rivalries have evaporated and been replaced by commercial and political competition. As political tensions have eased, domestic freedoms have increased to the point where citizens of the Russian Federation are free to travel abroad and in China an increasing number of citizens have access to independent overseas travel. A number of tourism researchers contend that tourism has been a major contributor to the development of peace, however, in the international relations literature the accepted view is that tourism has been one of the beneficiaries of peace, with development of bilateral tourism flows following, rather than preceding, the warming of relations between former protagonists (Bell and Kurtzer 2009; Calder 2006).

This chapter focuses on the Korean peninsula. After reviewing the arguments made for and against the view that tourism has contributed to the development of peaceful relations, the chapter examines the situation with particular emphasis on the regional geopolitical situation in the first decade of the 21st century. The chapter argues that in the political manoeuvrings between the Democratic People's Republic of Korea (North Korea) and the Republic of Korea (South Korea) tourism has been used as a policy instrument in a wider political context that both states view as critical to the their future survival. In the South, tourism has been used as a component of policy objectives aimed at winning support amongst domestic constituents, while in the North it has been used to collect foreign currency and achieve specific international policy goals. The chapter concludes that when peace does eventually occur, tourism has the potential to become an important instrument for nation building in a future united Korea.

A review of the literature on the role of tourism as a vehicle to promote peace between divided and warring nations reveals considerable agreement that tourism does promote peace while acknowledging that there are some circumstances where there are difficulties in this process. Authors including Butler and Mao (1995), Kim and Crompton (1990), Waterman (1987), Yu (1997) and Zhang (1993) have supported the view that tourism has some ability to reduce tensions between partitioned nations. Kim and Crompton (1990) for example introduced the concept of two-track diplomacy (discussed later in this chapter) while Yu (1997) built on previous contributions in the political science literature (Spero 1981; Zhan 1993) and suggested the concept of high politics activity (government-to-government) and low politics activity (person-to-person). A large number of researchers have promoted the view that tourism is able to exert a positive influence by reducing suspicion and tension (Hall 1984; Hobson and Ko 1994; D'Amore 1988, 1989; Jafari 1989; Matthews and Richter 1991; Richter 1989, 1994; Var, Brayley and Korsay 1989; Matthews 1978; Var, Schluter, Ankomah and Lee 1989; Kim, Prideaux and Prideaux 2007). A smaller number of researchers have raised concerns that the connection between tourism and peace is not supported by research (Anastasopoulous 1992; Litvin 1998; Milman *et al.*1990; Pizam *et al.* 1991). Few tourism researchers have taken the view suggested by Litvin (1998) that tourism is not a generator of peace but is instead the beneficiary of peace.

The international relations literature paints a different picture of the role of tourism as an agent for promoting peace. In general, tourism is not seen to play a major role in relations between the two Koreas, and where mentioned is generally examined as a product of the Sunshine policy (see below), rather than a factor for peace in its own right. A major factor in the relative silence about the role of tourism in the international relations literature stems from the perception that relations between the two Koreas are subordinate to global and regional security issues (although this has changed somewhat since the end of the Cold War). The following discussion examines the current situation on the Korean Peninsula from a broad national and geopolitical perspective and then seeks to identify where tourism is able to participate as a positive change agent to create peaceful relations between the North and South.

Background to current state of tension

The Korean War and the ensuing political divide between the North and South have been outlined in previous publications on this topic and need not be retold in depth in this chapter (Kim and Prideaux 2003). However it is important to understand the current political situation on the Korean peninsula for it is this situation that has created the current level of tension between the North and South and defines the opportunities that tourism has for promoting reconciliation and assisting in future moves to unification.

Since its unsuccessful attempt to forcibly reunite the Korean nation during the Korean War (1950–53) the North has continued to press for reunification on its own terms, and both the North and South have remained bitter enemies separated by the heavily fortified Demilitarized Zone (DMZ). Both states spend considerable resources on military preparedness and following a period of relative calm, tensions have again escalated following the North's announcement that it has nuclear weapons capability. Formal diplomatic relations between the North and South have not been established although the United Nations has mediated talks at the Panmunjeom Joint Security Area in the DMZ. Informal bilateral discussions did take place at Mt Gumgang, a South Korean-operated tourism resort in North Korea and in the Kaesong industrial zone.

The current state of North–South relations is a direct result of the ideological views that each of the divided states has of its role in the world, how it views the other and how it has chosen to organise domestic politics and its economy. The South has adopted the capitalist approach to economic organisation, has embraced democracy as the preferred method for political organisation. The nation can now be classed as a first world nation with an annual GDP of US$27,649 (the North's GDP is estimated to be US$1700 per person) (CIA World fact Book, accessed 20 June 2009). Citizens are not restricted in their ability to travel domestically or internationally and through the tightly controlled Mt Gumgang enclave have been able to travel into North Korea, although without the opportunity to mingle with Northerners. South Korea continues to maintain a strong military force specifically organised to repulse an attack from the North, while across the DMZ the North maintains an equally large military presence to protect it from a Southern invasion and to supposedly allow it to mount an invasion of the South if necessary.

The North has adopted a different approach to political and economic organisation than the South and can be described as a single-party state lead by the Korean Workers' Party. While nominally described as a socialist republic the country is widely regarded as a totalitarian Stalinist dictatorship where leadership has passed from father (Kim Il-sung) to son Kim Jong-il and possibly to grandson (Kim Jong-un) in the near future in what may be described as an emerging communist royalty. There is no ability for citizens to travel abroad and domestic travel is tightly controlled. From childhood citizens in the North are exposed only to the views of their government and are constantly fed the message that South Koreans are poor and have been enslaved by western capitalist nations (Yang 1999). In this way the government has been able to completely control and mould the views of its citizens, telling them that their national duty is to reunify the divided Korean nation (Hong 2002), through armed invasion if necessary.

In summary, each of the divided states wishes reunification but on its own terms. As Breen (2004) observed, unification in these circumstances can only be seen as a win–lose situation where the achievement of unification would mean victory for one and defeat of the other. Recent tensions (discussed below) indicate that the North has no desire to be the losing party in a possible future reunification of the divided states. It can be further argued that while the South maintains a policy of reunification on its own terms the North will continue to feel threatened, fearing that reunification on Southern terms would fatally undermine what the North Koreans see as the achievements of its 60-year struggle against the West.

Reunification from a Southern perspective would involve enormous costs, possibly greater then those encountered by the re-unified German nation as it continues to upgrade services and infrastructure in the former East Germany (Chul 2002). It is apparent that any unification lead by the South will entail travel freedoms of the type that are totally alien to citizens of the North. How these would be implemented will be important and it is in this area that tourism can be envisioned to play an important part in the reunification process.

There are a growing number of South Koreans who have visited the North but only under very restricted conditions that have precluded the development of unofficial person-to-person contacts of the nature theorised by Kim and Crompton (1990). In their view, tourism could assist reunification via Track Two diplomacy, described as unofficial people-to-people relations made possible by tourism. Such contact could then be built upon by Track One diplomacy, which is undertaken at the official government-to-government level. In a later paper, Butler and Mao (1996) suggested an evolutionary process based on the premise that as tourism increases between countries in dispute, tensions are reduced leading to peace and even unification. This seems unlikely for the Korean Peninsula in the foreseeable future.

Achieving reunification did not appear to be a possibility when this chapter was written in June 2009 but as the rapid collapse of the USSR in 1991 and the realignment of many of its former satellite states to full membership of the European Union and NATO in a little over a decade illustrates, the previously unimaginable is never impossible. Both Minghi (1991), and Nijkamp (1994) observed that political boundaries have moved from being lines of separation to being lines of integration, with the European Union being an example of this trend. While the actual path that will be taken to reunification is difficult to predict, it is apparent that tourism will have a place prior to unification if the North allows its citizens greater freedom to travel, and certainly after reunification once the restrictions on cross-border travel are removed. This chapter considers that the weight of history is on the side of a Southern-led reunification and it is from this perspective that the later discussion on tourism as a force for peaceful reunification is considered.

Recent developments

During the Presidency of Kim Dae-jung (1998–2003) in South Korea the so-called 'Sunshine Policy' was adopted as a method to increase engagement with the North with the ultimate aim of reunification. A significant development in this process was a historic summit between North and South Korea in 2000, where the two states committed themselves to reconciliation through signing the inter-Korean Joint Declaration (Snyder 2005; Sigal 2002). A number of economic and diplomatic exchanges and the reunion of divided families were agreed upon as measures to build trust between the two Koreas (Ha 2001). As part of this process a number of North–South commercial agreements were undertaken and the large Mt Gumgang tourist venture in the North was allowed to proceed with heavy financial support from the government of the South.

On the North Korean side, enthusiasm generated by the initial engagement soon cooled. Despite the delivery of food aid and fertilizer, and other forms of economic cooperation, North Korea began to disengage itself from the agreement (Oh 2002; 2003). As Martin (2002) notes, there remained scepticism on the part of the North over South Korean and US talk of reconciliation, which they viewed as a way of hiding their true, anti-North Korean intentions. A major part of the rationale behind this was that for the North to see the South as keeping its end of the agreements, it should stop collaborating with the US and Japan in its policy towards North Korea (Oh 2002).

The North's expulsion of International Atomic Energy Agency inspectors and withdrawal from the Nuclear Non-Proliferation Treaty in 2003 sparked a crisis on the Peninsula (Park 2005). The position of South Korea in negotiating with the North was further jeopardized by the United States' 'War on Terror' and specifically its linkage of North Korea with this war through President George W. Bush's reference to North Korea being part of an international 'Axis of Evil' (Editors' note, see Baum and O'Gorman, Chapter 15, this volume) during his 2002 State of the Union Address (Oh 2002).

In response to the worsening crisis, China took a key role in attempting to stabilise the situation, first through trilateral talks and later through six-party talks among the two Koreas, Japan, the USA, Russia and China itself (Park 2005). Despite a number of rounds of talks, little success was made as the North Koreans withdrew and continued the development of their nuclear weapons programme. Despite the continuance of the Sunshine Policy by Kim's successor Roh Moo-hyun (2003–08), US foreign policy continued to frustrate attempts by the South to engage the North (Park 2005).

The election of Lee Myung-bak in the South in 2008 and the subsequent reversal of many aspects of the Sunshine Policy has lead to increased North-South tensions, with almost constant calls by the North for its citizens to prepare for imminent invasion by the USA and South Korea. The Mt Gumgang project was amongst the causalities of the recent increase in tensions following the shooting of a South Korean tourist by a North Korean security guard.

The current geopolitical situation

It is not possible to understand fully the role that tourism may or may not play in the shaping of North–South relationships without considering the geopolitical context within which tourism operates. The relationship between North Korea and South Korea must be viewed within the broader geopolitical impacts of North Korea's development of nuclear weapons, the stability of the Northeast Asian region and the threat of reunification on Southern rather than Northern terms. Most vital to current understandings of the North–South relationship is the issue of the North's development of nuclear weapons technology. Also crucial from a broader geopolitical perspective is the impact a nuclear-armed North Korea is likely to have on the stability of the broader Northeast Asian region (Cha and Kang 2004: 97). Although South Korea has generally pursued an independent approach to North Korea, it still has to consider both the US and Japanese positions on this issue (Ha 2001). The situation is also further complicated by the future role China wishes to play, both in Asia and the world. Continuing Chinese support for North Korea may be viewed as a method of achieving its foreign policy objectives in the North Asia region and its goal of gaining global superpower status. In this sense, peace has become hostage to geopolitical issues that are unfolding in a manner beyond the control of either North or South Korea.

Given the seriousness of the situation, and the refusal of the USA to conduct bilateral talks with North Korea, the Chinese government sponsored the multilateral 'six-party talks' in a bid to bring stability to the region (Park 2005). The talks made some progress in the fifth and sixth rounds, where North Korea showed willingness to give up its nuclear programme in return for food aid and normalization of relations with the USA and Japan (Park, 2009). However, as a consequence of a UN resolution condemning a failed 'satellite' (possibly ballistic missile) test launch, North Korea has since withdrawn from the talks, tested a second nuclear weapon in May 2009 and suspended the 1953 Armistice Agreement.

Another important point, vital from both a regional and a South Korean perspective, is fear of economic and political collapse in the North. Unification of the two Koreas through the collapse of the North would be economically devastating for the South, and so the South has an interest in preventing the collapse of Kim Jong-il's regime (Park 2005). As a result, North Korea has been in a strong position to win concessions from both the international community, and particularly from South Korea. There is a general consensus emerging that the North Korean nuclear programme is a means by which the regime is able to exploit its one advantage to ensure its survival (Cha 2002) and in more recent years to ensure a smooth handover of power from Kim Jong-il to his son Kim Jong-un. Even in the period of thawing relations between North and South in the late 1990s and early 2000s, Soon-young (1999) commented that North Korean foreign policy consisted of 'threat and blackmail'.

In examining this history, it is clear that the nature of this problem is not merely a problem of interstate relations between the two Koreas but hinges on the failure of the Northern state to be able to sustain itself without international support, its quest to gain security vis-à-vis the United States and Japan, and its fear of a Southern-lead reunification. The Sunshine Policy, although having had for South Korea the favorable impact of helping prevent the implosion of the North Korea state, could not, by itself, resolve these underlying issues. To a large extent, relations between the two states are subject to broader political forces beyond the influence of person-to-person contacts or leader-to-leader contacts. For these reasons, the prospect of tourism in itself being a factor for peace between the two Koreas is unlikely, at least from the international relations perspective.

Tourism promoting peace on the peninsula

A growing body of research (Kim *et al.* 2003: Kim and Prideaux, 2006; Kim, 2002; Lee 2001)), mostly emanating from South Korea, has commented on the prospects of tourism promoting peace on the Korean Peninsula. Much of this research has focused on the development of the Mt Gumgang tourism resort by the Hyundai Corporation. According to Kim and Prideaux (2003) the symbolic value of the Mt Gumgang project is enormous, far outweighing the venture's commercial benefits. The project was a major issue in the 2003 South Korean Presidential elections and continues to be a significant political issue in the South. As Kim *et al.* (2007: 305) state the

> '*use of tourism for political purposes rather than for commercial reasons raises a number of important issues including the impact of non-tourism motives on visitor flows and the wisdom of using tourism as a foreign policy tool to achieve specific national political goals such as the peaceful reunification of South and North Korea.*'

The Mt Gumgang tourist resort in North Korea had its origins in the 1998 Sunshine Policy and was the first tangible success of the policy. The project was significant from a diplomatic perspective but failed to meet its financial objectives and incurred substantial losses that were later underwritten by the South Korean government. For the North, the resort offered the opportunity to generate foreign currency and as a place where further discussions could take place outside the orbit of the other parties involved in the ongoing conflict on the peninsula.

The July 2008 shooting of a South Korean tourist at Mt Gumgang by a North Korean security guard lead to the suspension of travel to the area by South Koreans. As of July 2009 the suspension has not been lifted. The ambitious Gaeseong Industrial Park, built in North Korea by South Korean investors as an example of inter-Korean business cooperation, is also in jeopardy because of North Korean demands for higher land lease payments and higher wages for North Korean workers at the site. Further, the detention of a South Korean worker for allegedly voicing derogatory remarks about the North Korean Government has also reduced prospects for achieving improved North–South cooperation via this mechanism.

In one of the most recent commentaries on the role of tourism in North-South relations Kim *et al.* (2007, 306) observed that

'...the Mt Gumgang project has reduced feelings of mistrust towards the North by Southerners and assisted in the peace process in several ways. It is also apparent that the North does not regard tourism as threatening and has increased the opportunities for South Koreans to visit the North in areas outside of the Mt Gumgang precinct.'

More recent events indicate that from the perspective of the North, a Northern-led reunification is more important than almost any other issue on its political horizon (*Weekly Chosun* 2002). The belligerent attitude of the North, expressed by its development of nuclear weapons and continual calls for an invasion of the South, indicate that the observations made by Kim *et al.* (2007) were overly optimistic. From the Southern perspective South Korean tourists visit Mt Gumgung for reasons that have little to do with a genuine interest by the North in developing tourism and more to do with internal political dimensions not fully apparent to external observers.

The weight of recent research (Go 2002; Kim and Prideaux 2006; Kim *et al.* 2007; Lee 2001; Kim *et al.* 2003) indicates that from the perspectives of South Korean tourists visiting Mt Gumgang, the experience has softened their views towards the North.

A role for tourism in post unification Korea: several scenarios

While there has been considerable discussion of the role that tourism projects such as Mt Gumgang are able to play in Korean reunification, less has been written about a possible role for tourism in a future post-reunification economy. Given the current level of tension and the attitudes both nations have towards reunification it is unlikely that reunification will follow a path similar to that which led to German reunification in 1990 (see Chapter 3 of this volume by Suntikul) or to the peaceful handover of colonies by the UK and Portugal to China in the 1990s (see Chapter 5 of this volume by McCartney). It is more likely that given the course of political developments over the last 60 years a different path to reunification will be taken. At least three plausible scenarios appear possible but their probability is not able to be predicted.

1   A dramatic economic and political collapse of the North as a result of famine and a post Kim Jong-il scramble for power by groups within the North's elite.

2   A peaceful negotiated integration based on the precedents established by Hong Kong and Germany.

3   A new generation of leaders in both the North and South quietly let reunification policies slide from the political agenda, agreeing to recognise each other as sovereign independent states and allowing increased inter-Korea trade and commerce to develop.

Scenarios 1 and 2 would create enormous problems for the South because of the poor state of the North's infrastructure. Promoting tourism from the South to the North is one strategy that could be used to quickly boost the Northern economy and promote social cohesion. It is also likely that large numbers of Northerners would want to travel to the South for employment, education and so on, which would pose specific problems for the South if large numbers of such economic migrantswere involved. The third scenario, now almost inconceivable, would create a new role for tourism where Track One and Two diplomacy could be a practical approach to developing more peaceful relations but only where each side recognised the right of the other to exist as an independent state.

Conclusion

This chapter has consistently argued that tourism and its role in the peace process must be considered within the larger geopolitical context as well as the national political agenda of each state. Prior to World War I (1914–18) there was extensive travel between the countries that became protagonists in that conflict, but this did not prevent the conflict between nations whose citizens had previously enjoyed reciprocal hospitality. The roots of conflict are often manifestations of deeper ethnic, cultural, religious and economic divisions that tourism alone is unable to heal. Healing occurs on a broader political and economic canvas and to take this metaphor further, tourism can provide the colour and form to complete the canvas.

We find a situation now operating on the Korean peninsula where tourism has been used as a tool by both protagonists to further domestic political objectives. The North appears to see the current state of tension as necessary to ensure its survival as a state and to ensure a smooth handover of power from Kim Jong-il to his son Kim Jong-un. It sees a South-led reunification as hostile and a threat to its survival. While these larger issues of state and national survival are paramount, tourism will continue to be a tool, not an agent, of change. Once relations normalise, or if reunification under any of the scenarios outlined previously occurs, tourism will assume a new role primarily as a tool for promoting North–South harmony and Northern economic development.

References

Anastasopoulous, P. (1992) 'Tourism and attitude change: Greek tourists visiting Turkey', *Annals of Tourism Research*, **19**:629–642.

Bell, M, and D. Kurtzer. (2009) 'Old city, new regime', *Foreign Affairs*, 88(2), 131–135.

Breen, M. (2004) '*The Koreans: Who they Are, What they Want, Where their Future Lies*', New York: Thomas Dunn Books.

Butler, R. and B. Mao (1995) 'Tourism between divided quasi-states: international, domestic or what?' in R. Butler and D. Pearce (eds), *Change in Tourism: People, Places, Processes*, London: Routledge, pp. 92–113.

Butler, R. and B. Mao (1996) 'Conceptual and theoretical implications of tourism between partitioned states', *Asia Pacific Journal of Tourism Research* 1 (1), 25–34.

Calder, K. (2006) 'Japan and China's simmering rivalry', *Foreign Affairs*, 85 (2): 129

Cha, V. (2002) 'Korea's place in the axis', *Foreign Affairs*, **81** (3), 79.

Cha, V. and D. Kang (2004) 'Can North Korea be engaged? An exchange between Victor D. Cha and David C. Kang', *Survival* 46 (2), 89–108.

Chul, Y. (2002) 'The implications for German Unification for Korea: legal, political and international discussions', in *Korean Politics: Striving for Democracy and Unification*, Korean National Commission for UNESCO, p 137–156. Seoul: Hollym.

CIA World Fact Book (2009), Available: https://www.cia.gov/library/publications/the-world-factbook/geos/KN.html (20 June 2009).

D'Amore, L. (1988) 'Tourism: a vital force for peace', *Annals of Tourism Research*, **15**, 269–270.

D'Amore, L. (1989) 'Tourism: the world's peace industry', *Journal of Travel Research*, **27** (1), 35–40.

Go, Y. (2002) 'Evaluation of Mt. Gumgang tour business', in Proceedings of Academic Forum of Mt. Gumgang Tour Project and Inter-Korea Economic Cooperation, Seoul: Hyundai Economy Institute.

Ha, Y-C. (2001) 'South Korea in 2000: a summit and the search for the new institutional identity', *Asian Survey* **41** (1), 30–39.

Hall, D. (1984) 'Foreign tourism under socialism the Albanian "Stalinist" model', *Annals of Tourism Research*, **11**, 539–555.

Hobson, J. and G. Ko (1994) 'Tourism and politics: the implications of the change in sovereignty on the future development of Hong Kong's tourism industry', *Journal of Travel Research*, **32** (4), 2–8.

Hong, H. (2002) 'Relations between North Korea and US', *Unification Economy*, March, 14–20.

Jafari, J. (1989) 'Tourism and peace', *Annals of Tourism Research*, **16**, 439–444.

Kim, S., and B. Prideaux (2003) 'Tourism, peace, politics and ideology: impacts of the Mt. Gumgang tour project in North Korea', *Tourism Management*, **24**, 675–685.

Kim, S., and B. Prideaux (2006) 'An investigation of the relationship between South Korean domestic public opinion, tourism development in North Korea and a role for tourism in promoting peace on the Korean Peninsula', *Tourism Management*, **27** (1), 124–137.

Kim, S., K. Chon and K. Kim (2003) 'Student tourists' perception of Mt. Gumgang tour in the Korean Peninsula', *Proceedings of 9th APTA Conference*. Sydney.

Kim, S-S, Prideaux, B. and Prideaux, J. (2007), 'Using tourism to promote peace on the Korean Peninsula', *Annals of Tourism Research*, 34 (2), 291–309.

Kim, Y. (2002) 'Evaluation of recent policies toward North Korea', *Unification Economy*, March, 21–26.

Kim, Y. and J. Crompton (1990) 'Role of tourism in unifying the Two Koreas', *Annals of Tourism Research*, **17**, 353–366.

Lee, J. (2001) 'Tasks of activation of Mt. Gumgang tour project', *Unification Economy*, November, 23–28.

Litvin, S. (1998) 'Tourism: the world's peace industry? *Journal of Travel Research*, **37** (1), 63–66.

Martin, C. (2002) 'Rewarding North Korea: theoretical perspectives on the 1994 agreed framework', *Journal of Peace Research*, **39** (1), 56–68.

Matthews, H. (1978) *International Tourism: A Political and Social Analysis*, Cambridge: Schenkman Publishing Company.

Matthews, H. and L. Richter (1991) 'Political science and tourism', *Annals of Tourism Research* 18, 120–135.

Milman, A., A. Reichel and A. Pizam (1990) 'The impact of tourism on ethnic attitudes: the Israeli-Egyptian case', *Journal of Travel Research* 29 (2), 45–49.

Minghi, J. (1991) 'From conflict to harmony in border landscapes', in D. Rumley and J.V. Minghi (eds), *The Geography of Border Landscapes*, London: Routledge, pp. 15–30.

Nijkamp, P. (1994) *New Borders and Old Barriers in Spatial Development*, Aldershot: Avebury.

Oh, I. (2003) 'Characteristics of North Korea's tactics toward South Korea since the South-North summit talk and its countermeasures', *International Politics Studies* (in Korean), **43** (3), 255–273.

Oh, K. (2002) 'Terrorism eclipses the Sunshine Policy: Inter-Korean relations and the United States', *Asia Society*. Available at: http://www.ciaonet.org/wps/ohk01/ohk01.pdf. (17 June 2009)

Park, J. (2005) 'Inside multilateralism: the Six Party talks', *Washington Quarterly*, **28** (4), 75–91.

Park, S. (2009) 'Clout behind US-North Korea policy', *JoongAng Ilbo*, June 15.

Pizam, A., A. Milman and J. Jafari (1991) 'Influence of tourism on attitudes: US students visiting USSR', *Tourism Management*, **12**, 47–54.

Richter, L. (1989) *The Politics of Tourism in Asia*, Honolulu: University of Hawaii Press.

Richter, L. (1994) 'The political dimensions of tourism', in J. Ritchie and C. Goeldner (eds), Travel, *Tourism and Hospitality Research: A Handbook for Mangers and Researchers*, New York: John Wiley, pp. 219–231.

Sigal, L. . (2002) 'North Korea is no Iraq: Pyongyang's negotiating strategy', *Arms Control Today*, **32** (10), 8–13.

Snyder, S. (2005) 'South Korea's squeeze play', *Washington Quarterly*, **28** (4), 93–106.

Soon-Young, Hong (1999) 'Thawing Korea's cold war: the path to peace on the Korean Peninsula', *Foreign Affairs*, **78** (3): 8–13.

Spero, J. (1981) *The Politics of International Economic Relations*, 2nd edn, New York: St Martin's Press.

Var, T., R. Brayley and M. Korsay (1989) 'Tourism and world peace: case of Turkey', *Annals of Tourism Research*, **16**, 282–286.

Var, T., R. Schluter, P. Ankomah and T. Lee (1989) 'Tourism and peace: the case of Argentina', *Annals of Tourism Research*, **16**, 431–434.

Waterman, S. (1987) 'Partitioned states', *Political Geography Quarterly*, **6** (2), 151–171.

Weekly Chosun (2002) 'North Korea leader who has deceived world and played with the Sunshine Policy', *Weekly Chosun*, October, 26-27:3.

Yang, S. (1999) *The North and South Korean Political Systems: A Comparative Analysis*, Seoul: Hollym.

Yu, L. (1997) 'Travel between politically divided China and Taiwan', *Asia Pacific Journal of Tourism Research*, **2** (1), 19–30.

Zhan, J. (1993) *Ending the Chinese Civil War: Power Commerce and Conciliation between Beijing and Taipei*, New York: St Martin's Press.

Zhang, G. (1993) 'Tourism across the Taiwan Straits', *Tourism Management*, **14** (3), 228–231.

17 The Opening of the Ledra Crossing in Nicosia: Social and Economic Consequences

David Jacobson, Bernard Musyck, Stelios Orphanides and Craig Webster

Introduction

Cyprus is divided along ethnic lines, with Greek Cypriots in the south and Turkish Cypriots in the north. The division is formalised by a Green Line, established by the United Nations in the aftermath of the war between Greek Cypriot and Turkish armed forces in 1974. The Green Line runs through the middle of Nicosia, the capital city, which has in fact been divided for an even longer period, following inter-ethnic unrest in the 1960s. There are huge consequences for the Cyprus economy, not least for tourism, which is a key contributor, accounting for significant amounts of employment and income (Jacobson et al, 2008).

Following agreement between officials on both sides, in April 2003 a number of crossings were opened between north and south. None of these, however, were in busy urban areas. The opening in April 2008 of Ledra Street, which runs north–south through the heart of the old city of Nicosia, was the first crossing directly connecting residential and commercial areas in one municipality.

For all these crossings, including the new Ledra crossing, individuals must show a passport or identity card. The Turkish Cypriot authorities check this, and date-stamp a visa form on crossing to and from the north. Many Greek Cypriots do not cross into the north because of this. "Why should I show my passport to anyone while moving around in my own country?" is a typical explanation for this reluctance.

Table 17.1 shows the number of people that used this crossing from its opening until February 2009, the latest month for which data are available.

The table shows that of the three categories of people using the Ledra crossing, the largest is the non-Cypriot, mainly tourist, category. Prior to the opening of the Ledra crossing, many tourists in the south did not know where or how to cross into the north. The new crossing is much more central and obvious.

Table 17.1: Crossings through Ledra Street/Lokmaci checkpoint. Source: Republic of Cyprus Police

Month	Greek Cypriots	Turkish Cypriots	Non-Cypriots	Total
April 2008	46,925	29,216	21,128	97,269
May 2008	37,129	22,560	41,458	101,147
June 2008	19,596	17,074	29,643	66,313
July 2008	19,851	18,716	33,838	72,405
August 2008	17,985	17,272	30,204	65,461
September 2008	15,978	18,593	31,383	65,954
October 2008	19,804	20,019	37,271	77,094
November 2008	18,932	18,612	32,749	70,293
December 2008	23,561	25,865	34,311	83,737
Total 2008	**219,761**	**187,927**	**291,985**	**699,673**
January 2009	21,769	18,651	31,622	72,042
February 2009	20,076	16,311	30,631	67,018

As we have argued elsewhere, the Cyprus problem has been reflected for tourism in the restriction on movement, both of tourists and of tourism professionals, across the Green Line (Webster *et al.*, 2009). Any diminution in that restriction on movement – arising, of necessity, from a relaxation in inter-communal tension – would therefore be reflected in an improvement in tourism.

The opening of the Ledra crossing is an example of such a diminution in restriction on movement. It is also, as will be shown below, a consequence of rapprochement between the leaderships of the two communities. The Ledra crossing is in the middle of Old Nicosia, a main attraction for tourists; they are therefore aware of it, and given how easy it is to cross, many do. Tourism is, moreover, not limited to non-Cypriots. Many Cypriots also cross for tourist and other purposes.

This chapter examines some of the causes and consequences of the opening of the Ledra Street crossing – known to Turkish Cypriots as the Lokmaci crossing. The chapter draws on research that was carried out by an international team, including Greek and Turkish Cypriots, in the summer of 2008 (Jacobson *et al.*, 2009). The rest of the information for the chapter is derived from secondary sources, including Greek and English language newspapers in Cyprus.

Having set the context in this introduction, this chapter goes on to briefly review the literature on divided cities. From this literature some key issues emerge that suggest that tourism may have an important role in the context of the Cyprus problem. Tourism in Cyprus is predominantly that of non-Cypriots. However, given the increasing ease with which Cypriots in Nicosia can go to the north of the city following the opening of the Ledra crossing, it should also be noted that particularly for Greek Cypriots, 'sightseeing' or tourism is one of the reasons why they visit the other side. The final section of the chapter considers the new crossing in the context of the literature and discusses the implications for the future of Nicosia and of Cyprus.

Divided cities

Nicosia and other ethnically, militarily, politically or culturally divided cities around the globe have been the subject of a variety of analyses in the international literature. Key among these is *Divided Cities* by Calame and Charlesworth (2009). In this book five divided cities are examined: Belfast in Northern Ireland, which has been divided since 1968; Beirut, Lebanon's capital city, in which a violent civil war raged for 15 years; Jerusalem, divided for almost two decades until it came under Israeli control in the 1967 war; Mostar in Bosnia Herzegovina, separated into Croatian and Bosnian halves; and Nicosia, the capital of Cyprus.

In his foreword to *Divided Cities*, Woods identifies characteristics that these divided cities share. First, behind the division is sectarianism. This is where a 'confrontation of differing, though not necessarily opposed, religious beliefs [leads] to widespread violence' (vii). Next, a 'stopgap solution' is found in which the conflicting communities are physically separated. Finally, this solution, initially intended to be an immediate means of preventing physical confrontation, riots and bloodshed, 'turns into more or less persistent, if not permanent, division' (vii).

According to Calame (2005), the partition itself, as symptom of the division that encourages and teaches 'one ethnic community to disdain and violate another', constitutes a disease with its own pathology and undesirable and sometimes predictable symptoms. It is the citizens in divided cities, where development is marked by institutionalised fear and suspicion, who bear the cost of partition by living a life under siege without options – unlike soldiers, who eventually leave the battlefield. This cost includes death; the construction and monitoring of dividing walls, checkpoints and transit stations; the creation of bureaucracies to address by-products of partition such as problems of jurisdiction, compensation, encroachment; investment in mechanisms to prevent the re-emergence of inter-communal violence instead of growth and prosperity; and damaged lives following the destruction of social networks and the loss of friends, relatives and property. Residents in divided cities, even those who have little to do with the partition, may suffer psychological trauma. Property prices and quality of life suffer along the boundaries, regardless or because of the presence of walls.

Such urban pathology is not sustainable; 'partition is not an effective long-term reply to discrimination and violence' (Calame and Charlesworth, 2009, xi). This raises the question as to whether the opening of peripheral crossing points in 2003 and again in the middle of Nicosia in 2008 constitute a permeation of partition, a sign of the beginning of the end of pathology, a revival of activity and prosperity. Does the increase in crossings by tourists have an impact? If so, does tourism increase or reduce the gap between the two communities?

Divided Nicosia

The impact of the division of Nicosia is self-evident along the Green Line. Within the Green Line the UN Buffer Zone is full of neglected, often crumbling buildings; this is also true of many of the adjacent blocks north and south. From a joint attempt by the two sides to improve the existing and future habitat and human settlement conditions for all inhabitants there emerged the Nicosia Master Plan. With the cooperation of the UNDP (United Nations Development Programme) this resulted in the successful restoration of places of cultural and historical interest on both sides of the walled city. This achievement did not come easily; Abu-Orf (2005), for example, concludes that communication between the two sides for collaborative planning was distorted by the power relations and the political agendas. Moreover, these interventions were insufficient to stall the process of degradation – Calame's (2005) urban pathology – of Old Nicosia.

Emerging from Calame's (2005) work, but also specifically addressed by Broome (2005), is identification of the problem that there is very little contact between members of the two communities in Nicosia. According to Broome (2005) contact between members of the two communities was limited after the 1963/64 events and almost non-existent after 1974. Apart from a small number of Greek Cypriots who had relatives in the Karpasia Peninsula in the northeast of the island, and a small number of Turkish Cypriots who remained in the south following the 1974 events, or who crossed to the south to work, contact between the two communities took place mainly abroad. Contacts between political parties, trade unions and civil society groups were maintained and encouraged by foreign diplomats. Measures impeding or restricting such contacts were, however, often imposed by local officials. Also acknowledging this problem, Sönmez and Apostolopoulos (2000) called for a strengthening of ties between members of the two communities. They argued that minimising obstacles to travel across the Green Line could help eliminate distrust and contribute to understanding between the two communities. Internal tourism, serving as an informal diplomatic channel between the two groups, could play a significant role in mutual understanding and thus help towards a settlement of the Cyprus conflict.

Some restrictions on movement were removed in 2003; in response, tens of thousands of Cypriots, members of both communities, have crossed the Green Line, in addition to many more non-Cypriot tourists. However, establishing substantial contacts between the two communities remains problematic. Webster and Timothy (2006) examined the motives underlying Greek Cypriots' decisions to cross/not cross, after the lifting of restrictions on movement in April 2003. They concluded that the new opportunities for contact have allowed the two communities to maintain more amiable and normalised relations. The new conditions allowing contact between the two sides created hope for reconciliation, but what Greek Cypriots consider to be ethical considerations prevent a significant proportion of them from crossing.

Webster and Timothy (2006) found that 57% of Greek Cypriots would not cross to the north. The most common reason for Greek Cypriots objecting to the idea of crossing to the north was the need to show a passport or an identification card at the crossings. Other factors related to the nationalistic sentiment among Greek Cypriots, whether one was a refugee or not, emotional reasons, and/or the reluctance to spend money in the north. A survey published in *Politis* in July 2008 (31 June 2008) shows a similar percentage of Greek Cypriots unwilling to cross to the north (58%); the main objection – obligation to show a passport or ID card – was also the same. That Greek Cypriots are more reluctant to cross than Turkish Cypriots is clear from the data (Table 17.2). It should be pointed out that there may also be practical and economic reasons why more Turkish Cypriots cross to the south than Greek Cypriots to the north. There are few if any Greek Cypriots working in the north, for example, but many Turkish Cypriots working in the south. Still, although 75% of the respondents said they were not intending to cross in the next twelve months, an equal percentage said that it is good to have contacts with the Turkish Cypriots even before there is a settlement.

Table 17.2: Crossings through the Green Line. Source: Republic of Cyprus Police

	2003	2004	2005	2006	2007	2008
Greek Cypriots	1,123,720	1,173,825	1,319,899	897,044	601,351	708,656
Turkish Cypriots	1,371,099	2,159,541	2,222,199	1,638,734	1,116,990	1,298,325
Total	**2,494,819**	**3,333,366**	**3,542,098**	**2,535,778**	**1,718,341**	**2,006,981**

If reaching a final peace settlement is the ultimate objective, Hadjipavlou (2007) argues that the reconciliation process has to be strengthened with new beliefs, attitudes, motivations, goals and emotions. A concerted effort at the political level – among other things – may be necessary to achieve this. Though they may be relatively isolated, organised acts of violence against Turkish Cypriots in the south do still occur (e.g., January 2009 (*Cyprus Mail*, 20 January 2009) and November 2006 (Cyprus Mail, 26 November 2006)) and they are indicative of the amount of ground that remains to be covered if reconciliation is to be achieved. They may also have a negative impact on tourism.

The opening of the Ledra crossing

As Table 17.2 shows, there have been millions of crossings at the five peripheral crossing points opened in 2003. These, however, had little impact on the nature and prosperity of the centre of Old Nicosia which continued to decline. The opening of the Ledra Street crossing seems to have resulted in delaying and perhaps partially reversing this process. Following the opening, thousands of Cypriots, and many more non-Cypriot tourists, flocked into Old Nicosia to cross to the other side (see Table 17.1). Businesses in the area saw a sudden increase in the number of passers-by and customers, a great many of them tourists. The new life in the area is reminiscent of the activity here when it was the city's main commercial area.

After remaining almost hermetically sealed for 34 years, and five years after the lifting of the restrictions on movement across the ceasefire line in 2003, the centre of Old Nicosia was re-opened on 3 April 2008. There can be little doubt that the change in the political situation in Cyprus contributed to the agreement finally to open the new crossing point.

Already in late 2004 there had been suggestions that the end of Ledra Street might be opened to pedestrian traffic. Nothing came of it, though plans seemed to be in place, on both sides, to facilitate the opening of the new crossing. Again in November 2005, both Greek and Turkish Cypriot politicians released statements to the effect that it was likely that it would be ready before Christmas. UNFICYP (United Nations Peacekeeping Force in Cyprus) on the other hand issued a statement making it clear that complete agreement was necessary before this could happen. UNFICYP pointed out that the Turkish Cypriot side had commenced building and clearing work and this involved some unofficial entry by Turkish Cypriots into the buffer zone. Unilateral initiatives, the statement continued, 'are incompatible with the spirit of the confidence building measures that have driven the carefully coordinated effort since April 2003 to promote and ensure the orderly opening of crossing points on the island' (UNFICYP, 2005).

The UNFICYP statement reveals only part of the problem. The absence of agreement – despite moves by both sides towards opening the new crossing point – was a consequence of a hard-line attitude particularly on the part of Greek Cypriot president, Tassos Papadopoulos. His intervention on the eve of the referendum on the Annan Plan for the reunification of Cyprus had been a crucial factor in the Greek Cypriot rejection of the plan in April 2004. That plan was named after its key sponsor, Kofi Annan, the then Secretary General of the United Nations. In the remaining years of Papadopoulos' presidency he continued to mistrust the Turkish Cypriots and insisted that agreement on the opening of Ledra Street could not proceed until all Turkish troops were completely removed from the area.

In the February 2008 presidential election, Papadopoulos was replaced by the AKEL party's leader, Dimitris Christofias. AKEL was already in the coalition with Papadopoulos's centrist and nationalist party, DIKO, but the change of president was an important political shift. AKEL is a communist party, and the views of Christofias were much closer to those of the left-leaning Turkish Cypriot leader, Mehmet Ali Talat. In addition, during the election campaign one of Christofias's planks was the promise to enter talks with the Turkish Cypriot leadership.

It is therefore not surprising that already by the end of February 2008 the two leaders had spoken on the phone and prepared the ground for the opening of the Ledra crossing. Much of the rubble had already been cleared by the two sides since the opening had first been mooted in 2004, and the only remaining obstacle was political. The leaders met personally on 21 March 2008 and formally agreed to the opening. The work of UNFICYP in liaising with all relevant municipal and military officials and getting agreement from all of them in time for the opening on 3 April is clear from the 2 June 2008 report of the UN Secretary General on the United Nations Operation in Cyprus (UNFICYP, 2008).

It is of particular interest that UNFICYP facilitated and monitored the withdrawal of Greek Cypriot National Guard and Turkish and Turkish Cypriot soldiers 'from their respective positions on either side of the crossing, escorting members of the political and diplomatic communities into the buffer zone for the opening ceremony and facilitating press coverage' (UNFICYP, 2008, par.13). Papadopoulos had refused to agree to the opening until the Turkish forces were removed. Under Christofias, agreement was reached and then, immediately prior to the formal opening, the Turkish forces moved back.

Immediately after the opening ceremony, hundreds of pedestrians who had flocked to attend it crossed to the other side. Suddenly, Nicosia's old commercial centre ceased to be yet another theatre of confrontation for the Cyprus problem but rather a link connecting the two communities. It rapidly became a popular destination for various purposes: shopping, leisure, walks, dining, meeting friends, on both sides. Already in the first month, more than 97,000 crossings were registered – most prominent among them was probably the leader of the Turkish Cypriot community Mehmet Ali Talat (*Cyprus Mail*, 12 May 2008). There were 20,000 on the first weekend alone. In May, the number of crossings exceeded 101,000, boosted by a surge in the number of non-Cypriot tourists (Table 17.1).

The increase in the flow of people in Nicosia's centre however, although it was rather like a pre-Christmas shopping frenzy, was not felt by all shops. According to some sources, restaurants and cafés – the number of which has been rising in the area in recent years (Drousiotis, 30 December 2006) – benefited most, while other establishments did not fare so well (*Cyprus Mail*, 08 May 2008). On the other hand, and especially north of the crossing on the Turkish side, clothing, footwear and textile retailers seem to have done very well, too, following the opening of the new crossing. Over the first weekend following the opening, 'thousands of Greek Cypriots and foreign tourists flocked into the north at Ledra Street, bringing a welcome boost to an area that had over the years been losing trade to out-of-town supermarkets' (Bahceli, 2008, n.p.). The opening repositioned Old Nicosia on the tourist map of Cyprus, as both sides of Nicosia's old centre became accessible to tourists who could now walk through the crossing. Aeolos, one of the leading tourist agencies in Cyprus, immediately after the opening launched a new sightseeing tour called 'Nicosia Match and Mix' that allowed tourists to walk from the south to the other side. The company organises 10 to 20 such tours every week. Demand for the tour is high as participants experience the diversity of Cyprus within a unified space (Webster *et al.*, 2009).

As part of the research for Jacobson *et al.* et al (2009), on 26 November 2008, a round table discussion was held in the library of the Goethe Institute (Nicosia), attended by entrepreneurs from both sides of Nicosia's old commercial centre. The Goethe Institute is in the buffer zone between the Greek and Turkish Cypriot checkpoints. The main interest of both sides was in how to attract more customers to the old commercial centre. Among Greek Cypriot entrepreneurs, there was an opinion that identification procedures at the crossing points reduce the willingness of the public to cross and thus limit the number of potential customers. Members of both groups acknowledged that this obstacle could only be lifted if the Cyprus problem was settled. There was accord among both Greek and Turkish Cypriot businesspeople who attended the round table discussion that some measures could and should be taken, even prior to settlement. These included: establishing a shopkeepers' platform to promote dialogue; organisation of a fair (Greek πανηγύρι, Turkish *panayir*) in the buffer zone at the Ledra Street/Lokmaci crossing to attract crowds; restoration of damaged and neglected buildings in the buffer zone at the crossing to host events such as exhibitions, meetings, etc.; promoting acceptance of the Turkish lira by Greek Cypriot shopkeepers; and printing and distribution of a Nicosia town map with advertisements from businesses on both sides. Turkish Cypriot businesspeople attending the discussion expressed their concern over the spread of propaganda on the Greek Cypriot side to prevent Greek Cypriots from shopping in the north. While many of the points made by the participants were focused specifically on problems in the relationship between the two communities, virtually all the suggestions for improvements would have, if implemented, a positive impact on tourism.

It is clear that the pursuit of a settlement of the Cyprus problem, both top-down by the leaderships of the two communities, and bottom-up by business people on both sides, has important implications for tourism in Cyprus. The change in presidency resulting in the opening of the new crossing, and the subsequent willingness of people on both sides to enter into discussions about ways of solving mutual problems, provide clear evidence of the tourism-enhancing potential of these developments.

Conclusion

Despite the lifting of restrictions on movement in 2003, the division of Cyprus continues, both politically and militarily as well as in the minds of Cypriots. The reconciliation process went into abeyance following the referendum on the Annan Plan in April 2004 and the opportunity for progress towards settlement that had arisen a year earlier remained unexploited. Thus, the opening of Ledra Street/Lokmaci in April, 2008 can be regarded as an attempt to recover lost ground.

The opening brought people from both communities together. It increased contacts between Greek and Turkish Cypriots and it broadened the channels of communication and opportunities for interaction. Despite the resumption of bi-communal talks in summer 2008, however, crossing to the north and establishing contact with the other side remains taboo for many Greek Cypriots. This reveals an impediment to Greek Cypriot reconciliation with Turkish Cypriots which needs to be addressed. One means of doing so is the sort of civil society initiatives to promote trade in Nicosia's traditional commercial centre suggested by the Greek and Turkish Cypriot local businesspeople from Nicosia who participated in the round table discussion (noted above).

The opening of Ledra Street/Lokmaci has revitalised Nicosia's old commercial centre, both in the north and in the south. There is a view, on both sides, that settlement of the Cyprus problem would be to the benefit of the tourist sector of the other side (Jacobson et al, 2008). The contribution of the opening of the Ledra Street crossing to the improvement of business on both sides goes at least some way towards dispelling this myth. Rather than one side gaining and the other losing from the new crossing, the opening provides evidence of a win–win scenario for Cyprus, because both Greek and Turkish Cypriot businesses in Nicosia's old centre have benefited from the increase in customers. These gains, moreover, have been made despite the global economic downturn. Tourism has enhanced these gains, on both sides.

This positive evidence must be seen in the context of the enormous challenge of the continuing division of Cyprus and of its capital. The positive effects of the opening are highly localised. Elsewhere Nicosia continues to be divided and to suffer from that division. This is obvious along the Green Line. As Calame (2005) points out, the consequences are more general, too, because in ethnically divided cities there are no coordinated design, planning, and conservation strategies or, where they do exist, they are very difficult to implement. Based on this, politicians may have to think 'outside the box' and start discussing not only the opening of further crossings within the old centre but also to consider other measures to reduce the militarisation all along the Green Line.

References

In English

Abu-Orf, H. (2005) 'Collaborative planning in practice: The Nicosia Master Plan', *Planning, Practice and Research*, **20** (1) (February), pp.41–58.

Bahceli, S. (2008) 'Arasta shops stunned by new trade book', *Cyprus Mail*, 8 April.

Broome, B. (2005) *Building Bridges across the Green Line: A Guide to Intercultural Communication in Cyprus*, United Nations Development Program, Nicosia.

Calame, J. (2005) 'Divided cities and ethnic conflict in the urban domain', in Nicholas Stanley Price (ed.) Cultural Heritage in Postwar Recovery, papers from the ICCROM Forum held at Rome on 4–6 October 2005, ICCROM Conservation Studies, pp. 40–50.

Calame, J. and Charlesworth, E. (2009) *Divided Cities: Belfast, Beirut, Jerusalem, Mostar, and Nicosia*, University of Pennsylvania Press.

Cyprus Mail, www.cyprus-mail.com.

Drousiotis, M. See the website www.makarios.eu. This contains the writings, mainly in Greek, of journalist and commentator Makarios Drousiotis.

Hadjipavlou M. (2007) 'Multiple stories: the crossings as part of the reconciliation efforts in Cyprus', *Innovation*, **20** (1), 53–70.

Jacobson, D., Musyck, B., Orphanides, S. and Webster, C. (2008) 'Cyprus settlement: a tourism zero-sum game?, paper presented at the Irish Academy of Management Annual Conference, DCU, September 2008.

Jacobson, D., Musyck, B., Orphanides, S. and Webster, C. (2009) The Opening of Ledra Street/Lockmaci Crossing in April 2008: Reactions from Citizens and Shopkeepers, PRIO Cyprus Centre, Paper 2, from: http://www.prio.no/Research-and-Publications/.

Sönmez, S. and Apostolopoulos, Y. (2000) 'Conflict resolution through tourism cooperation? The case of the partitioned island-state of Cyprus', *Journal of Travel and Tourism Marketing*, **9** (3), 35–48.

UNFICYP (2005) Ledra Street Crossing, from: http://www.unficyp.org/nqcontent.cfm?a_id=2087andtt=graphicandlang=l1 (29 Sept 2009).

UNFICYP (2008) Report of the Secretary-General on the United Nations Operation in Cyprus, from: http://www.unficyp.org/media/SG%20Reports/S.2008.353.pdf (29 Sept 2009).

Webster, C., Musyck, B., Orphanides, S. and Jacobson, D. (2009) 'Working on the other side. Cooperative tour organizers and uncooperative hoteliers: evidence from Greek Cypriot tourism professionals', *European Planning Studies*, **17** (10), 1485–1508.

Webster, C. and Timothy, D. (2006) 'Travelling to the 'Other Side': The Occupied Zone and Greek Cypriot Views on the Green Line', *Tourism Geographies*, **8** (2), 162–181.

In Greek

Δρουσιώτης Μ., 2005, Η πρώτη διχοτόμηση – Κύπρος 1963 – 1964, Αλφάδι, Λευκωσία, (Drousiotis Makarios, 2005, The first partition – Cyprus 1963 – 1964, Alfadi, Nicosia). See also www.makarios.eu

Politis Online, www.politis-news.com

18 Politics on Ice – Tourism in Antarctica

Thomas G. Bauer

Introduction

The Polar Regions form the northern and southernmost ends of the Earth. The Arctic is a frozen ocean surrounded by land that is under the governance of, and occupied by citizens of, the sovereign states of Iceland, Norway, Sweden, Finland, Russia, Canada, and the USA (State of Alaska), as well as the Danish dependency of Greenland. In contrast, Antarctica is an icy continent surrounded by the Southern Ocean, has no sovereign, and has never had a permanent human population.

Antarctica surrounds the geographic South Pole which is located 2825 m above sea level, and covers 13.9 million square kilometres, roughly twice the size of Australia. 98% of the continent is covered by a layer of ice which averages one and a half miles in thickness, (almost three miles thick at its maximum), and which holds some 70% of the world's fresh water reserves. Antarctica is the highest, coldest, windiest, driest, and remotest of all the continents and its landscape is dominated by ice sheets, glaciers, ice shelves, and mountains. Parts of the coastline and the offshore islands, in particular in the Antarctic Peninsula region, are areas where wildlife such as penguins, seals and flying sea birds congregate during the warmer summer months from October to March and where tourists, who mainly reach the continent aboard a variety of cruise ships, visit during the Antarctic tourism season, between late October and early March.

Antarctic history

For most of its 50 million years of ice-covered history Antarctica has not been subjected to any human interference with its natural processes. The earliest human interest in Antarctica dates back to the sixth century BC. As McGonigal (2008: 262) notes 'Antarctica is the only continent that, from the perspective of human thought, began as a sophisticated concept emerging from a series of deductions'. In the sixth century BC, Pythagoras calculated that the Earth was round and a century later Parmenides divided the world into five climatic zones and postulated that there were frigid zones at the poles. It was Aristotle in the fourth century BC who suggested that the landmasses of the Northern Hemisphere must be balanced a large landmass in the South: Terra Australis Incognita. On 17 January 1773 the *Resolution* and *Adventure* under James Cook became the first vessels to cross the Antarctic Circle but due to heavy ice they had to retreat and did not sight land. Cook is quoted as saying that 'no man will ever venture farther south than I have done, and…the lands which may lie to the South will never be explored' (quoted in McGonigal 2008: 266). As with many other predictions this one did not hold true but many years passed between Cook's comment and the first sighting of the continent in 1820 and the first landing on the continent by Bull, Borchgrevink and Kristensen at Cape Adare in 1895. The 'heroic' and largely nationalistic age of Antarctic exploration was to follow, culminating in the race to the South Pole between expeditions lead by the Norwegian Roald Amundsen and the Englishman Robert F. Scott. Amundsen reached the pole on 14 December 1911 and as is well known, Scott and his companions died on the way back from reaching the pole a little later in early 1912. As Damjanov (2006: 1) notes: 'The attempts of geo-political powers to reach the Pole and settle there created a climate of colonial competition over the continent that was only ended by the legal regulation of the Antarctic Treaty in 1959. The Treaty proclaimed Antarctica as international space and ended Antarctica's official colonial periods.' In its early human history prior to 1820, Antarctica was *terra nullius* – no man's land. Damjanov notes: 'Its legal status was an open invitation to nation-states to colonize it' (2006: 2). Today no visas or passports are required to enter Antarctica but such documents are necessary to leave the southern countries from whence ships to Antarctic leave.

Governenace of Antarctica

Unlike every other tourist destination there is no 'normal' political structure in Antarctica. There is no local, regional, provincial or central government that is responsible for the administration of the continent. Instead, Antarctica is administered under the Antarctic Treaty and its associated conventions, protocols and recommendations, collectively known as the Antarctic Treaty System (ATS). Bauer (2001: 53) notes that many of the complexities of Antarctic tourism have their origins in the unique legal and political situation of the continent. Seven countries (Argentina, Australia, Chile, France, New Zealand, Norway and the United Kingdom) claim territory, largely based on discovery and/or geographical proximity. These claims to territorial sovereignty are, however, not universally recognized. To reduce the dangers of international armed conflict, the twelve countries that had established scientific bases in Antarctica during the International Geophysical Year 1957/58 negotiated the Antarctic Treaty. The Treaty was signed on 1 December 1959 and came into force on 23 June 1961. Damjanov (2006: 2) notes: 'Complicated and conflicting political situations about claimed areas that were overlapping [in the Antarctic Peninsula, Great Britain, Chile and Argentina lay claim to the same regions], and the tendencies of claiming nations to physically explore the resources of their "nation-state extensions", ended with the Antarctic Treaty in 1959.' Under the Treaty (Article VI) the area south of 60 degree South latitude, including all ice shelves, is technically governed by none of the nation-states, but by an international regime established by the Treaty. At the core of this piece of international law is Article IV, which basically states that countries agree to disagree on the issue of sovereignty. It reads:

Nothing contained in the present Treaty shall be interpreted as:

- *A renunciation by any Contracting Party of previously asserted rights of or claims to sovereignty in Antarctica;*

- *A renunciation or diminution by any Contracting Party of any basis of claim to territorial sovereignty in Antarctica which it may have whether as a result of its activities or those of its nationals in Antarctica, or otherwise;*

- *Prejudicing the position of any Contracting Party as regards its recognition or non-recognition of any other State's rights of or claim or basis of claim to territorial sovereignty in Antarctica.*

- *No act or activities taking place while the present Treaty is in force shall constitute a basis for asserting, supporting or denying a claim to territorial sovereignty in Antarctica or create any rights of sovereignty in Antarctica. No new claim or enlargement of an existing claim, to territorial sovereignty in Antarctica shall be asserted while the present Treaty is in force.*

(Heap 1990)

Article IV makes it clear that whatever a signatory country does or does not do while the Treaty is in force (the next review opportunity is not until 2041) will have no influence on its territorial claims. As outlined later in this chapter, this does not stop some countries from trying to strengthen their claims by a variety of means.

The Antarctic Treaty was originally signed by 12 countries (the seven claimant countries and Belgium, Japan, the Soviet Union, South Africa and the United States of America) but the list of signatories has now grown to a total of 47 countries, 28 of which are Antarctic Treaty Consultative Parties (ATCPs), which means that they can participate in the decision making process and have a vote at the Annual Antarctic Treaty Consultative Meetings (ATCMs). It is interesting to note that 15 of the 35 accessions took place during the 1980s when the Minerals Regime was being negotiated. It could be argued that countries rushed to accede purely in case some commercial gains could be obtained from Antarctica. In contrast, interest in joining the Antarctic Treaty waned in the 1990s when the Protocol on Environmental Protection was introduced, with only seven countries acceding, a rate which has slowed even further since 2000 when only three countries acceded.

From CRAMRA to the Madrid Protocol

The Antarctic Treaty makes no direct reference to tourism and it is considered as a non-governmental activity. Several additions to the Treaty in the form of conventions and agreed measures, however, are relevant to tourism. They include the Convention on the Conservation of Antarctic Marine Living Resources, the Agreed Measures for the Conservation of Antarctic Fauna and Flora and the Convention for the Conservation of Antarctic Seals. The biggest change to the way tourism in Antarctica is conducted came from the failure of the Convention on the Regulation of Antarctic Mineral Resource Activities (CRAMRA) and the subsequent coming into force of the Protocol on Environmental Protection to the Antarctic Treaty in 1998. As Bauer (2001: 58) notes: 'In the late 1970s it was argued that because no large scale mineral reserves had been identified in Antarctica and that as a result mining in Antarctica would not be economically viable until at least the next century, there was no need to negotiate a minerals' regime'. The Treaty Parties nevertheless noted the possible negative environmental effects of potential mining operations in Antarctica and decided that: 'since there would be even greater difficulties in negotiating a minerals' regime if it was left until exploitable deposits were found and the necessary technology was available, the better course would be to conclude a framework regime which would cover all stages of prospecting, exploration and development' (Heap 1990: 4301). Throughout the 1980s the Treaty Parties worked on drafting a minerals' regime. During the final session of the Fourth Special Antarctic Treaty Consultative Meeting on Antarctic Mineral Resources held in Wellington, New Zealand from 2 May to 2 June 1988, the Consultative Parties adopted the 'Convention on the Regulation of Antarctic Mineral Resource Activities' (CRAMRA). The Convention was opened for signature on 25 November 1988. During 1989 the Australian Government decided that it would not ratify CRAMRA but instead seek support from other Antarctic Treaty parties including France, Italy and Belgium, for a full environmental protection for the continent and its surrounding seas (Haywood 1995: 230). Under the Antarctic Treaty all decisions must be unanimous – thus Australia's refusal to ratify it effectively rendered CRAMRA null and void. For the protection of the Antarctic environment and for the conduct of tourism the Australian action led to the most important addition to the Antarctic Treaty System, the Protocol on Environmental Protection to the Antarctic Treaty (Madrid Protocol). The Australian Antarctic Division summarizes the key provisions of the Madrid Protocol in the following fashion:

> *The Protocol places an indefinite ban on mining or mineral resource activity in Antarctica, designating the Antarctic as a natural reserve devoted to peace and science. It provides a multinational, codified set of environmental standards (Antarctica is the only continent for which this applies), and creates a new system of protected areas. The Protocol establishes environmental principles for the conduct of all activities, which must be assessed for their potential environmental impact before they are undertaken, and provides guidelines for conservation of Antarctic flora and fauna, managing and disposing of waste, and preventing marine pollution.*
>
> (Haywood 1995: 23)

The Madrid Protocol requires that tour operators provide evidence that their activities will not have more than a transitory impact on the Antarctic environment and prior to the start of each season they have to seek approval from their respective governments to carry out their activities. In addition, the International Association of Antarctica Tour Operators (IAATO) has developed its own guidelines for the conduct of tourists and operators, and since its establishment in 1991 has demonstrated that the private sector is able to self-regulate its activities. Haase *et al.* (2009) raise the question of the robustness of industry self-regulation of Antarctic tourism. This question is valid but it is difficult to see how a system other than a hands-on self-regulation by the tourism operators can be implemented under current ATS provisions. One option that this author suggests that the Treaty Parties could consider is to bring IAATO under the ATS umbrella in a formal way by making it a specialised agency responsible for the management of tourism in Antarctica (along the lines of UNWTO evolving into a specialised agency under the UN umbrella). To do this would probably require the negotiation and ratification of a 'Tourism Management Convention'. A precedent for such an agency is the establishment of the Hobart-based secretariat that administers the Convention on the Conservation of Antarctic Marine Living Resources (CCAMLR) that protects the marine resources in the Southern Ocean around Antarctica. If the Antarctic Treaty Parties want to make ship-based Antarctic tourism even safer, they need to focus on controlling vessels with very large numbers of passengers. Such vessels frequently sail under the flags of convenience of countries such as the Bahamas, Panama, or Liberia, that are not members of the ATS and hence it may be difficult to ban them from traveling south. One way to stop them is by reducing demand for such Antarctic tourism products by requiring citizens of ATS member countries to seek permission from their respective governments prior to sailing to Antarctica. Permission to nationals who wish to travel on large, non-ice strengthened vessels could be denied leaving operators with empty vessels and hence taking away the incentive to sail to Antarctica. Recent problems with tourist boats in Antarctica would almost certainly have arisen irrespective of the administration of tourism in Antarctica.

The case of CRAMRA is interesting because it demonstrates the power of the nation-state and its political leaders in influencing decisions at the international level. Herr, Hall and Haward (1990) compiled *Antarctica's Future: Continuity or Change* that reported on a conference organized by the Australian Institute of International Affairs in Hobart, Tasmania in 1989. The book's contributors represented the elite of scholars, Antarctic programme administrators, lawyers and politicians, with an involvement in Antarctic affairs. In Chapter 1, the then Prime Minister of Australia, The Hon. R.J.L. Hawke, defended the decision by his government not to ratify the Minerals Regime and to instead propose a comprehensive environmental protection regime for all of Antarctica. He noted: 'That Antarctica has become the focus of such current international interest should be no surprise. There is something about Antarctica that lifts the spirit and stimulates the mind. Antarctica is the only one of the seven continents that cannot sustain human life; the only one where a near-pristine environment remains. It is the last great wilderness' (Hawke 1990: 17). Hawke also provided an insight into why his government refused to agree to the Minerals Regime:

> *The most urgent and relevant action we can take is to ensure that the irreplaceable environment is never put at risk by mining. That is why Australia has decided not to sign the Minerals Convention...The Mineral's Convention might provide for some a dangerous illusion of environmental protection. But by permitting immediate prospecting and setting out a path by which mining might proceed, it will in fact be working in precisely the opposite direction. So with France, Australia is pursuing the initiative of a comprehensive environmental protection convention which will establish Antarctica as a 'Natural Reserve – Land of Science'.*
>
> *(Hawke 1990: 19)*

Addressing criticism of his Labour government's decision, Hawke continues:

> *I am aware that our decision has caused considerable anxiety amongst those Antarctic treaty members who believe that the coming into force of the Minerals Convention was not just a correct outcome but a foregone conclusion. And I'm also aware of assertions that our opposition to the convention is purely tactical, or has been adopted for short-term electoral reasons and will be reversed as soon as convenient. Let me urge anyone who might still harbour that fantasy to abandon it. Because the reverse is true.*
>
> *(Hawke 1990: 19)*

The Australian Labour Party under Bob Hawke won the subsequent 24 March 1990, election and proceeded with its ambitions to have the Antarctic environment protected. As a consequence the Protocol on Environmental Protection to the Antarctic Treaty was signed on 4 October 1991 and came into force on 14 January 1998, after all Consultative Treaty Parties had ratified it.

Challenges to the Antarctic Treaty system

The governments of different countries obviously have different opinions on the governance of Antarctica. Malaysia, under its former Prime Minister Mahatir bin Mohamad, was one of the strongest critics of the ATS. In their comprehensive analysis of the Antarctic position of Malaysia, Tepper and Haward (2005) note that Malaysia emerged as a vocal critic of the Antarctic Treaty and the Antarctic Treaty System in 1982. Malaysia's criticism was based on their perception that the continent was run by an 'exclusive club' (the Antarctic Treaty Parties) and argued that it should be managed by the United Nations for the benefit of all mankind, and re-iterated its position on many occasions in the General Assembly of the UN without achieving any change. By 2009 Malaysia had established an Antarctic Programme but it had still not acceded to the Antarctic Treaty. To his credit Dr Mahatir and a group of his senior ministers did at least visit the Antarctic Peninsula aboard a tourist cruise vessel from 5 to 13 February 2002, making him one of the very few Heads of State to have visited Antarctica.

Scientific stations in Antarctica: expressions of sovereignty

Since the coming into force of the Antarctic Treaty in 1961 the continent has been considered by scientists as their own 'playground'. Tourists who pay for the privilege of visiting it were often considered as undesirables who had the potential to interfere with scientific work. Under the ATS, tourism is classified as a non-governmental activity. While the continent is technically free from any form of ownership, the research stations that are scattered around it are funded by the taxpayers of their respective countries and are administered by the various Antarctic programmes (such as the British Antarctic Survey, Australian Antarctic Division, and US National Science Foundation). Since 1966 when Lars Eric Lindblad chartered the Argentinean Navy vessel *Lapataia* and visited the Antarctic Peninsula and the Argentinean station Esperanza at Hope Bay (Headland 1989), tour operators have sought to incorporate visits to scientific research stations into their itineraries to add a human touch to the Antarctic cruise experience. Being visited by tourists has its positive and negative aspects for station staff. On the positive side, tourists provide diversions from an otherwise fairly regimented daily routine, but they can also disrupt the routine of a station. The Antarctic summer is short and many researchers depend on this 'window of opportunity' to carry out their experiments. Interruption of their work is therefore not appreciated. Tourists also have the potential to inadvertently disturb areas that are under observation and they may bring infectious diseases ashore which may infect station staff. Time is of the essence and any illness-related downtime may jeoparise research projects.

Permission to allow tourist visits to research facilities is at the discretion of the respective country and the base commander, and unannounced visits are not welcome. There is a wide variety of attitudes towards station visits ranging from a very warm welcome at stations such as the Ukraine's Vernadsky (previously the British Faraday Station) and Poland's Arctowski to a friendly and commercial welcome at Port Lockroy where the former British Antarctic Survey base has been converted into a museum, gift shop and post office, resulting in it being the most visited site during recent Antarctic seasons.

Other countries are not as welcoming to tourists. The adventurer Mike Horn, who, in 2008 walked solo from the coast to the geographic South Pole where the United States of America maintains the Amundsen-Scott station notes:

> *When I reached the South Pole I was walking over the landing strip at the Scott-Amundsen American base and I didn't notice a red light flashing. This American guy comes out and yells, 'Didn't you see the light? A Hercules was about to land and you've broken the law. We'll sue you.' And I said, 'Who's law?' I was astonished. I had been alone for two months and now some jerk is asking me to stop at a red traffic light at the South Pole.*
>
> *(Horn quoted in Jeffreys 2009: 21)*

Other private expeditions have faced similar treatment. When Reinhold Messner, one of the world's most celebrated adventurers, arrived at South Pole Station in 1989 he was reportedly refused entry to the station and denied even a cup of tea.

In December 2006 when Jennifer Murray and Colin Bodill wanted to land their helicopter at Britain's Rothera station on their way to the South Pole they were advised that their visit was not welcome. Thus national rather than international policies determine visitations to 'inhabited' or occupied parts of this international continent. Underlying what appear on the surface to be hostile attitudes towards tourists in general and adventure tourists in particular, is the fear of liability and litigation and the possibility of being called upon to perform Search and Rescue operations. This fear arose out of the tragic events of the crash of Air New Zealand flight TE 901 on 28 November 1979, that killed all 257 people on board. The plane crashed on Mt Erebus in the Ross Sea sector near the US McMurdo Station and some family members of the victims accused the US government (as the operator of McMurdo) of not providing adequate weather forecasting for the flight. Some tried (unsuccessfully) to sue the United States Government for negligence. It was subsequently established by Justice Mahon that the crash of the plane was not due to poor weather forecasting but due to the re-programming of the flight plan by the ground crew who failed to advise the pilots of this change. This change provided the pilots with the illusion that they were flying further to the west of Mt Erebus than was actually the case. What they mistook for the flat Ross Ice Shelf in front of them was actually Mt Erebus.

Since that time the USA has had a 'tolerate but do not condone or support' attitude towards adventure tourism and also to a somewhat lesser degree towards more mainstream tourist visits to the continent and US research stations. Such visits are arranged on request but are limited to a small number each season to minimize disruptions at the facilities of the two coastal US stations. Palmer Station can be visited and tourists are shown around by a friendly staff. In the author's experience, visits to McMurdo Station are not as straightforward. Despite having received prior approval to visit what is the largest human 'settlement' in Antarctica, the vessel the author was travelling on was not able to carry out the visit because it may have required assistance from a US Coast Guard icebreaker in order to leave the turning basin (an area that is kept ice-free to allow ships to turn around and head back north through the artificially created channel of open water) near the station. The icebreaker was scheduled to leave the area and requests to delay its departure by a few hours were ignored and hence the planned visit to McMurdo Station had to be cancelled. This caused much displeasure among the passengers on board who had paid a lot of money in part for the privilege of setting foot on the continent, to visit McMurdo Station and the nearby Scott's Discovery hut. This incidence is a clear example of tolerating tourism (the visit had been approved) but not assisting it.

Other examples of attempts at strengthening territorial claims include an incident when a Russian flagged cruise ship was followed by an Argentine navy vessel for two days while carrying out a routine commercial cruise to the Antarctic Peninsula. (The Argentineans claimed to be checking the waste disposal practices of the Russian vessel but in reality were exercising their 'territorial rights' to control the sea in what Argentina claims to be their territory.) Other examples of attempts at exercising sovereign rights in Antarctica include requests by the Chilean 'harbour master' for ships to identify themselves and to report on number and nationality of passengers and crew on board before entering Maxwell Bay (King George Island, South Shetlands), where a high concentration of Antarctic research facilities, including Chile's Arturo Frei, can be found. There is no legitimacy to such a request in what are, in essence, international waters. Thus, while Antarctica is an international continent, the sometimes petty nationalistic attitudes of nation states still surface.

Antarctic tourism management

Tourism in Antarctica is unique because unlike in the rest of the world it takes place in the absence of a national government and without an indigenous human population. It is a remote destination with a fragile, and at times, hostile environment. To date tourism in the deep south has been managed in an exemplary way and Antarctica can serve as a model for other natural destinations of how tourism could be successfully managed in remote and extreme locations. Of particular importance have been the establishment of the International Association of Antarctica Tour Operators (IAATO) in 1991 and of the Protocol on Environmental Protection to the Antarctic Treaty that came into force in 1998. IAATO has demonstrated that in the absence of law enforcement agencies in Antarctica the industry is capable of self-regulation of its activities.

Compared to most other tourist destinations visitor numbers to the southern-most region of the world are still relatively small (Figure 18.1). The International Association of Antarctica Tour Operators (IAATO) collects data on visitor arrivals and reports them annually on their website www.iaato.org.

Figure 18.1 shows how tourism in Antarctica has grown since 1992. Despite the current financial crisis, the future outlook for cruise-based Antarctic tourism products remains positive. During the 2008/09 season a total of 27,082 seaborne and airborne passengers landed in Antarctica. An additional 11,818 passengers travelled to Antarctica by ship and air but without making landings (IAATO 2009). As of August 2009, IAATO provides the estimates for visitor arrivals in Antarctica during the 2009–10 season.

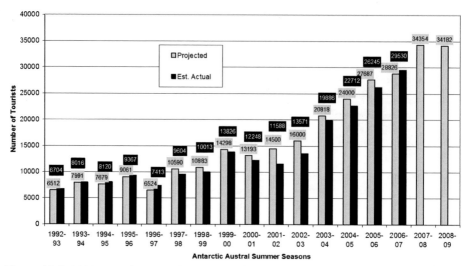

1992-2007 ANTARCTIC TOURIST TRENDS - Landed (Includes Ship and Land-based passenger numbers. 1997-98 onwards includes some commercial yacht activity)
March 14, 2008

Figure 18.1: 1992-2007 Antarctic Tourist Trends. Source:

Table 18.1: Total preliminary visitor estimates for 2009-2010 season. Source: IAATO 2009

Seaborne traditional tourism (with landings)	25,258
Seaborne tourism cruise-only (no landing)	16,631
Air/cruise	450
Air/land-based 'traditional' tourism	225
Overflights (no landing)	400
Total	**42,964**

Antarctic tourism is almost entirely ship-based but some adventurers do explore the interior of the continent and day flights that do not land are available from Australia and Chile. Limited air services are also available from Punta Arenas to King George Island in the South Shetlands and to a blue ice runway at Patriot Hills in the interior of the continent. Commercial cruising began in 1966 with cruises to the Antarctic Peninsula, the closest Antarctic region to any of the other continents, 1,000 km south of Cape Horn. Today most cruises depart from Ushuaia, the southernmost town in the world located on Tierra del Fuego in Argentina. Two types of cruises exist: those using smaller vessels that involve landings and those on large vessels that only cruise and do not land passengers. In the absence of port facilities operators depend on Zodiacs (inflatable rubber dinghies) to land passengers. Tourism activities are restricted to the warmer southern summer months (October to March) when the winter sea-ice has broken up and the region is relatively ice-free. This makes it possible for vessels to approach the coast. For much of the summer, daylight lasts 24 hours and this allows passengers to enjoy the beauty of Antarctica around the clock as landings can be made at any time of the day or night.

Conclusion

In the strictest sense it cannot be argued that Antarctica is a tourist destination that has been strongly influenced by political changes as described in other chapters of this book. In fact, with few exceptions, it is remarkable how much continuity there has been in the administration of the continent despite the great changes that have taken place in some of the Antarctic Treaty member countries. The Antarctic Treaty was negotiated and came into force during the period of the Cold War but even than there was a high level of respect for the Antarctic environment and a great focus on collaboration and openness. This has continued after the fall of communism in Eastern Europe where some of the places that were previously under Soviet influence are now involved in Antarctic affairs as independent nation states (Russian Federation, Ukraine, Belarus, Czech Republic, Estonia and Slovak Republic). The major lesson that other destinations can learn from Antarctica is that in tourism management there is a need for close co-operation between all stakeholders. Antarctic tourism is only possible because all stakeholders involved – national governments, Antarctic Treaty Parties, cruise companies, the industry association (IAATO), ship owners, crew, staff, tour operators, guides and tourists have a deep respect for the resource and hence are willing to work together to maintain it. Such cooperation is unique to Antarctica and other destinations are encouraged to adopt a similar approach to the management of tourism.

References

Bauer, T.G. (2001) *Tourism in the Antarctic: Opportunities, Constraints and Future Prospects*, New York : The Haworth Hospitality Press.

Damjanov, K. (2006) 'Tourism in the sublime: cultural colonization of Terra Australlis [sic] Incognita', Proceedings of UNAUSTRALIA, the Cultural Studies Association of Australasia's Annual Conference. www.unaustralia.com/proceedings.php (25 July 2009).

Haase, D., Lamers, M. and Amelung, B. (2009) 'Heading into uncharted territory? Exploring the institutional robustness of self-regulation in the Antarctic tourism sector', *Journal of Sustainable Tourism*, 17 (4), 411–430.

Hawke, R.J.L. (1990) 'Australia's policy in Antarctica', in Herr, R.A., Hall, H.R. and Haward, M.G (eds), *Antarctica's Future: Continuity or Change, Australian Institute of International Affairs*, Hobart: Tasmanian Government Printing Office.

Haywood, E. (1995) *Looking South: The Australian Antarctic Program in a Changing World*, Kingston, Tasmania: Australian Antarctic Division.

Headland, R.K. (1989) *Chronological List of Antarctic Expeditions and Related Events*. Cambridge: Cambridge University Press.

Heap, J. (ed.) (1990) *Handbook of the Antarctic Treaty System, Seventh edition*. Polar publications. Cambridge: Scott Polar Research Institute, University of Cambridge.

Herr, R.A., Hall, H.R. and Haward, M.G (eds), *Antarctica's Future: Continuity or Change, Australian Institute of International Affairs*, Hobart: Tasmanian Government Printing Office.

IAATO (2008) website www.iaato.org visited on 1 August 2009 but reporting figures for 2008

IAATO (2009) , from: www.iaato.org (1 August 2009).

Jeffreys, D. (2009) 'Changing tack', *South China Morning Post Magazine*, 26 July.

McGonigal, D. (2008) *Antarctica: Secrets of the Southern Continent*, NSW: Simon and Schuster Pymble.

Tepper, R. and Haward, M. (2005) 'The development of Malaysia's position on Antarctica: 1982 to 2004', *Polar Record*, 41(2), 113-124. Cambridge: Cambridge University Press

UNWTO (2009) World Tourism Barometer, from: http://www.world-tourism.org/facts/menu.html

Part VI
Conclusions

19 Conclusions

Richard Butler and Wantanee Suntikul

The preceding chapters in this volume have revealed the many ways in which tourism and political change have become increasingly interrelated. The rapid and extensive political changes in the world over the last quarter century have been unparalleled in terms of the fundamental changes that have taken place in the political geography and economics of the world without involving armed conflict. It is true that some of the changes discussed in this volume have come about following earlier conflicts – the Reunification of Berlin (and Germany as a whole) and the improvements in relations between the two communities in Cyprus, for example – while other changes have arisen from rebellions and coups, fortunately in most cases involving very little loss of life, even if considerable loss of liberty, such as in Libya and Fiji. In many other cases, however, massive change has come about in the most unexpected circumstances, often suddenly and apparently successfully, as seen in the emergence from the Communist yoke of Eastern European states following the dramatic fall of the Berlin Wall and from the horrors of apartheid in South Africa. One might also think of examples not covered here, such as Northern Ireland, where tourism is increasing, as it is in the republic to its south, after decades of 'Troubles', following a cessation of violence and a political settlement; and the tourist success stories of Croatia and Slovenia following the civil wars in the Balkans after the fragmentation of the former Yugoslavia.

It would be comforting to think that politicians and others have reached the stage of political development that they feel confident that non-violent means can be used to achieve political goals, as shown with the creation of new levels of government in Canada and Scotland for example, but one has to be aware that the risk of violence is still present in parts of the world and that tourism still has 'no go' areas, either because of insecurity and danger as, for example, in Afghanistan, or because of restrictions backed by the threat of force imposed by totalitarian regimes, such as North Korea. In such locations, tourism has not proved to be 'a force for peace', despite, for example, many years of efforts in the still divided peninsula of Korea. Even in locations that are popular international tourism destinations, political factors can restrict tourism, as the US embargo on travel to Cuba by its citizens demonstrates, a situation stemming from political events a half a century ago that are still not resolved.

In most parts of the world, however, tourism has been welcomed, even if it is recognised as being a sometimes controversial force of change in many areas, economic, social, cultural, environmental and political. Restrictions on tourist travel have diminished with fewer countries now requiring visas for tourists than in previous years, although some nations now appear to see visas not only as a means of exerting control over who visits them, but also as a source of revenue. Security measures enacted following the 'Twin Towers' terrorist acts in the USA have resulted in the 'home of the free' appearing increasingly unwelcoming to casual visitors from overseas, with increasing amounts of information being required before potential passengers are even allowed on an aircraft flying close to the United States, let alone landing there. In almost all countries now, as a result of terrorism, much closer checks are made on identity and items being transported by air, resulting in increased delays and travel times, although without much apparent impact upon tourist numbers. Perhaps only within the European Union (among those countries who have signed the Schengen Agreement in particular) has there been a reduction in air travel procedures, and an arrangement whereby travellers can drive from one country to another without passing through passport controls of any form.

Tourism in general has benefited greatly, therefore, from the political (and of course technological) changes that have taken place in recent decades. It has become easier, cheaper and mostly quicker, to travel internationally than ever before, and this is reflected in increased tourist numbers, both internationally and domestically, the current (2008–09) economic downturn not withstanding (in terms of total tourist numbers). The examples discussed in the preceding chapters suggest a number of themes and issues emerge when we examine the overall relationship between political change and tourism.

Vulnerability of tourism

As noted elsewhere (Aramberri and Butler 2005) tourism is an industry and an activity that is highly vulnerable to exogenous forces, one of the most important of these being threats to security. With an almost infinite choice of destinations in innumerable locations, tourists can and do easily and quickly respond to any real or perceived threat to security, mostly by avoiding any such destination. It has not been shown if there are various levels of concern about security, and it would appear likely that it is much more of a binary decision than a continuum of influence that shapes potential tourists decisions on whether to visit a particular destination or not. That is to say, if there is a perceived threat to security the destination is discounted and not considered in the decision-making process, rather than becoming less attractive, it ceases to be attractive at all. Only those few extreme risk takers (e.g. members of the 'Holidays for Maniacs' fraternity) are likely to seek out and visit places which are politically unstable and in which violence is present.

Thus destinations can be expected to experience rapid change in terms of declines in numbers of tourists when political situations worsen or reach a critical level, such as during or following coups, civil unrest or invasion as noted by Nepal (Chapter 13 of this volume) in the case of rebellions and riots in the Himalayan kingdom of Nepal. The decline in number of visitors and almost disappearance from the international tourism scene of places like Yugoslavia during the Balkan conflicts towards the end of the 20th century, the fall in visitor numbers in Fiji during its series of coups over the last 20 years, and reluctance of tourists to visit Egypt following attacks on tourists are all evidence of this trend. Numbers can increase fairly quickly following the resumption of normal relationships and the restoration of law and order, as shown by tourist numbers in Bali after the terrorist bombings there (Putra and Hitchcock, 2006), and convincing public relations and promotion exercises as performed by Fiji can persuade potential visitors that tourists are safe from local disturbances, as shown by Harrison and Pratt (this volume, Chapter 14).

It is clear that when restrictions on visitation to potential destinations have been removed by the destination governments concerned, tourists will flock to such new locations. The Baltic countries such as Estonia, Latvia and Lithuania, previously virtually unknown as tourist destinations to most of the world, have seen massive rises in numbers of international tourists once they gained freedom from Communist control by the former Soviet Union, a process particularly accelerated by the provision of low-cost air travel by budget carriers. One may deduce that if an inability to visit a destination is purely due to political constraints, tourists will rapidly seize the opportunity to visit that location once the political arrangements are changed, without fear or undue concern, as shown in Cyprus by Jacobson *et al.* (this volume, Chapter 17). It may take somewhat longer for them to be convinced that it is safe to do so if the reason for non-visitation was the existence or fear of violence. Undoubtedly much depends on the credibility of sources of information and the perception among potential tourists of their veracity and of the nature of the destination. It is clearly very much a one-sided situation, with tourism being highly vulnerable to political change, while political changes are rarely significantly influenced by tourism, as shown in Korea (Prideaux *et al.*, this volume, Chapter 16).

Inertia

The point made above about perceptions of destinations reflects the fact that much tourist travel is influenced by traditional emotions and feelings, often inaccurate and inappropriate, but nevertheless convincing to potential visitors. There is considerable inertia in attitudes towards destinations and their governments, some based on personal experience, for example Cuban émigrés in the United States who fled Castro's regime, or Greeks and Turks in Cyprus, some based on stereotypes and misunderstanding, a point noted by MacLellan in his discussion of Scotland and its image (this volume, Chapter 6). In the cases of Cuba, Cyprus and the Koreas, the origins of the issues affecting visitation to these areas lie up to half a century ago, and old habits are still dying hard in terms of attitudes between the two groups of neighbours in each case, with significant effects upon tourism to those areas and between the groups. In such cases, it is generally expected that significant political change would have massive implications for tourism. Much depends on whether the negativity in relations is external, e.g. Cuba and the USA, in which case change could result in massive and rapid changes in tourism, or internal, e.g. in the case of Cyprus, where complete reconciliation between the two parties might not have major impacts on international tourism to the island as a whole, and would have little impact on domestic tourism at all. In the case of Korea, the most likely analogy would be with the re-unification of Germany, and Nicosia for example, could well follow the pattern of change experienced by Berlin (Suntikul, this volume, Chapter 3).

Tourism image and management

In some cases, political change has meant a rapid expansion of tourism and visitor numbers and complete change in the management of tourism and the image of the destination, as noted above in the case of Eastern European countries by Hall (this volume, Chapter 8). In some cases, the rise of tourism has meant a change in image and adjustment in the way tourism is managed, perhaps best illustrated by the case of Antarctica (Bauer, this volume, Chapter 18), where the multinational Antarctic Treaty signatories have modified arrangements to accommodate the ever-increasing number of tourists visiting the continent.

In other cases, however, political change does not always prove sufficient to overcome traditional problems with the image of a destination or in the way that tourism has been managed. MacLellan (this volume, Chapter 6) discusses how devolved powers and a new Parliament have not significantly changed the image of Scotland, nor resolved some of the problems with the way tourism has been packaged, organised and supported, with duplication and conflicting messages still bedevilling the industry there. Dieke (this volume, Chapter 11) also shows that despite the massive political changes in South Africa following the abolition of apartheid, some problematic issues of image are still present and despite several initiatives and the lifting of embargos, tourism is still experiencing great difficulties in investment and development. In other situations, revolutionary change has created great possibilities for tourism in Libya in particular as Jones (this volume, Chapter 10) demonstrates, but the idiosyncratic nature of the government there combined with Muslim sensitivities and constraints has not yet delivered massive change in tourism. A somewhat similar situation exists in Iran (Baum and O'Gorman, this volume, Chapter 15), where great tourism potential has been prevented from being developed by a combination of fundamentalist and totalitarian viewpoints that are heavily politically inspired. Finally, the creation of a new political entity within Canada, Nunavut (Stewart and Draper this volume, Chapter 7), has not resolved the problems which tourism in Arctic Canada faces, and the new institution is still struggling to resolve a wide range of issues relating to overall development policies and priorities, one of which is the place of tourism in this vast remote and thinly populated area.

Conversion from Communism

One of the major political and economic changes over the past two decades has been the conversion of a number of political units from Communism to a capitalist economic system. This has meant that tourism within those countries has changed from being a heavily controlled, mostly domestic activity, with the only foreign visitors being guests of the state, operating in a non-competitive way, to becoming an emerging industry generally poorly prepared for its role in catering to foreign visitors in a highly competitive global market. Suntikul (this volume, Chapter 12) illustrates this clearly in the case of Vietnam, which, through its *doi moi* policy, has opened both the country and its tourist industry to foreign investment as well as foreign visitation, and seen massive changes in the industry as a result. Standards in services, infrastructure and facilities have improved greatly, the image of the country has been transformed from one of a site of intense conflict, both military and political, to one of a welcoming and exciting destination, albeit with some constraints still present.

A similar situation has developed elsewhere, in Eastern Europe as noted above, and particularly in Cuba, where Hinch (this volume, Chapter 9) has shown the way in which a revolutionary Communist government has gradually relaxed controls on tourism and not only welcomed, but actively sought capitalist investment, agreements and tourists for reasons of economic survival. Cuba's survival depended on such political and economic modifications as its traditional support from the Soviet Union declined severely over the decades from the 1960s onwards. In this case, perhaps more than any other, tourism has emerged as a key element in the political and economic survival of the Castro regime, enabling it to withstand the embargo and other attempts at removing its government by the neighbouring United States. Despite the difficulties noted above, a similar situation may develop in North Korea in the future, which has already experimented, albeit briefly and in limited circumstances, with allowing tourism development and tourist visitation from capitalist countries to occur within its borders.

Final comments

Political change affects tourism in a number of ways on a scale much larger than tourism appears to be capable of bringing about political change. Neighbouring countries, with earlier histories of tourist interaction between their residents, have waged wars against each other on many occasions, as seen in Europe twice in the 20th century. Thus, the presence of tourism appears to have little effect on international politics. Tourism does, perhaps, have the ability to initiate or be a factor in initiating contact between opposing nations but it would appear not to be able to do much more in terms of ending political stand-offs, let alone conflict.

On the other hand, as shown throughout this volume, political change often brings about major changes in tourist flows, increasing them when political stability and security is achieved, and shrinking or even stopping them completely, when politics gives way to conflict or a significant change in political regime occurs. Partly, as noted above, this is due to changes in security as far as tourists are concerned, not only safety from harm, but also fear of absence of freedom to travel into, around and out of countries in the process of political change. When political change has been completed, then almost inevitably different policies are enacted, and as Hall (this volume, Chapter 2) notes, such changes have effects in many areas and at many scales. It is, in most cases, the policies and their implementation which have the major effect on tourism. Tourists from Communist countries appear to have longed to travel to the capitalist Western countries but were not allowed the freedom to do so because of the policies of their own governments. Potential Western tourists to Communist countries were thwarted more often by restrictions resulting from 'closed door' policies than by an absence of desire to visit those countries, as shown by immediate increases in visitation to countries still Communist in name, such as Cuba, the People's Republic of China and Vietnam, once restrictions were eased. Fears of a decline in visitation to Hong Kong and Macau when these administrative units were ceded back to China did not materialise and tourism continued at the same or increased levels under Communist rule, albeit from a long distance and under special arrangements (McCartney, this volume, Chapter 5).

It would be naïve to imagine that the world will not see further political change and therefore subsequent changes in tourism in the years ahead. It is difficult to imagine changes as major as the ending of the Cold War, the decline in Communism, the change in regimes in the Muslim world, the rapid expansion of the European Union and the ending of apartheid in South Africa, along with the emergence of global terrorism, but doubtless observers will continue to be surprised in the future also. One might reasonably expect significant improvements in relations between Cuba and the United

States, and one can hope that North and South Korea might reunify, as might Cyprus, and that countries such as Libya, Iran, Iraq and Afghanistan could re-emerge as tourist destinations. Perhaps unfortunately less likely, the Middle East in general might secure peace and tourism could then grow in areas such as Lebanon, Gaza and the West Bank that desperately need economic development. Increased stability in African countries could see more of that continent gain tourist numbers and investment, and a change in political arrangements in Myanmar could see that country re-emerge onto the tourist itinerary. Finally, cessation of terrorism in all its forms could have dramatic effects on the distribution, the cost and the volume of tourism at the international scale.

One can only assume that the future will bring continued and often unanticipated political change, surprising in location, nature and speed of change and as a result, continued dynamism in tourism at the international and the domestic level.

References

Aramberri, J. and Butler, R.W. (2005) *Tourism: A Vulnerable Industry*, Clevedon: Channel View Publications.

Putra, N.D. and Hitchcock, M. (2006) 'The Bali bombs and the tourism development cycle', *Progress in Development Studies*, **6**, (2) 157–166.

Index

Act (of legislation) 16

Agreement 24-25, 35, 45-46, 51, 68, 70-72, 78, 85, 135, 154, 179, 180, 192-193, 199, 203-204, 222 224

Apartheid 3-4, 120-129, 221, 224-225

Attractions 23, 27-30, 50, 59, 72, 84, 88, 99, 100, 122, 124, 127-129, 133-134, 137, 141, 172, 200

Benefits 5, 9, 14, 24-25 27-28, 37, 52, 61, 64, 72, 74, 83 -84, 88, 100-101, 114, 120, 123, 141, 156, 167, 170, 194, 205-206, 213, 222

Blockade 22, 150, 152

Border 2, 23, 30, 35, 41-42, 49, 51, 53, 85, 87, 108, 110, 147-148, 150, 157, 177, 180, 182, 192, 225

Boundary 13, 138-142, 147, 163, 167, 179, 181, 183, 194, 203, 205-206

Capitalist/Capitalism 23, 29, 49, 83, 111, 121, 135, 141, 190-191, 224-225

Cold war 1, 3, 4, 21, 29, 30, 45-53, 101, 104, 109, 110, 113-114, 128, 134-135, 141, 160, 189-190, 195 217, 225

Colonial/colonies 1, 3, 52, 114, 128, 134, 135, 160, 195, 209

Communism/communist 1, 3-4 21, 29 82-83, 85, 87-88, 90, 99-101, 111, 133-135, 152-154, 191, 204 217, 221, 223-225

Competitiveness 9, 34, 37-38, 40-41, 43, 84, 137

Conflict 82, 88, 152, 154, 175, 177, 180, 194, 196, 201-202, 209, 221-222, 224-225

Consequence 1, 5, 10, 12, 27, 31, 43, 68, 76, 84, 89, 161, 168, 175-176, 193, 199-206, 212

Constitution 11, 15, 46, 60, 102, 121, 135, 148-149, 151-153, 161

Coup 4, 99, 110, 113-117, 161-171, 221-222

Crossing 23, 25, 182, 199-206

Culture 1, 5, 28, 40, 42, 49, 52-53, 57-58, 62, 64, 68-70, 89, 99, 101, 114-115, 136, 161, 167, 175, 178

Decision making 12, 16, 46, 50, 61, 210, 222

Dependents/dependency 1, 22, 28, 48-49, 53, 71 83, 85, 100 127, 161, 208

Devolution 4, 57, 59-61, 63-66, 84

Diplomacy 1, 189, 191, 196

Distribution 100, 112, 150, 153, 205, 226

Disturbance 4, 148, 161, 222

Economies 34-35, 51, 83-84, 89, 170, 178

Economy 1, 4 23-24, 33, 37-38, 52, 58, 64, 78, 83, 100, 103, 106, 108-109, 111, 113-114, 120-122, 125, 127-128, 136-137, 153, 156-157, 160, 162-163, 168, 190, 195, 199

Ecotourism 72, 133

Embargo 4, 97-99, 101-106, 112, 135, 221, 224-225

Ethnic (ethnicity) 83, 88-89, 153, 158, 160-162, 175, 180, 196, 199, 201

Foreign direct investment 2, 84, 89, 122, 137

Foreign exchange 34, 147, 150, 156, 157, 162, 168

Foreign policy 16, 97-98, 101, 103-106, 135, 141, 192-194

Funding 11, 29, 35, 38, 43, 61, 71, 77, 89, 139, 140, 167

Gambling 47-50, 52, 99, 114, 124

Global (globalisation) 1-2, 5, 10, 21-22, 31, 33, 37-38, 43, 45, 47, 69, 84, 89, 120, 122, 125, 127-128, 133, 135, 170-171, 189-190, 193, 206, 224-225

Identity 1, 13, 57-58, 65, 87-89, 191, 222

Ideology 4, 16, 111, 117, 133, 162, 176, 182-183

Image 4, 22-24, 42, 47, 57-58, 63, 66, 85, 88, 114-117, 123, 126, 167, 171-172, 176, 178, 182, 223-224

Indigenous (indigenes, natives) 68-70, 75, 78, 89, 129, 160-161, 167-169, 215

Inequality 120-122, 125, 169

Instability 4, 87, 134, 136, 148, 162

Disintegration/re-integration/ integration 2-3, 14, 23, 35, 38, 46, 60-62, 82-83, 85, 89, 98, 116, 125-128, 136, 154, 192, 195

Investment 2, 9, 11-12, 24, 29, 40-41, 47, 50, 59, 86, 88, 99, 101-103, 106, 110, 116, 118, 122 123, 127, 129, 137-138, 151, 153, 160-162, 167, 178, 201, 224, 226

Isolation 4, 98, 101, 103, 105, 108, 112, 117, 120, 135, 148

Labour 33, 35-37, 43, 51, 84-85, 89, 117, 121-122, 160

Land use 39, 70

Legislation (see also Act) 43, 53, 102, 111, 115, 137

Management 12-13, 15, 43, 48, 52, 61, 64, 68, 70, 72, 78, 106, 113, 116, 126-127, 139, 178, 211, 215, 217, 223

Market (markets, marketing) 4, 11, 21-24, 26, 30-38, 42, 49, 52-53, 58-59, 61-65, 68, 71-72, 82-89, 99-100, 103-104, 106, 111, 114-118, 121-122, 124-130, 133, 135-136, 138-141, 150-151, 153, 157, 158, 160-161, 166-168, 171, 179-180, 182, 224

Mass tourism 34, 83, 124

Migrants (migration/emigration) 23, 35, 52, 85, 89, 105, 148, 160, 168-169 196

Mobility 34-35, 42, 84-85

Parks (national) 71-72, 75-78, 88, 124, 139-141, 151

Parliament 4, 13, 29, 57, 59-62, 64, 148-150, 152, 224

Peace 35, 45, 154, 189-191, 193-196, 203, 211, 221, 226

Political party 148, 161

Politics 1-3, 5, 8-18, 46, 60, 106, 108-119, 133, 166, 171, 178, 183, 190, 208, 225

Population 9, 40, 43, 51-52, 57, 70, 73, 75, 105, 115, 121, 123, 160-161, 167-168, 171-172, 176, 208, 215

Promotion 11, 13, 29, 40-42, 59, 61, 63-68, 71, 84, 88, 99, 103, 117-118, 126-127, 135, 139, 150-151, 222

Privatisation 23, 27, 122

Racism (racist) 120, 161, 167, 169

Reform 47-48, 51, 58, 100, 103-104, 111, 117, 121, 135, 141, 180-181

Refugee 85, 176, 202

Regulation/deregulation 4, 33, 35, 38, 40, 42, 48, 70, 78, 88, 104-105, 121-122, 136-137, 209-211, 215

Religion/religious 1 , 114-115, 176, 179-181, 183, 196, 201

Residents/residence 29, 35, 46-47, 50-52, 69-71, 73-76, 78, 84, 101, 125, 129, 134, 148, 151, 163, 171, 178, 201, 225

Resources 15, 47, 52-53, 65-66, 68, 70, 72, 78, 88, 113-116, 118, 127, 129, 135, 139, 153, 158, 167-168, 176-177, 190, 209, 211

Reunification 3, 21-32, 134-135, 141, 190-196, 204, 221

Revolution 46, 97-101, 103-106, 111-112, 120, 122, 177-181, 183

Richter, L. 2, 163, 190

Sanctions 101-102, 105, 108, 112-113, 117, 124, 182

Strategy/strategies 8, 37-38, 40-41, 45, 47, 49, 51-53, 61-62, 65, 74-75, 77, 88, 97, 122-123, 126-127, 129, 151-152, 167, 195, 206

Sustainable/Sustainability 38, 40-41, 43, 62, 78, 85, 88-90, 121, 127, 129-130, 141, 162, 201

Terrorism/terrorist 1, 15-16, 112-113, 115, 117, 154, 221-222, 225-226

Territory 4, 46, 68, 71-72, 77, 175, 209, 215

Tourism development 2-4, 8-9, 15, 21-22, 24, 33, 38, 40, 42, 50, 52, 62-69, 72, 77-78, 82, 85, 88-89, 98-100, 108, 113, 115-120, 126-127, 129, 134-137, 141, 147, 149, 150-155, 157-158, 160, 162, 178, 181, 183, 225

Transport/transportation 9, 22, 24-25, 35, 38-40, 57, 60-62, 71, 73, 77, 85, 114, 128, 136, 140, 179-180

Treaty 33-35, 45-46, 152, 192, 209-213, 215, 217, 224

Unstable 90, 157, 162, 222

Urban 3, 25, 29, 30, 43, 57, 83-84, 88, 121, 134, 138, 199, 201-202

Value/value added 9, 13, 36-37, 40, 62, 64-65, 117, 127, 129, 151

Values 9, 12-13, 62, 64-65, 86, 106, 116-117, 178, 194

Violence/violent 48, 113, 121, 126, 151, 152, 154-155, 157, 161, 163, 166, 188, 201, 203, 221-223

Visa 23, 34-35, 49, 51, 84-85, 114, 118, 136, 141, 181, 199, 209, 221

War/wars 3-4, 21, 23-25, 28-30, 45, 47, 101, 104, 110, 112, 133-135, 141, 147-148, 150, 152-154, 176, 179, 180-181, 183, 189-190, 196, 199, 201, 217, 221, 225

Workforce (workers) 26, 34, 37, 39, 65, 84, 116-117, 121, 127, 133, 156, 177, 179, 194

Zone 112, 190, 201, 203-205, 208

Strategy for Tourism

by John Tribe, Professor and Head of Tourism, Surrey University, UK

Strategy for Tourism is an internationally focused text which explains strategic management, analysis and implementation specifically in the tourism industry. It covers strategic management in a variety of tourism contexts, such as organizations, destinations, governments, NGOs and IGOs, as well as for special purposes (e.g. ad hoc events, sustainability, inclusion, pro-poor). Using global case studies, it provides a complete overview of all the factors required when establishing a strategic plan.

ISBN: 978-1-906884-07-9

Hard copy: £29.99: €32.99:$48 E-Book: £22.59 E-Chapter: £2.50: March 2010

Tourism Research: a 20:20 vision

Edited by Professor Douglas Pearce is Professor Tourism Management, Victoria Management School, New Zealand and Professor Richard Butler, Professor in the Department of Hospitality and Tourism Management of University of Strathclyde

Tourism research continues to expand at a rapid rate and this explosion in output has meant it is more and more difficult to keep pace with what is being produced, as well as the quality of what is produced. Tourism Research: a 20:20 vision examines how research agendas have evolved and might develop in coming years, considers conceptual and methodological advances, discusses obstacles that have been encountered and suggests ways forward.

ISBN: 978-1-906884-10-9

Hard copy: £49.99: €49.99:$60 E-Book: £39.99 E-Chapter: £2.50: March 2010

Global Geotourism Perspectives

Edited by David Newsome, Associate Professor, Environmental Science and Ecotourism, Murdoch University, Australia and Ross Dowling, Foundation Professor of Tourism, Edith Cowan University, Australia

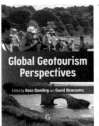

The field of geotourism is a rapidly emerging one. It expands and develops a new area of natural area tourism. This edited collection is divided into four sections to cover the globe, encompassing Australasia, Europe and Scandinavia, USA, and Asia. With chapters authored by international experts in the field from industry and academia, it examines specific sites to discuss best practice, issues of sustainability, planning, sensitive development and active management.

ISBN: 978-1-906884-09-3

Hard copy: £29.99: €29.99:$40 E-Book: £22.50 E-Chapter: £2.99 : April 2010

The Origins of Hospitality and Tourism

by Dr Kevin D O'Gorman, Lecturer in Hospitality and Tourism Management, Strathclyde Business School, University of Strathclyde, Glasgow

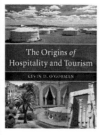 An exciting new text about the true origins of hospitality and tourism, identifying how an understanding the past can inform modern approaches to hospitality and tourism management. *The Origins of Hospitality and Tourism* covers the study of, and the development of understanding of, the origins of hospitality traditions within the domestic, civic and commercial contexts of hospitality, and develops this into the presentation of a new Dynamic Model of Hospitality.

ISBN: 978-1-906884-08-6

Hard copy: £29.99: €32.99:$49.99 E-Book: £22.50 E-Chapter:£2.50: March 2010

Tourism and Crime: Key Themes

Edited by David Botterill, freelance academic and higher education consultant and Professor Emeritus in the Welsh Centre for Tourism Research, University of Wales Institute Cardiff, and Trevor Jones, Reader in Criminology and Criminal Justice at the School of Social Sciences, University of Cardiff

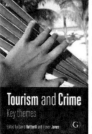 The tourist as victim or offender? With contributions from international experts *Tourism and Crime: Key Themes* is the first text to addresses the tourism-crime nexus, including issues such as drugs tourism, sex tourism and alcohol-related crime and disorder among holidaymakers, the 'naming and shaming' of specific 'danger travel spots', the governance of safety in 'stateless' spaces, cooperation between justice authorities in different jurisdictions, and much more.

ISBN: 978-1-906884-14-7

Hard copy: £34.99: €34.99:$40 E-Book: £25 E-Chapter: £3.99 : May 2010

For more details on these and other Goodfellow Publisher products, and to order inspection copies, visit the website at www.goodfellowpublishers.com
or email us at customerservice@goodfellowpublishers.com.

Also available from all good book retailers.

WWW.GOODFELLOWPUBLISHERS.COM